The Essential CORBA:
Systems Integration
Using Distributed Objects

The Essential CORBA:
Systems Integration
Using Distributed Objects

Thomas J. Mowbray, PhD

Ron Zahavi

John Wiley & Sons, Inc.
New York • Chichester • Brisbane • Toronto • Singapore

Publisher: Katherine Schowalter

Editor: Robert Elliott

Managing Editor: Micheline Frederick

Text Design & Composition: Integre Technical Publishing Co., Inc.

Figures 6.1–6.4 are reprinted courtesy of Microsoft Press from *Inside OLE2* by Kraig Brockschmidt, © 1994, Microsoft Press, Redmond, WA.

Figure 9.1 appears courtesy of IEEE. IEEE Micro, Vol. 13, No. 6 *Camp Development: The Art of Building a Market Through Standards* by Chris Halliwell, 1993.

ISBN 0-471-10611-9

Printed in the United States of America

10 9 8 7 6 5 4 3 2 1

This book is dedicated to our
lovely wives and lifelong friends:
Susan Zahavi and Kate Mowbray, C.P.A.

Let us raise a standard to which the honest and brave will repair.
—George Washington

Preface

Both of us have had a number of systems integration experiences before we started working together on a project called DISCUS (Data Interchange and Synergistic Collateral Usage Study) at The MITRE Corporation. We had the good fortune of working for a program management team that gave us the freedom to draw on our past experiences and develop a well thought out approach to a challenging problem: general application interoperability.

These ideas were based on the need for a carefully designed, well-documented software architecture, one that was designed with simplicity, extensibility, and cost implications in mind. We discovered through talking to our colleagues that these ideas, which seemed obvious to us, were not part of their training or backgrounds. In fact, these approaches are not adequately covered in the literature and not generally understood, even by experienced computer scientists. To transfer this knowledge, we put together this book, including a full coverage of the required background material, design approach, and implementation techniques.

Our approach builds on the standards foundations created by the Object Management Group (OMG). Our technical goals and the OMG goals are very much in sync. The OMG has made truly remarkable progress in generating quality standards and cultivating acceptance for its standards across industry, standards groups, and consortia. We want to see this vision realized even faster; hence, this book transfers our knowledge and approach for successful systems integration.

T.J.M.
R.Z.
McLean, Virginia
January 1995

Acknowledgments

Although this book was written on our own time, we must thank our project management for their visionary support, in particular: Webster Anderson, Dwight Brown, Steve Brown, Tim Daniel, Jeff Fleisher, Dolly Greenwood, Diane Haberstich, Gene Jarboe, Geoff Lipsey, John Polger, John Robusto, and Bill Ruh.

We sincerely appreciate the help and contributions provided by our friends and colleagues, including: Howard Cohen, Donna Cornwell, Jonathan Doughty, Ray Emami, Julie Gravalesse, Tom Herron, Michael Josephs, Melony Katz, Paul Klinker, Rafael Malveau, Emanuel Mamatas, John Marsh, Diane Mularz, Chibuike Nwaeze, Craig Prall, Bill Quigley, Andy Reho, Jeff Rogers, Hank Seebeck, Lisa Strader, Shel Sutton, John Tisaranni, Doug Vandermade, and Kendall White.

The Object Management Group has been essential to the publication of this work, thanks to Cheryl Bissonnette, Bill Hoffman, Kelly Kassa, Jon Siegel, John Slitz, Dr. Richard Soley, Geoff Speare, Chris Stone, and Lydia Thomas.

Special thanks to Steve Black, Mark Bramhall, David Chappell, Reggie Counts, Joe Croghan, John Eaton, Norman Eko, Alan Ewald, Charlie Green, Jim Green, Jed Harris, Jack Hassall, Ellis Horowitz, Andrew Hutt, Ole Jacobsen, Neil Jacobson, Huet Landry, Eric Leach, John Leary, Marie Lenzi, Jacob Levy, Geoff Lewis, Denise Lynch, Cliff Mauton, Todd Pelfrey,

Marty Polluconi, Michael Powell, Richard Probst, Yllona Richardson, Bob Rockwell, Mark Roy, Mark Ryland, John Rymer, Dave Seres, Cathy Sloan, Craig Thompson, Fred Waskhewicz, Andrew Watson, Dave Zenie, and all the others who helped us in our quest for understanding. These people gave us inspiration, motivation, and important ideas.

Finally, we wish to thank our wives and families for their patience, love, and unconditional support while writing this book.

Contents

Executive Summary

In this book, we introduce the theory and practice of systems integration using standard object technology, Common Object Request Broker Architecture (CORBA). The purpose of systems integration is to provide interoperability between software components and to provide for system adaptability as the system evolves. This book goes beyond the basics of systems integration and CORBA to show readers how to maximize the benefits of these technologies and practices throughout the system life cycle.

PROBLEM DEFINITION

Today's software systems comprise islands of automation. Each software component performs some limited range of useful functions, but components do not interoperate effectively. The integration that exists is insufficient and does not evolve gracefully with the component technologies. The scale of this problem ranges from the the user's desktop, to interuser, interdepartment, and interorganizational levels. Key consequences of poor systems integration include:

- *Stovepipe systems*. These systems are poorly integrated systems that have ad hoc or proprietary integration solutions. Poorly integrated systems have high maintenance costs, resist adaptation to changing user requirements, and cannot evolve with commercial technology.
- *Organizational productivity impacts*. Poor integration leads to substantial organizational inefficiencies, such as redundant data entry, multistep data conversion, and ad hoc file transfers. These processes are

1

costly, time consuming, and error prone. Poor systems integration requires users to be knowledgeable about multiple disparate applications. Users trained on one system cannot transfer skills to other systems.

CORBA — THE BASIS FOR A SOLUTION

CORBA is an industry standard technology infrastructure for systems integration. Some of its key benefits include:

1. CORBA simplifies distributed computing and application integration. It is easier to use than other distributed computing and integration mechanisms; therefore, it saves time and reduces software costs. CORBA also provides many useful new flexibilities compared to other mechanisms.
2. CORBA is object oriented. This means that architects and developers can improve their software structure, make their software more flexible, reuse software, seamlessly integrate legacy software, and develop new capabilities rapidly. CORBA provides a uniform layer encapsulating other forms of distributed computing and integration mechanisms.
3. CORBA is a stable technology supported by a growing coalition of commercial software vendors. CORBA is a standard from the world's largest software consortium, the Object Management Group (OMG), and supported by X/Open, the Open Software Foundation (OSF), the Common Open Software Environment (COSE), CI Labs, X/Consortium, and others. The core elements of CORBA have been stable since 1991. With CORBA, OMG has reengineered the standards process to allow suppliers and end users to create new standards for interoperability efficiently.

SYSTEMS INTEGRATION USING CORBA — THE OPPORTUNITY

CORBA is an enabling technology. Bad systems integration practices can lead to stovepipe systems regardless of whether CORBA is used. This book is a guide on how to follow good architecture principles that utilize CORBA for maximum benefits.

Key benefits of our approach to CORBA-based systems integration include: faster system delivery, enhanced software reuse, increased system adaptability, reduced maintenance costs, focused research activities, enhanced system interoperability, enterprise systems integration, and other benefits.

A FRAMEWORK FOR CHANGE

In Chapter 4 we define an integration capability model, which enables organizations to assess their current systems integration practices. This model allows organizations to discover the substantial benefits of improved systems integration compared to current practices. The integration capability model includes the following levels:

Level 6.   Standard Architectures
Level 5.   Frameworks
Level 4.   Distributed Objects (CORBA)
Level 3.   Mature Remote Procedure Calls (OSF DCE)
Level 2.   Miscellaneous Mechanisms
Level 1.   Commercial Off-the-Shelf Solutions

The capabilities range from organizations that do no value-added integration (level 1) to organizations that drive industry standards (level 6). Most organizations today practice systems integration at levels 2 and 3. When an organization first adopts CORBA, it begins at level 4. Substantial benefits result from level 5 practices, and technology leadership is demonstrated at level 6. This book teaches readers how to perform systems integration in order to achieve level 5 and 6 benefits. The capability model is described in detail in Chapter 4.

SYNOPSIS OF THE BOOK

Chapter 1, "Introduction," introduces the paradigm shift that motivates the increasing role of systems integration. It provides a detailed introduction to systems integration problems including commercial technology integration, legacy systems integration, and other key issues. It establishes a vision for the organizational use of good systems integration practices and CORBA.

Chapter 2, "Standards Strategy," defines what standards mean and how they are used effectively. It provides guidance for understanding and exploiting available standards and shows how an organization can leverage the work of government organizations and standards groups to define a comprehensive standards strategy.

Chapter 3, "An Introduction to CORBA," provides essential tutorial information about OMG standards: CORBA, OMG's Interface Definition Language (OMG IDL), CORBAservices (Common Object Service Specifications), and CORBAfacilities (OMG Common Facilities).

Chapter 4, "Software Architecture Design," includes the foundational theories of systems integration. It describes the integration capability model and defines architecture and framework concepts. It establishes an integrated software architecture design process and defines details of how to use OMG IDL for controlling design trade-offs. It also compares the architectural patterns that support the theory and shows the quantitative impact of each architectural approach.

Chapter 5, "Security," discusses one of the most challenging aspects of systems integration. This chapter surveys key security technologies that contribute to an overall security solution and establishes a vision for how they will interact in future systems constructed with OMG standards.

Chapter 6, "Framework Examples," describes Microsoft Object Linking and Embedding (OLE), OpenDoc, and X11R6 Fresco. These are some of the key commercial software architectures that will impact future systems integration.

Chapter 7, "In-Depth Example: The DISCUS Framework," discusses DISCUS, one of the most mature CORBA-based application architectures. It is presented here as a detailed example of systems integration practices. DISCUS incorporates many useful design examples, techniques, and lessons that can be transferred to new system designs and implementations.

Chapter 8, "Object Wrapper Techniques," discusses object wrapping, the core competency in systems integration for developers. This chapter is an essential tutorial about wrapping techniques for architects and developers. The chapter gives examples of object wrapping for the most commonly occurring integration challenges.

Chapter 9, "Systems Integration Guidance," summarizes the whole book in terms of six key guidelines.

Appendix, "ORB Products," contains product overviews of some of the major CORBA Object Request Brokers: Digital Equipment Corporation's ObjectBroker, SunSoft's DOE, IONA's Orbix, and IBM's System Object Model (SOM).

THE PRINCIPLES
OF SYSTEMS
INTEGRATION

Introduction

In this introductory chapter, we identify the key issues that motivate this book. In particular, we wish to heighten the contradictions in current systems integration practice. In this way, we can summarize all of the key technical and related nontechnical issues. In the balance of the book, we will explain Object Management Group (OMG) standards and other key concepts needed for successful systems integration. OMG's core standard, the Common Object Request Broker Architecture (CORBA), provides many technical benefits. We provide added value by addressing how to use the OMG standards effectively in systems integration. This chapter focuses on systems integration issues prior to the adoption of CORBA and prior to the application of the techniques presented in this book.

While most of the book focuses on the technical issues, this chapter will identify some of the factors outside the technical realm that influence systems integration. For example, software architectures often mirror our organizational structures, and systems integration success is dependent upon organizational support for the architects and developers.

Not long ago, a stand-alone program comprising a command-line interface and a few specialized functions was sufficient for a successful software application. Since then, end users' expectations have changed dramatically; the scope of requirements also has changed. Today it is expected that software systems will have graphical user interfaces; software systems will incorporate complex data types such as imagery, graphics, and multimedia; and software systems will have integrated database capabilities. Heterogeneous computing environments are a reality in most organizations where differences between platforms reinforce the need for multivendor integration solutions.

Systems integration requirements will become even more challenging in the near future. For example, universal data interchange between applications will be expected; applications will need to support computer-assisted human collaboration, and these capabilities will be needed in mobile distributed environments, supported on a wide range of platforms and networks. Standards support will be a key software product discriminator for end users; however these standards might not guarantee interoperability.

For most organizations, it is not feasible to build systems of this scope using custom software. As a result, the practice of building systems has changed from custom programming to systems integration from preexisting components. Custom applications have a role in meeting highly specialized needs, such as organization-specific user interfaces. As the diversity and capabilities of commercial software increase, the need for custom software decreases. For complex functions, it is usually more cost effective to reuse existing software than to create custom software. The majority of software in future systems will be preexisting, obtained from commercial vendors and other sources. Systems integration has a role in providing interapplication interoperability and system customization beyond the off-the-shelf capabilities; design and development of this custom software is a key focus of this book.

The growing supply of preexisting software is displacing the need for custom software. Preexisting software sources include in-house software, commercial software, public domain software, freeware, and shareware. In-house software can include legacy systems software, prototype software, and software designed for in-house reuse, such as class libraries. Commercial software is available directly from suppliers, retail outlets, industry conferences, and other advertising events and media. Public domain software is freely available software that is not copyrighted and can be used without restrictions. Freeware is similar, except that it carries a copyright notice. Shareware is software that is available for a nominal fee and also carries a copyright. Copyright can restrict the reselling of freeware and shareware, but the copyrights generally allow the usage of the software in end-user systems. Public domain, freeware, and shareware can be obtained from users' groups, from vendors, and from public networks (including the Internet and commercial computer networks).

The practice of systems integration can range from informal ad hoc programming to formal structured methodologies. In many organizations these practices coexist: the formal practices creating the documentation and the informal practices creating the working system.

The difficulties of integrating preexisting components create a need for highly creative programmers. Many successful programmers are masters of scrounging software components and integrating components in ingenious ways. These skills are essential to virtually every software engineering activity; ad hoc integration is expedient and leads to demonstrable results.

Often these integration solutions are brilliant, but these achievements are seldom sustainable. Ad hoc integration usually produces undocumented brittle systems that are expensive to maintain and costly to upgrade. When staff turnover occurs, organizations find themselves with cryptic code that is extremely difficult to understand. This code is practically unmodifiable and at some stage must be thrown away, possibly to be replaced by another programmer's undocumented code.

Formal design methodologies generally are not supportive of preexisting software integration. Methodologies typically address subsystem level issues that are relevant to the design of a single custom application. In addition, change to requirements during the system life cycle are a major system cost driver, perhaps involving up to 50 percent of all software costs [Horowitz, 93]. Most methodologies do not address the issues of integrating independently designed components and maintaining systems through long life cycles entailing requirements changes and multiple system extensions.

In this book, we offer some alternatives to the shortcomings of ad hoc integration and formal methodologies. We show how to leverage practical systems integration skills into the creation of documented, extensible, standards-based systems. This book offers a new way to think about systems integration and a new way to package the integration solution. Much of the ad hoc integration code will still reside in the resulting system, but it will be incorporated in a way that enables the reuse of integration solutions as well as the component software. We believe that our approach enables the development of robust software architectures that support enhanced reusability and extensibility. These software architectures contain an appropriate balance between the need for formal documentation and the realities of programming with preexisting components.

In this chapter we introduce the key issues of computing technology and systems integration. Then we overview the key concepts in our software architecture design and integration approach.

ISSUES IN COMPUTING: TECHNOLOGY, MARKET, AND ORGANIZATIONS

The following are some important factors in computing that tend to exacerbate systems integration challenges. These issues are challenging to resolve because they combine business, human, and technological factors. Each systems integration organization should be aware of these issues and possible approaches for mitigating the consequences.

Stovepipe Systems

A stovepipe system is a set of legacy applications that resists adaptation to user and organizational needs. To the user, stovepipe systems appear to be unfriendly legacy applications that lack interoperability. These deficiencies become obvious when compared with inexpensive PC software. Stovepipe systems are brittle; they do not tolerate change. In contrast, computing technology and facilities are changing rapidly. As systems change and age toward obsolescence, users experience an increase in bugs and system failures.

Some key characteristics of stovepipe systems include:

- Monolithic, vertically integrated applications
- Closed system: custom proprietary solution
- No discernible software architecture
  –system structure poorly understood by developers and maintainers
- Lack of provision for reuse and extension
- Slow development and deployment
- Expensive maintenance and evolution

Stovepipe systems are the source of many problems for end users, developers, maintainers, and management. Even though the problems are obvious, the solutions are not obvious, even to computer industry experts. We have consulted with many senior technologists and experts in the computer industry who believe that there are no effective solutions and that even the best next-generation systems of today will be the stovepipe systems of the future.

We believe that there are two fundamental causes of stovepipe systems:

1. The way that systems are acquired.
2. Lack of architectural focus.

New systems are typically acquired in a manner that facilitates the creation of a stovepipe system. Many acquisitions are driven by external system requirements, such as the user interface functionality. Most requirements documents are snapshots of user needs. Changing requirements are the major cost drivers in software development and maintenance. [Horowitz, 93]

Acquisitions typically involve organizational relationships that maximize the negative characteristics of stovepipe systems. For example, an inventory system for a parts supply department might be acquired from the outside contractor who submitted the lowest bid. The contractor's interest may be to deliver a minimal cost system that meets the requirements. To cut costs, the system may contain various ad hoc integration solutions and the presence of these may benefit the contractor with more work later, as the customer's requirements change. The parts supply department, focused on its own internal needs, may acquire the system without much consideration of how the new system will interoperate with the rest of the enterprise. Later, it may be discovered that integration with the parts consumer's systems is highly desirable, but difficult to achieve. In this example, the new inventory system becomes a stovepipe system primarily because of the way it is acquired.

The other fundamental cause of stovepipe systems involves a lack of architectural focus. Throughout this book, we present the principles and practices of how to use CORBA with a strong architectural focus in order to overcome the deficiencies of stovepipe systems. Architectural focus can be derailed in many ways. Inadequate training and experience is the most significant problem. Few university curricula include software architecture training. Architecture-level design is not widely practiced and taught by computer industry experts.

Individuals and organizations can easily lose their architectural focus to external influences, such as marketing information from commercial software vendors. Due to their substantial marketing expenditures, commercial vendors are the dominant sources of information for users and developers. Not all, but some marketing information is biased, and much of the information contradicts information from other vendors. These contradictions are the source of much confusion for users and developers. Architectural focus is strictly a user/developer concern that vendors may address in product-specific ways.

Proprietary Lock-In

A widely accepted practice of commercial vendors and systems integrators is to build proprietary integration solutions among software components that they develop and sell. Virtually all office automation packages are integrated in this manner. We call this practice proprietary lock-in. Proprietary lock-in can be the result of a specific marketing strategy. More likely, it is the natural result of an isolated system design and development. By default, independently developed computing systems will lack interoperability and adaptability.

Proprietary lock-in inhibits system extension. System extensions are the most commonplace of software activities and the most expensive driver of software costs [Horowitz, 93]. Once an organization commits to a proprietary solution, it is very difficult to extend the system without the vendor's involvement. Most end-user organizations have very little control over software vendors; hence software costs are driven by external organizations that have no direct interest in minimizing software costs.

Adaptability is the key quality of a system designed to minimize software costs. Software architecture is the functional structure of the system that provides adaptability.

Good software architectures are based on only two types of design elements: things that are stable and things that can be controlled. Standards represent the stable technology elements. If a standard is actively supported by multiple vendors, then the standard is likely to be the most stable, lowest-risk technology choice, compared to any proprietary technology. Controllable design elements are those that are under the direct control of the user organization as well as system characteristics that can be changed inexpensively.

A key part of the problem is that very few end users have identified software architecture as a deliverable part of a computing system [Horowitz, 93]. Traditionally, the focus of system acquisition has been on predefined user interface requirements. Other types of requirements are difficult to verify except at the computer-user interface. Since software architecture is the internal structure of the system, user requirements have little or no relationship to software architecture. Without a deliverable software architecture, the end user invites an undocumented lock-in integration solution.

Large-volume end users are beginning to demand open systems compliance, including conformance to standards profiles. (See Chapter 2.) Standards groups such as the Object Management Group (OMG) are making excellent progress creating multivendor interoperability standards, but available standards are far from addressing all of the end user interoperability needs. Systems integration and software architecture are needed to fill the gap between available standards and end user interoperability needs.

Another way vendors enforce lock-in is through data formats. Many packages provide data format translators for importing data from competitor's packages but no corresponding filters for exporting data to other applications. Once the end user imports data into a lock-in application, it becomes effectively trapped in the vendor's proprietary data format.

As a least common denominator, plain ASCII text usually can be transferred between applications, with compromise of data quality, such as pictures and formats. A number of third-party vendors, such as KeyPack and BlueBerry, sell high-quality filter packages to support multivendor data interchange. A software architecture in the end-user system can leverage these technologies to mitigate the lack of export filters in some commercial packages. In addition to application lock-in, vendors may hamper interoperability through platform lock-in.

Although decreasingly common among UNIX vendors, platform lock-in is still an active practice among PC operating systems vendors. In effect, platform dependencies restrict portability of third-party software and end-user software to foreign platforms. Many vendors need to maintain several independent versions of their products. A common description of this problem is that vendors need to maintain one version for Microsoft Windows platforms and another version for the Macintosh, RISC, and other platforms.

The cost of maintaining software with proprietary platform application program interfaces (APIs) is prohibitive for most volume end users, who find these platform API's unsatisfactory as de facto standards because they are beyond their development resources to use effectively. This excess cost has two aspects: excess complexity and technology stability.

Complex proprietary APIs often require highly trained development staff to utilize them effectively. These skills are not directly transferable between open systems and proprietary platforms. Training of programmers can take several years, and maintaining this separate skill base is a prohibitive cost factor for volume end users.

A key element of technology instability is technology evolution. Technology evolution requires maintenance costs, such as product version upgrade, upgrading integration code, testing, training, help-desk support, and so forth. The maintenance costs are increased due to the continual technology evolution and obsolescence of proprietary technologies.

At the desktop level, there are likely to continue to be several incompatible APIs, including Macintosh, Microsoft Windows, Common Open System Environment (COSE), Common Desktop Environment (CDE), OPENSTEP, and Taligent. In heterogeneous environments, there is likely to be some need for platform-dependent custom software. In the section titled Advanced Architecture Pattern: Separation of Facilities on page 97, we describe an architecture strategy for minimizing the potential costs supporting those platform dependent APIs.

Inconsistencies between Design and Implementation

The traditional waterfall system development process comprises a top-down design process starting with end-user requirements. The waterfall concept is implicit in most formal system design processes. Regardless of whether the analysis and design methodology is based on structured programming, object orientation, or design patterns, many methodologies rely exclusively on top-down analysis of the application problem. Waterfall methodologies assume that the application problem can be fully understood before implementation begins. We believe that this is a fundamentally flawed assumption. Implementation experience is essential to the creation of good software architectures.

The application problem (derived from end-user requirements) and the technical problem (for the software architect) are different. When the integration of preexisting components is the dominant development paradigm, we have found that the essential understanding of the technical problem is gained during the integration process. It is very difficult to scope this type of effort because the implementation requirements do not become apparent until each subsystem is integrated. Project planning involves substantial guesswork. Project managers cope with this uncertainty by employing highly talented programmers who can bail out a project, regardless of the complexity that is discovered during implementation. In practice, lessons learned during integration seldom bubble up to the formal system design.

There is a basic disconnect between formal development methodologies and the informal process of system implementation. Due to their respective roles, managers and senior staff are engaged in the formal process while programmers conduct the informal process. The authors have participated in projects where there is minimal communicationbetween these formal and

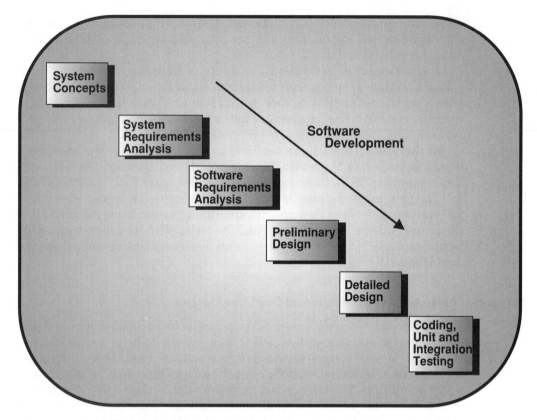

Figure 1.1. Traditional waterfall process.

informal processes, except for formal process documents that programmers are required to produce. Many programmers view the formal process as a burden and view their real task in the context of the informal process that produces the actual system implementation. Many managers are willing to relax conformance of the implementation to the formal specification in favor of successful implementation demonstrations.

Because the formal process appears to not provide substantive benefits to the informal process, senior staff and programmers have little motivation to maintain consistency between the design and the implementation. There is also a general lack of tools that can enforce consistency and reveal inconsistencies between implementation and architecture. At best, rigid conformance to formal methodologies is uncorrelated to project success, and there are many examples of projects where formal methodologies have had an adverse impact on project success [Coplien, 94]. What is needed is a balanced approach that can allow programmers the freedom to pursue informal integration processes within the context of a formal system architecture that is consistent with the implementation. Our guidance for this approach is summarized in Chapter 9. The balance of the book provides the details of the approach for software architects and developers.

Two non-waterfall-based methodologies include the *incremental development process* used in artificial intelligence and *Rapid Structured Prototyping* [Connell, 87]. These methodologies are called spiral development processes, in contrast to the waterfall-based processes.

Both methodologies recognize that the problem is poorly understood at the beginning of the project and that understanding of the problem grows as prototypes generate feedback from end users. The end-user involvement reduces overall project risk by giving the user experience with the new system and impacting the development process as it unfolds. The incremental development process involves knowledge gathering from a domain expert, the creation of a prototype knowledge base, and the refinement of the knowledge with end-user involvement. Rapid Structured Prototyping is a phased methodology where each phase defines system extensions, builds the extensions, and gathers end-user feedback. The process is iterated with each

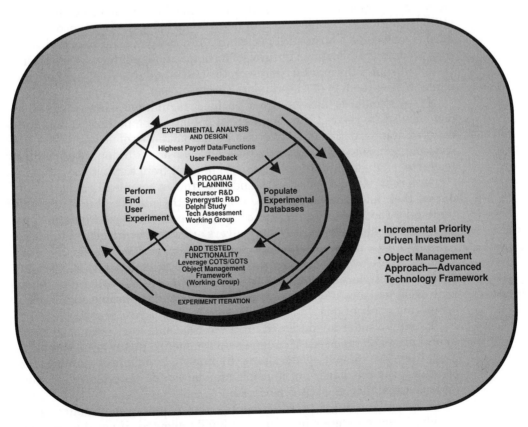

Figure 1.2. Spiral development.

experiment providing the planning for the next phase. Unfortunately, spiral processes do not produce system architectures as a natural outcome; nevertheless, they assume that programmers can reimplement and extend major features of the system at any time during the life cycle.

Standards Issues

Standards and the standards development process have been evolving over many years. Standards and their processes that precede OMG and CORBA have demonstrated some key strengths and weaknesses.

In general, standards hold out the promise of interoperability and component interchangeability. Current standards cover virtually every aspect of computer systems, and many organizations have compiled comprehensive profiles of standards that attempt to make some sense of the usage of standards in the context of system design. (See Chapter 2.)

Standards as a whole have not been effective in delivering the promised benefits of interoperability and interchangeability. Part of the reason is due to the organization of formal standards bodies. Formal standards are authored by representatives from profit-making industrial firms that have strong proprietary motivations. For many companies, the creation of a standard is viewed as a strategic opportunity. If a company can standardize its own product specifications in favor of a competitor's product specifications, then it can enter the market early with the first standards-compliant product while waving the flag of the standards organization.

Many standards play the role of business regulations—laws installed by one business to restrict the commerce of potential competitors. Excessively complex standards can effectively inhibit market entry of new products. For example, some have estimated that it would cost on the order of $100 million to create a standard relational database product from scratch.

In formal standards bodies, standards grow in complexity dramatically during their adoption process. One wonders if the size of a standard is only limited by the authors' ability to carry it. Large, complex standards have many technical loopholes. Various waivers are written into many standards to allow a wide range of compliant products. For most standards, there are products at all levels of compliance, and vendors can selectively support any part of the standards and ignore others. Compliance tests are useful, where they exist, but they do not cover the broad range of applicable standards in computing applications.

Even if standards addressed all these issues, a single standard is unlikely to meet all the needs of end-user environments. In any given standards area, there are competing standards. In order to build effective integration solutions, the coexistence of multiple standards and proprietary solutions for each capability must be considered.

A formal standards process requires four or more years; many formal standards are obsolete when they are finally adopted. Innovative vendors can easily outpace a formal standards process, providing significant new proprietary capabilities.

If traditional formal standards do not provide portability and interoperability, what is their purpose? One explanation is that standards play an essential role in establishing technology markets. A standard lends an air of credibility to a technology that translates into market growth. For example, without the Structured Query Language 1989 (SQL89) standard, supported from its inception by IBM, the relational database market would not have developed into the industry-dominating force that we know today. At both marketing and technical levels, standards reduce risk for both suppliers and consumers.

Prior to OMG, standards benefits were at the marketing level. For many consumers, the marketing level is equivalent to the political decision-making level. With OMG's focus on multi-language API specifications, OMG standards also potentially provide real technical benefits, such as interoperability and portability.

Lack of Tools for Creating Effective Abstractions

The creation of higher-level machine abstractions is a fundamental concept of computer science. For our purposes, an abstraction is a simplified interface that provides access to some underlying lower level mechanism. Programming languages are abstractions of the underlying machine code. Databases are abstractions of persistent storage. User interfaces are abstractions of computer programs. Abstractions are useful for managing complexity, and effective abstractions can reduce system cost by simplifying integration.

Object orientation is essentially an abstraction-building paradigm. A fundamental characteristic of objects is encapsulation, which is an abstraction for some combined unit of software and storage that hides internal data representations, algorithm choice, and other implementation details. At the level of systems integration, effective tools for creating abstractions are lacking with the possible exception of Object Management. As we discussed, system design and system implementation tend to diverge early in the life cycle. When the system design and the system implementation are completely separate descriptions, keeping the two in synchronization is a fundamental problem. Auditing of code and reverse engineering might reveal some consistency issues, but these techniques have not been widely applied in practice. Consider this question: What project manager would risk breaking a working system to enforce architecture consistency and would be willing to pay for it?

What we describe herein is an approach based on Object Management that addresses many of these issues. There is a machine verifiable relationship between the software architecture and the system implementation. To create highly effective abstractions of complex system components (so-called black box abstractions), an implementation-independent way to specify these abstractions is needed, such as that provided by the OMG's Interface Definition Language (IDL).

Lack of Security Facilities

Security is a pervasive issue in computing systems. The importance of security is exacerbated by the popularity of networking, since networking enables large groups to access vulnerable computing resources. For example, security is a critical issue on the current Internet because network hackers have penetrated and disrupted many systems that are directly connected, including systems containing vital operational functions, such as payroll or classified data.

Security is a requirement that most end users acknowledge, but few organizations are able to realize any workable solutions. Computer security in a networked interoperable environment involves both horizontal and vertical issues. Security must be enforced pervasively across all services and communication interfaces (horizontal). Security also must apply to every level of the system, from the applications down to the core of the operating system kernel. In practice, computer security is very difficult to achieve, short of complete system isolation.

Commercially available security technology is lacking. Technologies such as Remote Procedure Call (RPC) based Security Service are useful but only a partial solution. Effective solutions must be enforced pervasively across every type of integration technology, not just distributed RPC. Security technologies, such as special-purpose operating systems and Compartmented Mode Workstations, have never achieved the expected commercial success.

We believe that CORBA provides new opportunity for the creation of secure software architectures and commercially viable security technologies. Chapter 5 contains a discussion of computer security, including issues, standards activities, and security architecture approaches.

HETEROGENEOUS SYSTEMS INTEGRATION

Systems integration is an increasingly important discipline. As software technology continues to evolve, there is a growing trend toward the construction of systems from preexisting components. This trend is due in a large part to readily available high-quality commercial software packages that perform most major functions in today's information systems. In the 1970s, complex software systems were configured almost exclusively from custom software components, with the exception of perhaps a major component, such as a commercial database package. In the 1980s, the availability of bitmapped graphics workstations led to the development of all-in-one software packages so that complex systems could be configured around a major package, such as a Geographic Information System (GIS) or a document processing system. Other components were custom integrated as needed. In these systems, there remained a gap in interoperability from the end users' perspective; the system integrator's role was to provide a level of interoperability for the end user that was unavailable in the off-the-shelf software packages.

Users' expectations for interoperability have increased dramatically, due to the readily available highly interoperable platforms such as Microsoft Windows and Apple Macintosh. Unfortunately, vendor-specific solutions do not solve today's heterogeneous systems integration challenges. Information systems are increasingly heterogeneous; it is rare to find any organization with a monolithic computing base (all users on the same platform). Increasingly, an organization's interoperability needs span its customers' and suppliers' networked offices. Heterogeneity will increase as software becomes more portable and the role of computing becomes ubiquitous, with computing resources ranging from wireless notepads to massively parallel super computers.

Vision for Systems Integration

Ideally, systems integration should be as simple as plugging together a home audio system. In practice, it is a challenging activity and rarely results in a good software architecture. Systems integrators face problems with, among other things, different

- Hardware platforms
- Software languages
- Compiler versions
- Data access mechanisms
- Component/module interfaces
- Networking protocols

Custom integration approaches usually yield point-to-point integration solutions, and the system becomes difficult to extend due to the complexity and brittleness of the solution.

Our vision for systems integration is founded on the need for system adaptability through the system life cycle. In this book, we introduce software architectures (integration frameworks) as the core concept for realizing adaptability. We use the terms architecture and framework interchangeably.

Common interfaces is a key property of good software architectures. Ideally, the same common interfaces are supported by custom components and commercial software. Unfortunately, commercial interfaces are not always the most appropriate solutions; they may mismatch the cost, complexity, portability, or stability needs of the application system. The role of the soft-

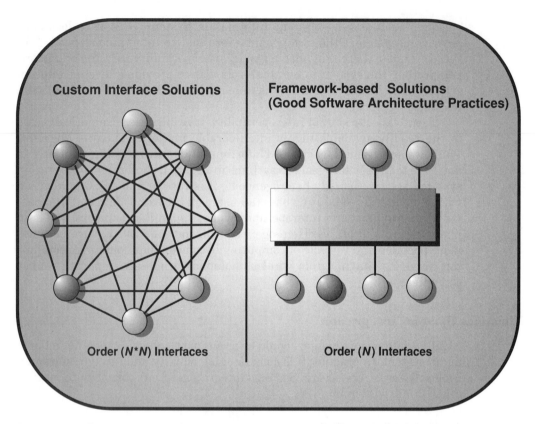

Figure 1.3. Custom interfaces vs. framework based.

ware architecture is to provide the right system-specific abstraction that can be interoperable with commercial interfaces.

The framework should conform to the object-oriented paradigm, for some practical reasons. For example, the object paradigm provides encapsulation that enhances component isolation. Object orientation supports design reuse through inheritance. Polymorphism supports component interchangeability. Object Management is a particularly appropriate technology for implementation of these concepts, although simply practicing these principles alone can yield measurable benefits. All of the characteristics of the object paradigm are potentially beneficial, but the realization of these benefits is closely tied to the design of the software architecture.

In this book, we emphasize that architectures should exploit methodology paradigms (such as structured programming, object-oriented analysis and design) instead of being driven by them. Methodologies are perhaps the fastest changing of any aspect of technology, and methodologies will go through many generations during a system life cycle. Good architectures must transcend ephemeral methodologies in order to provide their benefits consistently during the system life cycle.

In the implementation of an architecture, all the software subsystems support the integration framework. A layer of integration code called an object wrapper may be added to preexisting modules to provide the mapping between framework operations and application operations. A well-designed framework will require a minimum of integration code in this layer.

Adaptability comes from the ability to modify or add modules without having to modify the other components or their integration solutions. The system should be self-describing, containing sufficient metadata so that new subsystems can be discovered dynamically by preexisting subsystems. Semantic and data format translations should be layered into the system at the level of the integration framework, not tightly integrated to individual applications. These mappings can be installed incrementally as part of the system evolution, ensuring that legacy interfaces will be maintained as the system evolves and providing a graceful evolution path from initial prototypes throughout the system life cycle. Legacy systems provide a special integration challenge since they often are closed and may provide no access API or documentation. In Chapter 8 we present various object-wrapping techniques and examples that can be used during the system's migration and integration with other legacy or new systems.

THE ROLE OF CORBA

Interoperability between applications presents similar problems to that of interoperability between systems, just at a different scale and layer. Many advancements have been made in the area of systems integration and global networking.

Today communication networking capabilities are widely available between systems. Communication networks, phone lines, cables, and fiber are available; the necessary hardware also is available to connect systems to local area or wide area networks, hubs, and switches.

We also have well-defined protocols that allow systems to communicate by agreeing to certain standards that will be used. The Open Systems Interconnection (OSI) 7 layer model provides the definition of each layer and the services that it must perform.

The lowest layer, the *Physical* layer, describes how the physical network is accessed. The *Data Link* layer is concerned with reliable transmission across a physical link. The *Network* layer deals with connection establishment and routing. The *Transport* layer deals with reliable end-to-end transmission. The *Session* layer provides connection control. The *Presentation* layer is concerned with data syntax and transparency to the applications. Finally, the upper layer, the *Application* layer, provides end-user functional-

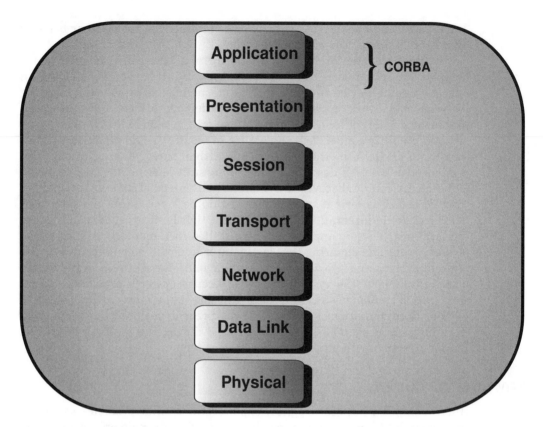

Figure 1.4. OSI 7 layer model.

ity. Much research also has been conducted in the area of security to provide the protection of data and to provide privacy and data integrity.

CORBA represents the next generation of client-server facilities that provide highly distributed systems and applications. Conceptually, CORBA sits in the application layer.

CORBA insulates the client and actually the programmers from the distributed heterogeneous characteristics of the information system.

- OMG IDL provides an operating system and programming language independent interface.
- Due to this higher level of abstraction, the programmer does not have to be concerned with the lower layer protocols.
- The programmer does not have to be concerned with the server location or activation state.
- The programmer does not have to be concerned with the server host hardware or operating system.

- Certain integration issues are simplified; for example, no longer does a client or server have to be concerned with byte ordering of data when transferring data between different platforms.

The Object Request Broker (ORB) provides a seamless infrastructure for distributed communication across heterogeneous systems. OMG IDL provides a common language and syntax for client and server access. A remaining issue is the selection of APIs used between applications. Technology has provided excellent connectivity between hardware platforms, but there is no analogous interoperability at the level of application functionality and application data interchange. CORBA paves the way for component object systems. A system builder should be able to select objects from several vendors and connect them as easily as we connect audio components at home today.

If commercial objects use OMG IDL interfaces and are otherwise CORBA compliant, we are a step closer to integrating the applications. CORBA enables objects to discover each other at runtime and invoke each other's services. Standardized APIs provide another level of interoperability. OMG has a growing set of API standards, called Object Services and Common Facilities. (See Chapter 3.) The Object Service definitions cover fundamental APIs, and the Common Facilities provide higher-level API standards.

Another level of specialization beyond standardized APIs addresses the interoperability needs of individual application systems. In the OMG architecture, these are called application objects. Systems integration concerns the design, implementation, and integration of application objects.

In this book, we describe the system-level design of these objects, which we call software architectures and frameworks (Chapter 4). We provide many important examples of architectures and frameworks (Chapters 6 and 7). We also describe how to implement these system-level designs given preexisting components, a practice that we call object wrapping (Chapter 8).

COMMENTS

This book is divided into two parts. Part I comprises Chapters 1 through 5 and covers the principles of systems integration. Here we present the concepts on which we have based our approach to the integration problems at hand. Chapter 2 covers strategies for using standards effectively through technical reference models and standards profiles. Chapter 3 presents a detailed introduction to CORBA and related standards. Design approaches for designing architectures and frameworks are covered in Chapter 4. We conclude Part I with an introduction to security problems and concepts (Chapter 5), and we discuss security issues as they relate to the CORBA distributed architecture.

Part II, comprised of Chapters 6 through 9, presents detailed integration examples, lessons learned and various integration methods used in different situations. Chapter 6 provides framework examples from the commercial world. Chapter 7 contains a detailed example of a desktop-independent and platform-independent interoperability framework developed using our approach. Chapter 8 discusses various object-wrapping techniques and gives program examples. Chapter 9 provides guidance both to managers and developers on using CORBA and system architecture. The appendix contains summary descriptions of key CORBA products.

2

Standards
Strategy

In order to design a successful, long-lived software architecture, software engineers must have an understanding of standards. Selecting and implementing a standards strategy is the first step in our systems integration approach.

A standards strategy is a plan for how to develop and evolve information systems toward support for open systems standards and strategic standards creation. Standards strategies can have multiple levels, including reference models across multiple projects and project-specific standards profiles.

A key part of the standards strategy is a guidance document, called a standards profile, that influences choices of information system components based on their support for the right standards. As systems evolve, through component upgrades, extensions, and error correction, the standards profile identifies the standards objectives of the future system and guides the migration toward a goal architecture. Another key part of a standards strategy involves the development of new specifications, which are a part of the development of any new system or system extension. The organization must consider the role that these specifications play in a larger community context.

In essence, a standards strategy involves making sense out of the complex, dynamic arena of open systems standards and exploiting standards activities as opportunities to save costs and realize organizational goals. The cost of implementing the standards strategy can be highly leveraged by exploiting readily available information and harmonizing the organization's standards initiatives with emerging trends.

STANDARDS BACKGROUND

Historically, suppliers have been the key drivers of standards processes. For example, the fundamental concept behind "open systems" is standards. Most open systems standards have portability as their primary objective. This goal is motivated by a traditional view of the computing industry as driven by hardware suppliers; narrowly defined, portability means independence from particular hardware suppliers. An expanded view of portability also considers the full range of software APIs, such as operating systems, windowing interfaces, and higher level services.

The industry is experiencing some important new trends in the standards arena. There is a growing awareness of the need for areas of cooperation between organizations through standards because standards create markets for products. We are seeing the creation of many new industry alliances, consortia, and special interest groups that are forums for standardization. We are also seeing many strong alliances between major standards groups, such as the Common Open Software Environment (COSE) with the Open Software Foundation (OSF) and the Object Management Group (OMG) with X/Open, the International Standards Organization Open Distributed Processing (ISO ODP), X/Consortium, and so forth. End users are playing an increasing role in standardization, primarily in high leverage vertical market areas. The OMG is the only consortium defining standards for distributed systems based on Object Management technology. (See Chapter 3 for more details on the OMG.) OMG has done much to fuel these trends by streamlining the standardization process and making standardization much more accessible. Interoperability is an important standards goal that is a key focus of the OMG.

The establishment of a standard enhances the credibility of a technical specification, reduces risks for clients and implementors of the interface, and enables reuse. The scope of the standard defines the scope of reuse. Probably the smallest useful scope of reuse is across a multiproject organization. This is a minimal organizational scope to consider when designing software architectures. (See Section Basic Architecture Patterns.) If we extend the scope across company boundaries, we can characterize the standards as applicable to a vertical or specialty market. Countless specialty market alliances and consortia groups provide forums for these standards. Standards at the specialty market level and larger scopes are essential for establishing commercial software markets. The standard becomes the common, stable element that reduces risks and provides technical benefits to both suppliers and consumers.

The OMG has reengineered the business process for standards creation and made it much more feasible to create new standards to fill gaps in specialty markets. (See Chapter 3.)

We can think of standards as the product of an organizational process promoting reusability, stability, reduced risk, and interoperability. Standards may take on different levels of formality, depending on our goals and strategy. The process of standards creation is an extension of system design and development. The standards process differs principally in the intended scope of impact. Whereas an ad hoc integration may solve an interoperability problem between two specific subsystems, an integration standard might be a reusable solution across a project, organization, industry, or larger context. Management is responsible for defining the standards context of a new specification and establishing the intended standards role in the target community.

From a traditional perspective, there are three principal types of standards: formal standards, de jure standards, and de facto standards. Formal standards are specifications that are formally adopted by accredited standards bodies such as the Institute of Electrical and Electronics Engineers (IEEE), the Consultative Committee International Telecommunications (CCITT), the American National Standards Institute (ANSI), and the International Standards Organization (ISO). There is a hierarchical relationship between national standards groups such as ANSI (for the United States) and ISO (encompassing an international community of national standards groups). De jure standards are those mandated by legal authorities. Federal Information Processing Standards (FIPS) are an example; these are standards approved by the United States for use in government information systems. In another example, a company can select and mandate de jure standards for its own organization. De facto standards are informal standards resulting from popular usage. X Windows and Network File Server are examples of de facto standards that became established through popular usage. Dominant vendors and vendor alliances frequently establish interfaces that become de facto standards through usage.

Standards are a broad category of specifications that encompass a great deal more than just the approved releases of formal standards organizations. Some standards are established by other forms of standards groups, such as industry consortia. In the past, de facto standards could be established by a single dominant company; today, multivendor support is essential for establishing de facto standards. De facto standards can also be established through informal means, for example, by popular usage.

In this chapter, our definition of the term standard is broad and closely related to software reuse. Standards are recognized technical agreements between people or organizations. The constituency of the group defines the appropriate forum for standardization. It may be effective for informal standards to be established across a single organization or project. Standards that are international in scope should be addressed in international forums, such as ISO, X/Open, and the OMG. Informal standards can be established at any organizational level between these extremes. It is simply a question of the appropriate organizational forum recognizing the specification at its standard. If the right forum does not exist, many groups have created new organizations explicitly for this purpose.

Some vendor alliances that create standards include X/Open, the OMG, the X Consortia, the OSF, the COSE alliance, and the Open GIS Foundation (OGF).

BENEFITS OF STANDARDIZATION

Some of the key benefits that standards provide include:

- *Portability.* Standards can provide portability of software between hardware and operating systems platforms, windowing systems, networking protocols, and a variety of other hardware and systems dependencies. The benefit is the ability to move and access software among multiple platforms in a heterogeneous environment. Portability also can support transparent upgrade of underlying hardware and networks.
- *Interoperability.* Standards define common formats and interface conventions that provide interoperability between software systems. Interoperability benefits might include data interchange, event notification, object embedding, application control, browsing, and others.
- *Risk reduction.* Use of standards is an essential approach that frees software architectures from implementation-specific dependencies. Use of standards can facilitate multisource alternative components, which reduces risks in system development, maintenance, and future system extensibility.
- *Interchangeability.* Standards promote product and subsystem interchangeability. Interchangeability can be used in several ways. It can be used to allow a wider choice of system components, selection of which may optimize cost, legacy leverage, performance, or other factors. And interchangeability can support deployment of multiple system versions, customized to site-specific user requirements. In addition, interchangeability supports system upgrade, as commercial and proprietary technologies evolve.
- *Cost reduction.* Commercial support of standards and their subsequent use for system integration implies a cost reduction for the end user. Commercial vendor's support of standards results in economy of scale. Cost reduction also can be realized through competition between alternative vendors conforming to the same standard.
- *Deferred obsolescence / Life cycle extension.* Conformance to standards can reduce the risk of system obsolescence. Standards can be used as a hedge against obsolescence, since many standards represent the most stable technology interfaces, which in most cases are supported continuously as technology evolves into upwardly compatible products.

As systems become more complex, standards become increasingly important. Standards provide one of the most accessible ways of assuring component compatibility.

SELECTING A STANDARDS STRATEGY

Available standards are quite numerous and individually complex. A strategy is needed to manage this complexity and diversity. Thousands of potentially applicable standards exist to cover the issues in most application systems. An effective standards strategy involves careful selection of standards among the many alternatives and selective use of parts of individual standards. After the selection, typical organizational standards profiles involve about 300 standards. Evaluating standards can be a complex and expensive task. The costs of strategy selection and implementation can be minimized by leveraging the efforts of standards groups and other organizations.

Application of a standard is not a simplistic decision. Most standards need to be utilized thoughtfully in order to yield their benefits. For example, most standards are very complex, and this complexity needs to be abstracted or subsetted in order to expose the desired functionality at the desired implementation cost. Standards also are designed for general applicability for multiple applications; many details must be added to the standard in order to make it useful within an application. For example, most standards are more general purpose and do not include any predefined data or metadata schemas (the schema is usually an application-specific profile); these schemas must be added to make use of the standard in the application system.

There are five potential goals to consider for your standards strategy.

Reducing Dependence on Custom Software   A key goal of a standards strategy involves the migration of high-cost custom software functionality into low-cost-commodity commercial software functionality. For most organizations, this goal cannot be realized overnight; it involves a longer-term strategy to evolve system interfaces toward replaceable software components provided by commercial vendors. We can think of custom software playing several roles.

Custom software for systems integration fills interoperability gaps not supported directly by commercial packages. For example, we might need custom software to automate the process of moving data between two application programs. Originally, the custom software may have eliminated some rekeying and data entry operations, but as the system evolves and programming staff turns over, custom software can become a maintenance burden. As the system evolves, we can add support for standards in the application systems, which can ease the data transfer problem between the systems.

Custom software for applications might entail functions that are fully replaceable with commercially developed software, such as databases. Other custom applications, such as user interfaces, might be migrated to commercial application generators, which could reduce the cost of system modifications and new user interface development. The standards strategy provides the guidance and rationale to architects and developers for making these choices.

Leverage Current and Future Commercial Technology   The standards strategy should identify commercial technology trends and place the organization in position to exploit support for standards as they become available. An important part of every standards strategy is knowing the mapping between commercial support to standards and predicting where commercial support is evolving.

Synergy with Standards Groups   Standards activities are long-term public processes. Ascertaining their direction and predicting their progress is relatively easy to do by attending meetings, reading about them in the press, reviewing their publications, or talking to representatives. A highly effective standards strategy involves exploiting the products that the standards groups are producing as well as positioning internal development efforts to leverage emerging standards. Such products include:

- Reference implementations
- Vendor product disclosures
- White papers
- Plans and road maps
- Architecture

Your organization may be able to exploit some plans or preliminary specifications that standards groups will produce in the course of their process. Alternatively, your organization may be pursuing designs that you may consider proposing for standardization. A middle-ground strategy consists of designing architectures to accommodate emerging standards, instead of waiting for final approval.

Influencing Industry and Organizations   A benefit of an effective standards strategy is the influence that the strategy asserts on commercial developers and other organizations. When a well-conceived strategy is explained clearly, it has significant impact on whoever is exposed to it. In our experience, we have noted positive changes in the product directions of many commercial firms after exposure to our standards approach. Many of the standards and technology issues that we identify are shared by other consumer organizations. Every time an issue is raised or concern is expressed about standards compliance, it has a measurable influence on suppliers. When many organizations are voicing their concerns, common themes emerge that raise the priorities for change. In a sense, each organization can play an activist role in shaping the standards strategies of other organizations. There are also direct ways of catalyzing technical change, such as reference technologies.

Reference Technologies   If your organization is interested in establishing or promoting a new standard, an effective standards strategy involves developing reference technologies. If an implementation of the proposed standard that leverages support across a community can be built and disseminated, then it's adoption is greatly accelerated. Some successful examples of this strategy include X Windows, MOTIF, and Network File Server (NFS). In each case, technology access was provided either free or for a nominal fee, so that the technology could be transferred as rapidly as possible. The Internet greatly enables this kind of technology transfer, because it provides "free" electronic dissemination of software and "free" advertisements of software availability through bulletin boards and e-mail lists. Reference technologies can be built by individual companies, by academic institutions, by the government, and by consortia.

STANDARDS REFERENCE MODELS AND PROFILES

Because so many standards apply to computer systems, various well-organized lists of standards and rationale have been compiled as technical reference models and standards profiles. A technical reference model is a standards guideline for multiple computer application systems. A standards profile is a specific set of standards, which may apply to a particular computing system. Whereas a technical reference model will identify multiple alternative standards for each category, a standards profile will provide limited standards choices.

New standards reference models and profiles can be based on work that is already available. For example, IEEE Portable Open Systems X (POSIX) is a standards reference model that is generic enough to be a baseline reference model for most application domains. Tailored reference models are often extensions of generic reference models.

The X/Open Portability Guide (XPG) is a standards profile. XPG identifies specific standards choices for generic applications systems. X/Open goes further in certifying compliance of products and licensing a brand seal to products that meet XPG guidelines.

Regarding standards reference models, we believe that your organization should publish one and that it should be consulted as a normal part of decision making during computer system design, component selection, system extension, and purchases of commercial software. Creating your own standards reference model can be relatively inexpensive, given that multiple generic models exist. You must ask how your organization's application domain differs from the generic model and focus your attentions on adding more detail to the generic models in those areas.

Technical reference models and profiles should be used as guidelines, not rigid regulations. Rigorous standards compliance can be very costly, and a decision maker should balance the model's guidance with practical considerations. For example, if a function can be procured much cheaper or faster or with less risk without strict compliance, then it is wise to disregard the standards model; however, the rationale for this deviation should be documented and revisited later when the system is upgraded.

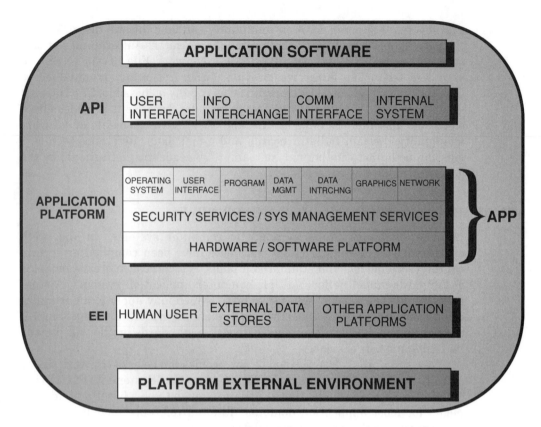

Figure 2.1. NIST Application portability profile (APP).

Another aspect of these models is that they need to be updated regularly. A standards model portrays a snapshot of a changing standards picture. The standards themselves can change or be replaced, such as when ISO adopted Structured Query Language 1992 (SQL92) to replace SQL89. Evaluating industry support for a standard is very important, and the situation can change as the market changes. Indirect changes occur when standards are added or deleted from XPG or POSIX that can have an affect on industry and standards support. Typically, these types of changes occur to one-third of the standards every year. This indicted that new standards are being introduced frequently, but does not impact the stability of individual standards.

IMPLEMENTING A STANDARDS STRATEGY

If utilized inappropriately, standards can increase costs in system development dramatically. In practice, only a handful of standards will have a direct impact on software development. In particular, major standards relating to the operating system, windowing system, and networking interface are the most critical. Many other standards are useful only as general guidelines, and their importance is quite subjective.

It is important to have a standards strategy and to leverage ongoing standards activities, particularly those that are attempting to catalogue the overall environment, those that directly impact software development, and those that impact your organization's specialty areas. This strategy starts with the selection of a generic profile, such as POSIX or X/Open XPG4. Then the particular specialty areas that are not adequately addressed by the generic profiles need to be identified. The profile should include expanded detail in these high-priority areas. Technology road-mapping is a useful exercise with respect to the specialty areas—for example, prediction of future industry trends based on past technology evolution and high-potential research. Any standards gaps that are identified should become strategic targets for the creation of organization-level standards, with future potential standardization in larger forums.

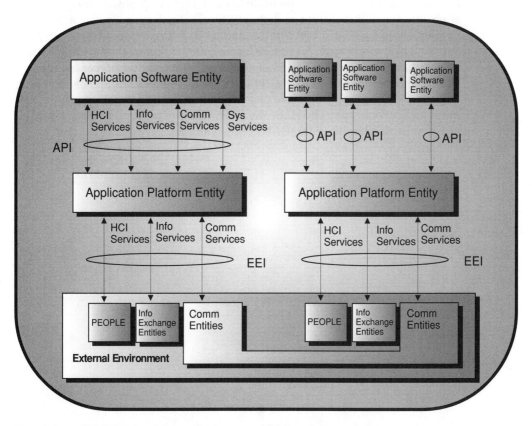

Figure 2.2. POSIX Open System Environment (OSE) reference model.

It is important to evaluate the reality of each standard and to assess what the real advantages are of its utilization. Detailed guidelines for utilization of key standards should be documented.

Standards creation and revision is a dynamic process that must be tracked. As much as a third of a comprehensive standards profile can change in the course of a year.

Standards are important to overall decision-making and development practices. Standards represent the long-term multiparty technology agreements that are the stable basis for software architectures and life cycle support.

COMMENTS

Weighing short-term needs against long-term needs is one of the most difficult problems that an organization faces. Often, decisions are based only on currently available technology and standards. While an organization may be able to answer some of its immediate needs using available market products, such decision making could be detrimental. Technology is moving at such an accelerated pace that often what is available today is already outdated by the time it is integrated. An organization must look into the future to determine its long-term needs and plan ahead using a combination of technology that is available today and a collection of emerging new standards. By using reference technologies for these new standards, an organization can experiment and collect experience that would enable it to position itself to leverage new products when they finally become available.

3

An Introduction to CORBA

Every major new distributed computing technology has held out the promise of interoperability between disparate systems and applications. Today connectivity between most types of operating systems platforms is readily available. However, interoperability at the application level remains elusive. Key factors include the inherent difficulty of distributed application programming and the lack of standard interfaces between applications. Since its introduction ten years ago, remote procedure call (RPC) technology has generated few popular interfaces, with Network File Server being perhaps the only widely used RPC interface definition.

The Object Management Group (OMG) is an industry consortium whose mission is to define a set of interfaces for interoperable software. Its first specification, the Common Object Request Broker Architecture (CORBA), is an industry consensus standard that defines a higher-level facility for distributed computing. CORBA simplifies distributed systems software in several ways. The distributed environment is defined using an object-oriented paradigm that hides all differences between programming languages, operating systems, and object location. CORBA's object-oriented approach enables diverse types of implementations to interoperate at the same level, hiding idiosyncrasies and supporting reuse. This interoperability is accomplished through well-defined interface specifications at the application level. CORBA provides a portable notation for defining interfaces called the OMG Interface Definition Language (IDL). The OMG participants are defining a comprehensive set of standard OMG IDL interfaces called object services and common facilities. Whereas CORBA simplifies the distributed software environment, object services and common facilities address the need for interface standards supporting application-level interoperability.

OBJECT MANAGEMENT ARCHITECTURE

The OMG's object management architecture is defined in a reference book which we highly recommend [OMG, 93]. The central component of the architecture is the object request broker (ORB). The ORB functions as a communication infrastructure, transparently relaying object requests across distributed heterogeneous computing environments. The CORBA specification covers all the standard interfaces for ORBs. Common facilities are the set of shared high-level services, such as printing and e-mail. Object services are a shared set of lower-level services, such as object creation and event notification. Application objects comprise all the remaining software including developer's programs, commercial applications, and legacy systems.

Much of the OMG standards activities centers around the three architecture areas: ORB, object services, and common facilities. CORBA Version 1.1, covering ORBs, was adopted in December 1991 [OMG, 92a]. The CORBA revision process comprises upwardly compatible extensions. CORBA Version

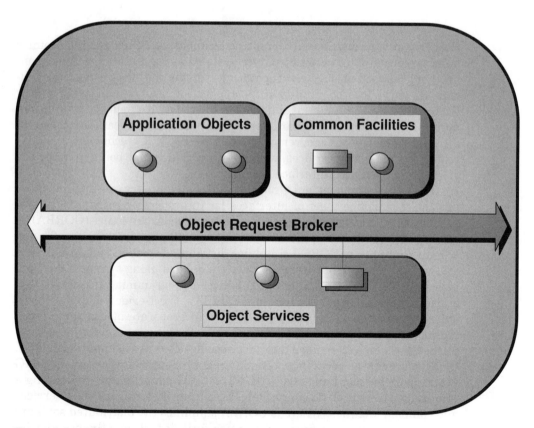

Figure 3.1.   Object management architecture.

1.2, primarily a typographical revision, was adopted in June 1994. Extensions to CORBA, under the umbrella of CORBA 2.0, include ORB interoperability and further specification of the Interface Repository. Future CORBA 2.0 activities include additional language bindings such as Ada, Cobol, and Smalltalk. Approved object services specifications include event notification, object naming, and object life cycles. The OMG has released a comprehensive road-map schedule for the adoption of additional object services [OMG, 92b]. The adoption process for common facilities is under way. Whereas object services are fundamental enabling service specifications, common facilities are high-level service specifications that will provide high leverage to application developers.

Object services and common facilities supply interfaces for application-to-application interoperability as well as commercially supplied services. These standard interfaces have a dual role: Suppliers may supply implementations of standard services, but application developers also can reuse standard interfaces.

OBJECT REQUEST BROKER

CORBA is a specification for an application-level communication infrastructure. It provides communication facilities to applications through two mechanisms: static interfaces and the Dynamic Invocation Interface (DII). An Interface Repository stores on-line descriptions of known OMG IDL interfaces. Any interface can be used with either mechanism. The Basic Object Adapter (BOA) is an initial set of ORB interfaces for object implementations. CORBA also specifies a set of basic system objects, such as general purpose name-value lists.

CORBA is a peer-to-peer distributed computing facility where all applications are objects (in the sense of object orientation). Objects can alternate between client roles and server roles. An object is in a client role when it is the originator of an object invocation. An object is in a server role when it is the recipient of an object invocation. Server objects are called *object implementations*. Most objects probably will play both roles. More flexible architectures can be implemented using CORBA rather than the pure client-server architectures imposed by remote procedure calls.

Interface Definition Language

OMG IDL is a technology-independent syntax for describing object encapsulations. When used in software architectures, OMG IDL is the universal notation for defining software boundaries. In OMG IDL, interfaces that have attributes and operation signatures can be defined. OMG IDL supports inheritance between interface descriptions in order to facilitate reuse. Its specifications are compiled into header files and stub programs for direct use by developers. The mapping from OMG IDL to any programming language could potentially be supported. Vendors have implemented mappings to many languages, such as C, C++, and Smalltalk. OMG IDL mappings to many other languages are under construction. OMG IDL compilers are bundled with ORB products and allow programmers to define portable compiler-checked interfaces.

In addition to header files, the OMG IDL compiler generates stub and skeleton programs for each interface. The client program links directly to the OMG IDL stub. From the client's perspective, the stub acts like a local function call. Transparently, the stub provides an interface to the ORB that performs marshalling to encode and decode the operation's parameters into communication formats suitable for transmission. The OMG IDL skeleton program is the corresponding server-side implementation of the OMG IDL interface. When the ORB receives the request, the skeleton provides a callback to a server-supplied function implementation. When the server completes processing of the request, the skeleton and stub return the results

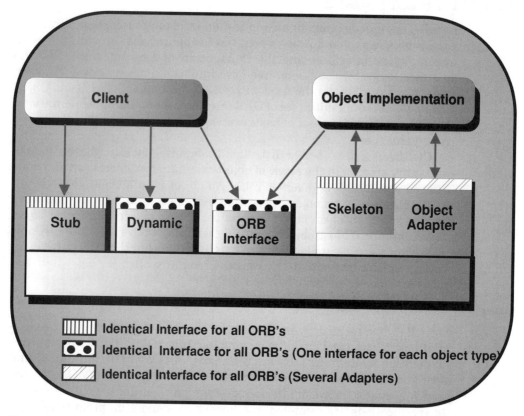

Figure 3.2. CORBA interfaces.

to the client program, along with any exception information. Exceptions can be generated by the server or by the ORB in case of errors.

The OMG IDL language is defined in CORBA Chapter 4 and the C language mapping is defined in CORBA Chapter 5. [OMG, 92a] The following is an example of OMG IDL and its mapping to the C language. This OMG IDL specification is for an interface with one operation. The interface name is example1, and the operation name is operation1. This operation has one user-defined parameter, param1. It also has clauses specifying a user-defined exception and a context expression.

```
// OMG IDL
exception USER_EXCEPTION1 { string explanation1; };
interface example1 {
    void operation1(inout long param1)
        raises (USER_EXCEPTION1)
        context( "CLIENT_CONTEXT1"); };
```

The corresponding C language mapping follows. The user-defined exception is mapped into a struct. The interface itself is a renamed type of CORBA-type Object. In the function prototype, the operation name is concatenated to the interface name with an underscore. This naming convention indicates the scoping of the names from the OMG IDL. The first three parameters are implicit parameters generated by the OMG IDL compiler. The first parameter is the implementation object handle; this indicates the destination object implementation for the example_operation1 message. The second parameter is the Environment parameter, which is an exception value returned to the client. The exception may be generated by the object implementation or the ORB to indicate operation failure. In addition to the user exception defined in the example, CORBA provides a comprehensive set of predefined exceptions [OMG, 92a]. The Context parameter is a set of attribute values specified by the client for usage by the ORB and object implementation. In general, these are a set of string values, associated with the attribute names in the context clause of the OMG IDL specification. Context is useful for the application programmer in order to pass default information about the client's environment. Following the implicit parameters is the list of user-defined parameters. For C, there is a complex set of conventions for how these parameters are passed, depending on whether the parameter is in, inout, or out and on the parameter's type.

```
/*  C Mapping */
typedef struct { char *explanation1; } USER_EXCEPTION1;
typecode Object example1;
void example1_operation1(
    example1 o,
    environment *ev,
    Context *ctx,
    long *param1);
```

The OMG IDL specification contains more documentation for the object interfaces. The header files and stub codes generated by the OMG IDL compilers are somewhat cryptic in comparison. For example, all of the following OMG IDL constructs are mapped into C struct definitions: OMG IDL structs, exception values, and union types. In addition, most OMG IDL compilers do not pass through the OMG IDL's comments. Programmers should use the OMG IDL for comprehension of the interfaces and use the compiler-generated header files as a reference for parameter handling and naming conventions.

Other OMG IDL language mappings appear quite different from the C mapping. Although the renaming of type Object does not seem to be an important factor in C, the specialization of type Object is an important factor in object-oriented languages such as C++ and CLOS, which depend on object type specialization in their runtime binding algorithms. The mapping to object-oriented languages is quite natural from OMG IDL, and the header files generally include native object class definitions corresponding to the OMG IDL interfaces.

Implementing OMG IDL Specifications

The standard specification defining OMG IDL is only 35 pages long [OMG, 92a], but it has a fundamental importance analogous to Backus-Naur Form (BNF). Like BNF, OMG IDL is a specification language. Where BNF is universally used to specify new language grammars, OMG IDL is universally applicable to the specification of APIs.

OMG IDL can be used in several ways: as built-in library interfaces, ORB interfaces, or RPC interfaces. An OMG IDL interface does not have to be used with an ORB product, or vice-versa. OMG IDL can be used separate from the balance of the CORBA specification, as a notation for specifying APIs implemented with CORBA and non-CORBA technologies.

In the built-in library interface case, OMG IDL provides the advantage of an implementation-free interface (Figure 3.3). However, the application is not distributed. The client and server are compiled and linked in as a single program. The ORB or RPC mechanism provides system distribution. The client still makes a local function call. However, the stub call is sent via the ORB or RPC to the remote skeleton function that in turn activates the server implementation (Figure 3.4).

IDL is language independent and supports multiple language mappings. Several mappings are already standardized by OMG: C, C++, and Smalltalk. When IDL is mapped into a programming language, for example, C, three arguments are generated automatically and the rest are user-defined parameters. These implicit parameters are the object handle, the environment, and the context (Figure 3.5).

The object handle specifies the handle of the server that is to be activated. The Context can contain system- or user-specific properties that can

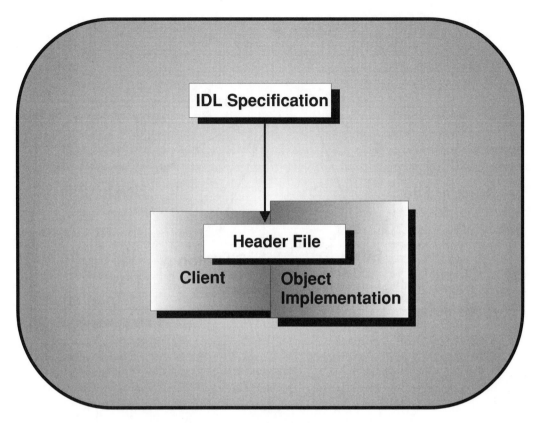

Figure 3.3.   Built-in library interface: same compilation module.

impact ORB decisions or information for the server, such as window system preference, that may not be suitable for argument passing. Context
objects contain a list of properties that consist of a name and a string value.
Like environment variables, the properties represent information about the
client, environment, or information about a request that can be passed as
parameters [OMG, 92a].

Clients can pass this information to the server, which in turn can query
about them. The information can be used for policy and binding decisions.
Context objects may be chained. CORBA defines operations for creating,
deleting, setting values, and getting values of properties.

The environment variable is provided to return exception information.
The environment type is partially opaque and includes a major error type,
minor code, and error identification string components. The major error
type indicates whether an exception occurred, a system exception occurred,
or a user exception was set. The minor code is a value that identifies the
particular exception in a form easily utilized by programmers in a case
statement. The identification string is a human-readable explanation of the

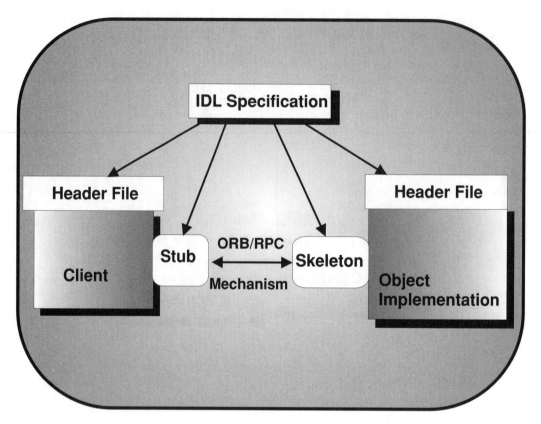

Figure 3.4. ORB or RPC mechanism.

error. CORBA defines a comprehensive set of standard exception types that can be returned by the ORB and by application object implementations. The predefined exceptions should be used wherever applicable.

For special exceptions unique to a particular architecture, user exceptions can be readily defined in OMG IDL. User exceptions contain the basic environment attributes, and user-defined properties can be added to the exception structure. Exception handling is an important aspect of software architecture specification that is well supported by OMG IDL.

Dynamic Invocation Interface

Early ORB products were based almost entirely on the DII, which is an alternative to compiled OMG IDL static interfaces. The DII is a generic facility for invoking any operation with a runtime-defined parameter list. A runtime interface description of the operation signature can be retrieved on-line from the CORBA Interface Repository. Using the metadata, a legal request can be constructed to a previously unknown operation and unknown object type. Use of the DII instead of an OMG IDL static interface is transparent to the object implementation. In general, programming with OMG IDL static interfaces is much simpler and results in more robust code for the developer. However, the DII provides a level of flexibility that is necessary in some applications, such as desktops and operating systems.

Object Adapters

An *object adapter* comprises the interface between the ORB and the object implementation. Object adapters support functions such as registration of object implementations and activation of servers. There are many potential types of object adapters. There could be different adapters for general-purpose uses, for object database integration, for legacy integration, and so forth. CORBA 1.1 defines only the Basic Object Adapter (BOA), but it recognizes the need for these other types of adapters.

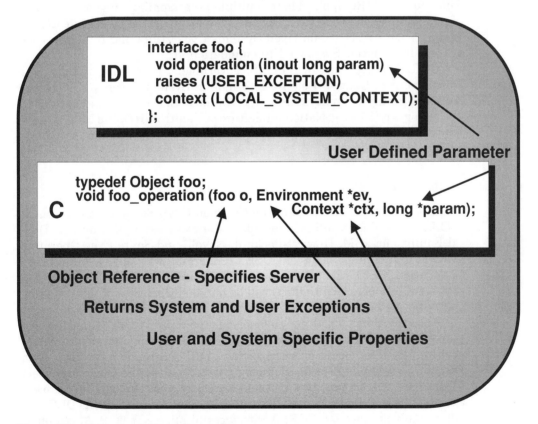

Figure 3.5. Example of IDL-to-C mapping.

The BOA is a general-purpose object adapter. When a client request specifies an inactive server, the BOA automatically activates the server process. The first responsibility of the server is to register its implementation with the BOA. The BOA stores this registration to use in future object requests. After an object is activated, it may receive client requests through the method callbacks in the OMG IDL skeleton. BOA services include exception handling and object reference management, among others.

CORBA Acceptance

CORBA and OMG IDL have gained wide acceptance by industry and consortia. OMG membership exceeds 500, including virtually all platform manufacturers and major independent software vendors. X/Open copublishes the CORBA specification and has included CORBA in the X/Open Portability Guide Release 4. OMG IDL is the Application Program Interface (API) specification language for the next release of X Windows, called X11R6 FRESCO. This makes X11R6 applicable to multiple programming languages instead of being tied exclusively to C. CORBA also is supported by specification of groups, such as Petroleum Open Systems Consortium and the Open Geographic Information System (GIS) Foundation.

CORBA acceptance in the U.S. government is growing rapidly. The Department of Defense Defense Information Systems Agency (DISA), the National Security Agency (NSA), the National Institute of Standards and Technology (NIST), the National Institute of Health (NIH), and MITRE have joined the OMG, and CORBA is included in several government standards profiles.

Product Availability

CORBA is a future standard of the Common Open Software Environment (COSE), an industry alliance including companies such as SunSoft, Digital Equipment, IBM, Hewlett-Packard, Novell, and Santa Cruz Operation (SCO). Successful elements of COSE are merging with the Open Software Foundation (OSF). All of these vendors have committed to deliver CORBA-compliant products, and CORBA will be bundled with most of their existing operating systems.

Several vendors are already delivering productized CORBA implementations including: IONA, DEC, HP, and IBM. Apple has announced future support for CORBA. Microsoft is supporting CORBA through its alliance with DEC in a cross-platform development product called the Common Object Model. DEC will support two APIs for developers, CORBA and the Microsoft Common Object Model, a more primitive alternative to CORBA. DEC and others have productized CORBA interfaces to Microsoft OLE. Microsoft is spearheading an OMG standards initiative to provide a standard definition of CORBA/Common Object Model (COM) interoperability. Available CORBA implementations cover most operating systems environments including Solaris, OS/2, AIX, HP-UX, DG UNIX, Virtual Memory System (VMS), OSF/1, IRIX, Macintosh, Windows, and Windows-NT.

Third-party vendors, such as Integrated Computer Solutions, WordPerfect, and Paragon Imaging, have announced future CORBA-compliant applications products. Expersoft, FORTE, and other companies are developing CORBA interfaces to major database products. As the common facilities standards are released, we anticipate direct CORBA support from most major independent software vendors. These companies are already actively involved in the OMG standards processes.

Underlying CORBA

CORBA is an abstract specification that does not constrain its underlying implementation. The ORB could be implemented as a linked library function interface, a layer directly over RPC, or as a higher-level communication facility. This flexibility allows vendors to utilize their existing networking facilities. Some vendors (such as IONA), are basing CORBA on ONC-compatible RPCs; some vendors (such as HP), are using OSF DCE; and some (such as Sunsoft) are bypassing the RPC layer and implementing CORBA at lower layers. Most vendors also provide developer support for implementing linked library code using OMG IDL interfaces.

The inherent flexibility underlying CORBA allows the software architect to separate design from implementation decisions. Relevant implementation decisions include process allocation and performance trade-offs. Because CORBA makes these implementation properties transparent, it is unnecessary to hard-code these details into the architecture design. This frees the designer to use OMG IDL to specify all architectural software boundaries and then choose the underlying communication mechanisms later. Many implementation decisions can be deferred until installation time, so system adaptability is maximized.

Today's CORBA products are like Ethernet products in the early days; the vendors are building to a common standard, and they are actively working toward interoperability with CORBA 2.0. Using earlier CORBA versions, if you want to build a multiplatform ORB application, you must choose an ORB vendor that runs on all the target machines. When CORBA products are bundled with operating systems, the CORBA 2.0 standard will enable multivendor ORB implementations to interoperate transparently. Most ORB vendors have announced and demonstrated interoperability between their platforms.

CORBA 2.0

CORBA 2.0 is a set of upwardly compatible standards that complete and augment the CORBA 1.2 specification. The key elements of CORBA 2.0 are:

- ORB-to-ORB interoperability specification
- Client and server initialization specification
- Additional programming language bindings: C++ and Smalltalk
- Interface repository specification

Among these, the interoperability specification is the most significant for the CORBA market. The specification provides for cross-ORB services between multiple vendor's products. The OMG adopted the Combined Submission for Interoperability, which is a merger of the major submissions. The core of the specification is a general architecture for interoperability called Universal Networked Objects (UNO).

Within UNO, there are two types of interoperability specifications: General Interoperability Protocols (GIOPs) and Environment Specific Interoperability Protocols (ESIOPs). The GIOPs are fully specified protocols that are mandated to provide for out-of-the-box interoperability. An initial GIOP called Internet Interoperability Protocol (IIOP) was included in UNO. IIOP is based on Transmission Control Protocol/Internet Protocol (TCP/IP), the ubiquitous protocol of the Internet. IIOP is a simplfied subset of an RPC mechanism that is specifically directed at ORB-to-ORB interoperability. The initial ESIOP specified within the Combined Submission is based on the Open Software Foundation's (OSF's) DCE, called the DCE Common Interoperability Protocol (DCE CIOP). Vendors can support ESIOPs and still be CORBA-compliant, as long as their products also support the GIOP. New ESIOPs and GIOPs can be added to the specification later through OMG technology adoption processes.

It is interesting to note that the choice of ORB interoperability solutions does not impact application software. Interoperability is an issue between the ORB vendors, not between vendors and users. Few, if any, application developers will ever be involved in programming with GIOPs and ESIOPs. Now that the ORB interoperability standard is in place, vendors can proceed to implement interoperable products with minimal risk. This standard also reduces risks for CORBA users, and it will soon provide for ubiquitous interoperability between ORB products.

The CORBA 2.0 initialization specification has much more direct impact on developers. The initialization specifications resolve important portability issues for application software. Initialization defines how clients and servers using CORBA establish initial communication with the ORB and obtain initial object references, such as the naming service handle. With CORBA 2.0 initialization, the interfaces and calling sequences will be consistent and portable between ORB products.

The language bindings for C++ and Smalltalk were standardized in CORBA 2.0. These bindings define how OMG IDL specifications are mapped into the API specifications of these programming languages. The bindings will provide consistent, natural support for these languages across ORB products. These bindings also provide for seamless interoperability between objects written in different languages. Several ORB products are supporting multiple language bindings.

The Interface Repository specification standardizes the access and management of on-line metadata describing all known OMG IDL interfaces. The CORBA 2.0 Interface Repository completes the specification in CORBA 1.2, which defined the basic retrieval interfaces.

OBJECT SERVICES

Object services comprise a fundamental set of system service interfaces. The adopted OMG Object Services comprise the Common Object Service Specification (COSS). COSS is a multivolume series, with one volume corresponding to each Object Services Request for Proposal (RFP). To date, the OMG Object Services Task Force has released four of the five planned RFPs: RFP1, RFP2, RFP3, and RFP4.

The RFP1 services include:

- Object Event Notification Service
- Object Life Cycle Service
- Object Naming Service
- Object Persistence Service

The RFP2 services include:

- Object Concurrency Service
- Object Externalization Service
- Object Relationships Service
- Object Transaction Service

The RFP3 services include:

- Object Security Service
- Object Time Service

The RFP4 services include:

- Object Licensing Service
- Object Properties Service
- Object Query Service

Each RFP takes about a year to complete the process and results in technology adoption. RFP1 and RFP2 have already been adopted at the time of this writing. RFP3 and RFP4 processes will be complete in 1995. RFP5 is due to be released in mid-1995 and complete in 1996.

The RFP5 services will likely include:

- Object Change Management Service
- Object Collections Service
- Object Trader Service
- Object Startup Service

It is anticipated that the International Standards Organization (ISO) will submit it's OMG IDL binding to the Open Distributed Process (ODP) Trader Service, which is in advanced stages of formal standards adoption.

The RFP5 services are the final services identified in the Object Services Architecture [OMG, 94]. Thus, RFP5 will complete the Object Services Architecture. By the end of RFP5, the standardization processes for both CORBA and Object Services will be essentially complete.

The first services to be standardized included the Object Naming Service and the Object Event Notification Service. The Naming Service enables the retrieval of object handles based on the string-valued name of an object server. Hierarchical naming contexts can be defined for groupings of objects. The Event Notification Service is a general facility for passing events between objects. Event interfaces are defined for administration and alternative forms of event posting and retrieval.

Servers that implement COSS interfaces can be constructed by the ORB vendor or by application developers. Allowing developers to build services is a very useful feature of the object management architecture called *generic objects*. Generic objects that reuse standard interfaces can interoperate transparently with any application supporting the standards and can be tailored for specific application needs. Generic objects can provide a common interface layer on top of noncompliant services. For example, Naming Service interfaces could be layered on top of various directory standards (such as DCE Cell Directory Service, X.500, or Internet naming) to provide simple consistent access to multiple services. Object services interfaces are designed to be extended through specialization. For example, a developer might specialize the standard event interface with facilities for a real-time application, while retaining interface compatibility with standard event clients and servers.

Other services adopted from RFP1 include the Object Life Cycle Service and the Object Persistence Service. The Life Cycle Service comprises operations for managing object creation, deletion, copy, and equivalence. The Persistence Service comprises facilities for storage of objects.

Some of the most commonly used object services, the Object Naming Service, the Object Event Service, and the Object Relationship Service, are summarized in the next sections.

Object Naming Service

The basic operations for accessing the Object Naming Service include bind, unbind, and resolve. Bind adds a (name, object handle) pair to a naming context. Unbind removes the pair. Resolve retrieves an object handle given a name. Some basic operations for accessing Naming contexts include: new_context, bind_context, and destroy. These correspond to creating a context, associating two contexts hierarchically, and removing a context.

Figure 3.6 is an example of a set of names and naming contexts. Names are defined as an OMG IDL sequence type, which allows the description of a hierarchical list of identifiers without imposing implementation-specific syntax. This is useful because the major directory standards all use different hierarchical naming syntax.

The naming service is one of the most basic and generally useful services. CORBA users should expect to have an Object Naming Service bundled with the ORB and layered over the native directory service. Most CORBA-based programs should use the naming service to locate other basic services, such as the Object Trader Service.

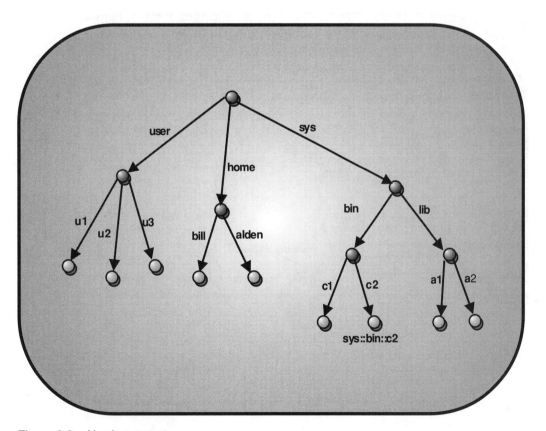

Figure 3.6. Naming contexts.

Object Event Service

The Object Event Service is a general-purpose, reusable set of interfaces for event posting and dissemination. The roles of the objects involved in event notification include suppliers, consumers, channels, and factories. The suppliers and consumers are usually application objects, and the event channel and the event channel factory provide the event services. Event channel interfaces operate in either push mode or pull mode. The IDL Consumer interface provides the push() operation. In push mode, a supplier can push() an event to the event channel object, and a consumer application will receive a corresponding push() invocation from the event channel object. Alternatively, applications may utilize the IDL Supplier interface, which provides pull() and try_pull() operations. The try_pull() operation polls for ready events, and the pull() operation retrieves the event. Using the administrative interfaces, applications dynamically register themselves as consumers indicating their interest in receiving event notification. The event channel

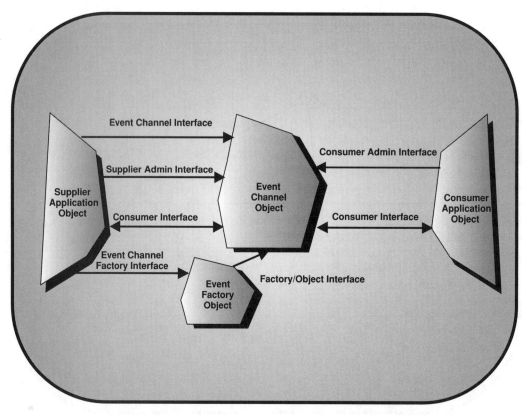

Figure 3.7. Event notification.

can support both push mode and pull mode interfaces with both supplier and consumer applications. This provides flexibility in selecting the event channel integration approach.

Object Relationship Service

The Object Relationship Service provides a capability for managing associations and linkages between objects. The service utilizes dedicated relationship objects that retain the object handles of the associated objects. Relationships are a fundamental service that can be used to implement many types of object linkages. For example, relationships can be used for desktop object linking and embedding. The relationship service is useful in combination with other services such as events, life cycle, and externalization.

The Object Properties service is a facility for attaching dynamic information to an object. A set of properties of any type can be attached to an object without changing the object's implementation. Among other uses, properties could be very useful for managing desktop objects, such as attaching icon representations to arbitrary objects.

COMMON FACILITIES

Common Facilities is the newest area of OMG standardization. Whereas CORBA and Object Services standardize the enabling infrastructure and services, Common Facilities represents higher-level specifications that complete the OMG's vision for interoperability. Now that CORBA 2.0 is finalized and most Object Services are standardized or near adoption, the OMG's focus is moving toward the standardization of the higher-level Common Facilities.

Common Facilities will provide richness and application-level focus to the ensemble of OMG technologies. Whereas ORB and Object Services are fundamental technologies, Common Facilities extend these technologies up to the application developer and independent software vendor level. Common Facilities may become the most important area of OMG standards because it is the level that most developers will utilize.

Common Facilities include specifications for higher-level services and vertical market specialty areas. Horizontal Common Facilities are application domain independent. Some examples include system management and compound documents. In addition, there are more specialized Vertical Market Facilities, such as geospatial data processing and financial services. Common facilities is an appropriate area for standards providing interoperability between independent software vendors' products.

The Common Facilities Task Force (CFTF) is the third permanent OMG Task Force. It complements the areas addressed by the ORB Task Force and the Object Services Task Force (OSTF). Common Facilities relates to the other OMG technology areas in that it is closer to the application level.

Ideally, the Common Facilities will include many specializations of the Object Services, specializations that extend the primitive Object Services into richer interfaces that directly address the needs of many applications and independent software vendors. Both Object Services and Common Facilities are intended to be reused by developers in application software and commercial software products.

The CFTF was created in December 1993 by vote of the OMG Technical Committee. CFTF is following the precedents established by the OSTF. The task force has released an industrywide request for information (RFI) and received many responses. The RFI responses are the source material for three key documents: the Common Facilities (CF) Architecture, the CF Road Map, and the first CF Request for Proposal (RFP). The Common Facilities Architecture identifies and describes the major categories of Common Facilities. The Common Facilities Road Map groups the CF categories by priority and establishes a schedule for facilities adoption through the RFP process. The first Common Facilities RFP (Compound Documents) initiates the technology adoption process by soliciting the first set of facilities specifications.

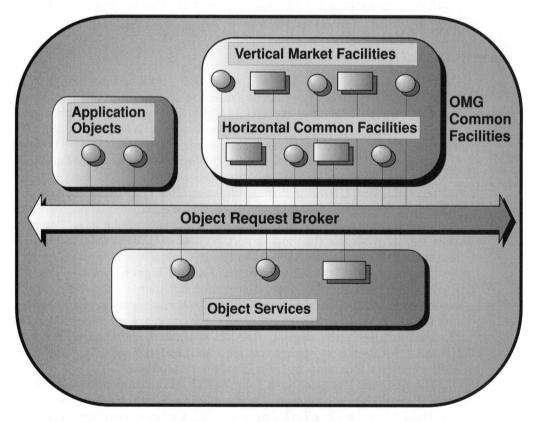

Figure 3.8.   Common facilities in object management architecture.

In comparison with the other task forces, Common Facilities has a more diverse charter. Many Common Facilities probably will be important only to particular specialty markets. The OMG has a fast-track Request for Comment (RFC) process that can be used for technology adoption in areas where industry consensus already exists. For those high priority areas that require an RFP process, the CFTF has documented the schedule for RFPs in the Common Facilities Roadmap. [OMG, 95b]

As development budgets increasingly require system life cycle extension, reengineering, and multisystem consolidation, Common Facilities will support system migration. For application developers, standards are needed that mitigate long-term risks and increase leverage from commercial technology. For commercial software developers and R&D innovators, standards are needed that create entry points in applications systems for value-added products. We envision Common Facilities bridging these needs, by establishing standards that are mutually supportable by both application developers and independent software vendors.

COMMENTS

ORB technology is an infrastructure technology area that is near maturity. Many CORBA implementations are available today, and platform vendors are investing substantially in bundled CORBA products. (See Appendix.) CORBA will be ubiquitous in the UNIX market, with bundled implementations on most platforms. CORBA also will be widely available on volume platforms (Apple, Windows), bundled with packages (such as OpenDoc) from major software vendors such as Claris, WordPerfect, Lotus, and Taligent.

Because it is independent of computer language and operating system, OMG IDL is universally applicable. One does not have to have an ORB or even use CORBA in order to obtain the benefits of the OMG IDL. OMG IDL compilers can be used independently from other parts of the system in order to allow the system architect and software developers to produce clean, well-defined interfaces.

There are many ways to prepare for the impending technology transition to CORBA. Most ORB vendors and some independent consultants offer comprehensive training courses covering CORBA products that offer insight into the standard and the technology. The OMG has published the Object Management Architecture Guide [OMG, 93], the CORBA Specification [OMG, 92a], and the Common Object Services Specification [OMG, 94b]. These publications are John Wiley & Sons books that are generally available. Finally, OMG IDL is a stable language that can be used for structuring architectures today. OMG IDL is the specification language for the next generation of X Windows, X11R6 Fresco from the X Consortium. A public domain OMG IDL compiler toolkit is available from the OMG (via ftp from omg.org); the toolkit readily supports OMG IDL syntax checking and can be extended for additional applications of OMG IDL.

4

Software Architecture Design

The important decisions in design are not what to put in but what to leave out.
—Attributed to Tony Hoare by Per Brinch Hansen, U.S.C.

There exists a range of alternative solutions for most application problems. It is well known that object-oriented design processes do not yield unique solutions. Design alternatives will vary in cost effectiveness. Designers should be aware of the alternatives, and cost should be a key consideration in design trade-offs.

When we talk about design alternatives in this chapter, we are discussing trade-offs in the design of software architectures. There is no consensus in the computing literature on the definition of the phrase software architecture. In our view, software architecture defines the boundaries between the major components comprising a software system. The boundaries are interface specifications that can be expressed in Object Management Group Interface Definition Language (OMG IDL) with appropriate sequencing constraints and semantics. Sequencing constraints define the conventions for the ordering of operation invocations. The semantics define the operation meanings (usually in prose). These definitions are comparable to a typical OMG specification. By defining software architecture in this way, OMG standards can be applied directly to application software architectures, and elements of high-quality architectures can be migrated into standards.

There are many other issues beyond software architecture in the design and implementation of an application system. We categorize the other relevant design information as comprising the system architecture; everything else is captured in the system implementation. Software architecture is a subset of system architecture; software implementation is a subset of system implementation. The software implementation comprises the major subsystems, which we sometimes call applications or components.

We use the terms software architecture and framework interchangeably. An architecture is also a collection of frameworks, where at a minimum a framework comprises an Application Program Interface (API) and sequencing constraints. In our view, a framework also includes metadata and other interoperability conventions, such as supported data formats.

The design concepts that we present are applicable directly at the level of the software architecture design. We avoid presenting higher-level issues requiring formal Computer Aided Software Engineering (CASE) methodologies and notations; instead we refer readers to one of the many existing methodologies [Hutt, 94]. In this chapter we focus on design at the OMG IDL level, a level that is language and methodology independent but has a straightforward mapping to both of these other levels. An increasing number of useful OMG IDL standards are available and provide many useful design patterns.

Typically, about 70 percent of the cost of a software system is incurred for operations and maintenance (O&M) after the system is operational [Horowitz, 93]. Of the O&M expense, about two-thirds is due to system extensions needed because of changes in requirements. These figures indicate that *adaptability* is the key characteristic of cost-effective software architectures. Our discussion of software architecture focuses on system-level strategies that can minimize these substantial costs by enhancing system adaptability.

Savings due to having well-structured software architectures versus unstructured architectures typically exceed more than 50 percent [Horowitz, 93]. When using CORBA-based software architectures, we believe the savings can be even greater. CORBA has simplified the creation of good software architectures by providing architecture notations such as OMG IDL, useful API standards, and the inherent system-level flexibilities built into Object Request Brokers (ORBs).

This chapter covers many effective design elements of highly adaptable systems. Perhaps the most powerful (but underutilized) concept for building adaptable systems is *metadata*. Metadata is any self-descriptive information contained in the software architecture and implementation. Typically, metadata describes attributes of the components of the architecture, so that it enables more adaptability, by allowing certain attributes to be determined at runtime. Many helpful metadata standards exist to aid in the implementation of metadata knowledge that a wide community of programmers can utilize. Metadata is the key to resource discovery in distributed, adaptable systems. It enables the system to configure itself, and to adapt to system extensions and changes automatically.

ESTABLISHING ARCHITECTURAL VISION

There are two major types of organization for designing software architecture: design by individual "chief" architects and design by teams. Individuals can design conceptually coherent and elegantly simple architectures. Most successful architectures are based on a strong architectural vision. The vision is generally due to one chief architect, and it is difficult to maintain a consistent vision across teams of designers.

Communication of the architectural vision to the team of developers is a very important element of a successful architecture. About half of software development activities involve system discovery, or trying to understand the system's structure. If developers do not understand the architectural vision, then they can easily make implementation choices that violate architectural assumptions.

With no direct relationship between separate design processes and implementation processes, the implementations rapidly diverge from the designed architecture. CORBA provides some important tools, such as OMG IDL, for communicating design information in a way that can be verified in the system implementation. Communication of vision must go beyond OMG IDL to include other documentation. Creation of a tutorial-format architectural walkthrough is an excellent way to communicate vision to a team of developers. Capture the tutorial on videotape, and use it as a mandatory part of each new developer's and maintainer's training.

Design by teams is an approach used more widely than design by an individual architect. Team design can result in robust architectures that incorporate the contingencies envisioned by a whole group of architects. Many team designs are large and complex because it is often easier to include additional complexity than to compromise and merge viewpoints. Design complexity exacerbates the problem of maintaining a consistent architectural vision that developers understand.

Both approaches require iterative design and revision. An effective architecture can seldom be designed in a top-down manner with a priori knowledge. To yield architecture benefits, an architecture design needs to be prototyped, then utilized and updated through experience and knowledge gained in the prototyping process. This process is most effective if changes are made on a predictable release cycle, where the architecture is stable between releases. Architecture revision is essentially a code cleanup task on a systemwide level. As experience is gained with an immature architecture, lessons learned can be used to create a new improved architecture that will reduce O&M costs for future system extensions.

ROLE OF CORBA IN SOFTWARE ARCHITECTURE

CORBA is an enabling infrastructure for good software architectures. Its architecture benefits are derived from two primary sources: OMG IDL and the CORBA-based ORBs.

OMG IDL is an important notational tool for software architects. Because it contains no implementation information, it provides a clean separation between design and implementation. In the developed system, this provides encapsulation of components and isolation between subsystems. Component isolation is an important property of a good software architecture because it enables the reconfiguration and replacement of components during the system life cycle.

OMG IDL is a universal notation for specifying APIs. It can be used without a commercial ORB product; for example, it can be used as a layer directly on top of the Open Software Foundation Distributed Computing Environment (OSF DCE). OSF has provided a guideline for this mapping in its CORBA interoperability proposal [OSF CORBA 2.0]. APIs denote system-level software boundaries. Defining good software boundaries is the primary goal of a good software architecture. OMG IDL is the best standard notation available for this purpose. It defines APIs concisely and rigorously, covering important issues such as error handling.

By using OMG IDL for specifying all architectural boundaries, good software architectures support a uniform abstraction layer with uniform access to services. Where to place OMG IDL interfaces and where to use a commercial ORB are two different decisions. The former is a design decision; and the latter, an implementation decision. OMG IDL can support library function interfaces just as well as distributed objects across a network. CORBA allows the deferral of many allocation decisions to installation time.

OMG IDL can be layered on top of virtually any communication layer. Many different communication layers are available from standard, de facto, and proprietary sources, and they are rapidly evolving; software architects should consider an approach that isolates the application software from these underlying layers. Direct integration of application software puts the architecture at risk of obsolescence as the technologies evolve and are replaced with higher-level layers. There are successor technologies on the horizon for virtually every communication layer available today, such as DCE, ToolTalk, and so forth.

An alternative approach is to define a custom API layer encapsulating the communication-layer software. Commercial vendors use this technique routinely to enable them to substitute mechanisms for different system builds. If this custom API layer is defined in OMG IDL, then the API specification can support multiple language bindings and be easily upgraded to utilize an ORB product. This technique also can be used to mask differences between layers if multiple communications layers must be supported within an architecture. In this case, the OMG IDL defines the uniform service access layer, independent of mechanism.

Stability is a key characteristic of good software architectures. No specification is more stable than a commercial or de facto standard with multivendor support. Among standards, OMG IDL is a very stable standard because

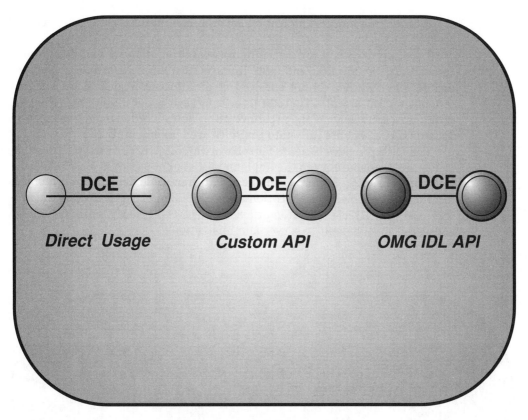

Figure 4.1. Three ways to utilize a low-level communication layer.

it is the basis for the OMG's standards process and many commercial ORB products. An adopted OMG standard comprises an OMG IDL specification and a description of the sequencing constraints on the interfaces. By using OMG IDL, software architectures gain these same benefits: conciseness, rigorousness, stability, and commercial support.

In addition, a reusable software architecture specified in OMG IDL is an informal standard for an organization. High-quality architectural specifications that address industrywide interoperability problems can be upgraded to standards. OMG IDL supports the migration of a specification from software architecture to organizational reuse to industry standard. This process may eventually enable general interoperability between applications.

OMG IDL provides a compilable linkage between the software architecture and the implementation. As OMG IDL is pure design information, it is part of the software architecture design. OMG IDL also is compilable to header files and stub programs, which the compiler uses to verify architectural constraints in the application software. These architectural constraints include enforcement of encapsulations, parameter type checking, and so forth.

This approach is a dramatic improvement on analysis and design processes that provide no compilable linkage between design and implementation. The compiler cannot check some architectural constraints, such as sequencing constraints. Therefore, the approach is not bulletproof; the programmer's knowledge of the architectural vision is needed to incorporate the architecture's benefits fully into the software implementation.

The ORB provides benefits for software architectures by supporting flexibility and transparency in the implementation. For example, CORBA's location transparency eliminates the need for direct code dependency on object location and enables the relocation and replication of services after the system is coded. Its use of automatic server startup greatly simplifies client software's involvement in server administration.

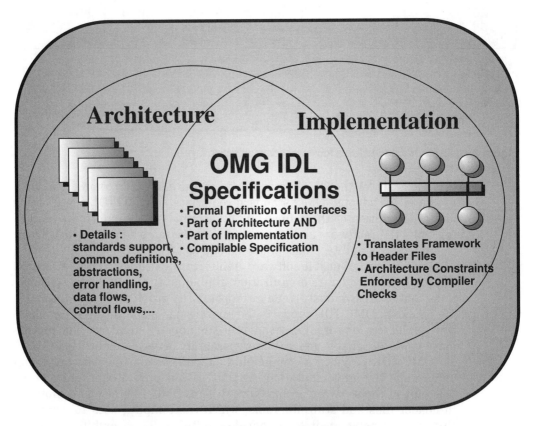

Figure 4.2.   OMG IDL role in software architecture and implementation.

CORBA is a great enabler of software architectures, but it does not design or define the software architecture. CORBA is a very general-purpose mechanism that supports almost any form of architecture. Many design decisions are the responsibility of the software architect and the implementors.

ARCHITECTURE PROCESS COMPARED TO METHODOLOGY

Many processes are involved in creating a software architecture. The overall process is difficult to define, because the architect's intuitive vision plays a more important role than any particular methodology. This fact is becoming more widely recognized as the methodology community shifts its focus from object-oriented design to "design patterns" [Gamma, 94].

In practice, formal design methodologies have had mixed results. More than two dozen documented methodologies based on object orientation currently exist. The OMG has published a comprehensive review and comparison of these methodologies [Hutt, 94]. In general, the quality of the people working on a project is much more critical to success than the methodology employed. The Hillside Group, a group of design patterns researchers, states that successful software architectures have been designed in spite of formal methodology. This group intends to study and document the successful software architect's expertise. In this book, we are relaying this expertise directly, bypassing the methodologists.

The process of software architecture design goes beyond people and methodology. We have met many competent people who have no concept of what a good software architecture is and why it is needed. This indicates that there is a serious educational gap. Software architecture is a top priority mainly for technology consumers such as corporate developers, systems integrators, and government organizations.

INTEGRATION CAPABILITY MATURITY MODEL

The architectural awareness of an organization can be characterized in terms of a capability model, as shown in Figure 4.3. The model provides categories for organizational use of systems integration technologies. It is useful as a self-assessment model or for gauging the awareness of architecture and development groups. This model applies primarily to corporate developers and systems integrators, but it is interesting to gauge these categories against technology supplier organizations in terms of how they support the practice of software architecture concepts.

At Level 1, the organization performs no value-added integration and produces no custom software; it is a straightforward user of commercially available software. At Level 2, the organization does produce software for its own needs, but it is indifferent to the integration technology utilized. Level 2 organizations use whatever integration technologies are readily available,

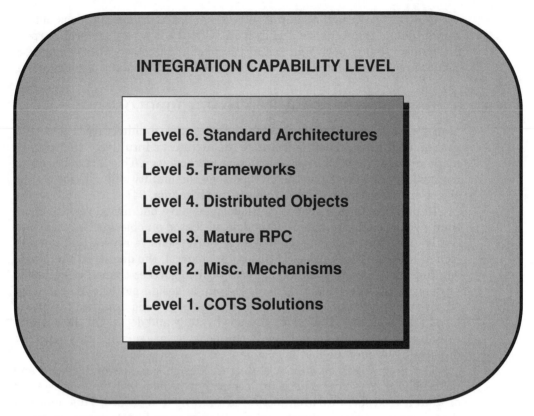

Figure 4.3. Integration capability maturity model.

such as Transmission Control Protocol/Internet Protocol (TCP/IP) sockets and Object Network Computing Remote Procedure Call (ONC RPC), which are available or bundled on most platforms. Level 2 organizations typically implement ad hoc software architectures because they have no real concern for creating a consistent architectural abstraction in the implemented system.

Level 3 organizations recognize the need for a uniform integration approach and have adopted a "mature" RPC technology, such as OSF DCE. OSF DCE adds security, naming, and other basic services to the RPC model, which provides advantages compared to Level 2 users. Level 3 organizations are technically conservative and are at risk of obsolescence. They are risking being caught on a nonmainstream technology base that may be expensive to support over the life cycle. Since these Level 3 organizations are not exploiting new technology advances, they are paying a high cost for software development based on the use of lower-level communication layers.

Level 4 organizations use CORBA technology actively, generally in a product-dependent manner. These organizations are primarily benefitting from the inherent advantages of the ORB technology as a higher-level RPC mechanism. Level 4 organizations insert the ORB only at distributed or heterogeneous system transitions. They do not have a concept of a software architecture other than to provide distributed processing capabilities. Their architectural interfaces utilize other legacy mechanisms when distributed processing is not required. Most of these groups do not rely on the CORBA specification, and they use the ORB products in a product-dependent manner. Level 4 groups are at risk of technology obsolescence wherever they are using vendor-dependent interfaces and do not realize any real software architecture benefits. Basically, they are using an ORB product as an improved form of RPC technology.

Level 5 organizations have developed software architecture frameworks for project-specific needs. Their frameworks include both local and remote uses of OMG IDL interfaces. Their frameworks embody sound software architecture principals. They realize software architecture adaptability benefits and cost savings over the entire system life cycle. Level 5 groups still have problems with intersystem interoperability, and they have minimal reuse across projects and systems. Level 5 groups have minimal external impact on their industry and the commercial market.

Level 6 organizations produce high-quality software architectures and services for reuse across multiple projects. They rely on the CORBA standard in preference to vendor-dependent interfaces. This gives these organizations the ability to support multiple platforms and ORBs and eliminates the risk of vendor-driven technology obsolescence. Level 6 organizations drive the limits of CORBA beyond the immediate support by the ORB vendor. For example, level 6 groups layer OMG IDL interfaces on a variety of mechanisms, including alternative protocols to address specialized application performance needs. These groups have external impact across systems and their industry. They are the generators of interoperability standards for their industries and enjoy business success by being industry leaders.

Level 6 organizations are superstar performers. Not every organization can produce technology at the world-class level. We believe that most organizations are capable of Level 5 performance. With the proper interoperability standards in place, level 5 organizations can produce level 6 results. It is the responsibility of the level 6 technology leaders to create the interoperability standards needed to make this possible.

In this book, we define a general process, provide some important examples, and give a set of techniques for software architecture design and implementation. Software architecture design is different from and not in competition with formal methodologies and CASE tools. The methodologies and tools have their roles within the process; these concepts are covered extensively by other authors. [Hutt, 94] In defining the process, we are most interested in the practical strategies that lead to good software architectures and system success.

SOFTWARE ARCHITECTURE DESIGN PROCESS

The software architecture design process comprises a number of heuristic steps. The process defined here is not a fixed methodology but an eclectic, flexible process that guides the architect on a path of learning necessary insights to create an effective architecture. We do not believe that good architecture can be created in a purely top-down manner. Good architecture involves experimentation and should be pursued in an environment that can tolerate some initial failures (or wrong turns). Overall, the pursuit of good architecture is a risk-reduction activity that builds robustness into the system design and adds adaptability that will save substantial costs over the system life cycle.

Software architecture design is more like an art than a science. Formal notations may provide the architect/artist's media, but in pursuing a formal methodology, it is important to keep the focus on the real source, the artist, not the media. Formal methodology constraints should take second priority to the creative directions of the architect. In this process, the architect uses his or her learning ability and creativity to formulate a strawman solution, then refines the working design through experience. In this description, we use metaphors from various industries to describe the creative processes (Figure 4.4).

At the start, the key learning activities include farming and mining. In farming, the architect pursues various domain analysis activities to create abstractions of the system requirements. In mining, the architect studies previous solutions and legacy systems to create generalizations of the component subsystems. These first two steps serve as exercises for edifying the architect, and the resulting artifacts might not be used directly in the architecture. In the composition process, the architect (as artist) synergizes the lessons learned to create an initial software architecture (the strawman architecture).

The balance of the process involves a series of iterative refinements to the architecture. The strawman architecture should be reviewed by the developers and refined by the architect a final time before prototyping begins. During prototyping, the architecture design should be frozen into stable versions. The fixed architecture provides a stable basis for parallel development of applications. As the architecture matures, the frequency of changes should decrease and the impact of any changes should decrease dramatically.

When the architecture is immature, prototyping should be relatively small scale. Limiting the commitment of prototype software at this phase enables more frequent and dramatic upgrades to the architecture.

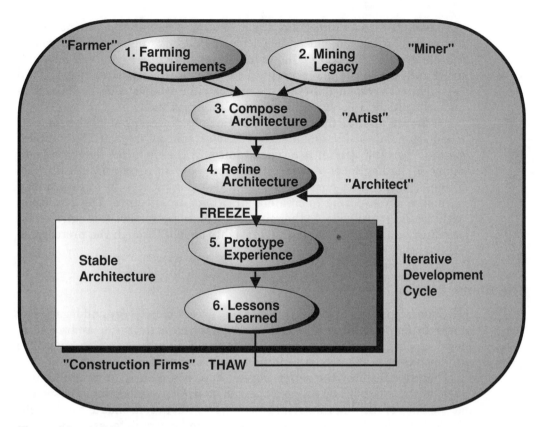

Figure 4.4. Architecture process.

Architecture refinement decisions may involve substantial project resources. Each time the architecture is modified, most or all of the component subsystems are impacted. This may be expensive if the changes are
dramatic. The primary goal of the architecture process is to accommodate
future change.

The architecture is the stable basis for the system. As technology evolves,
components are added, interchanged, and upgraded while the architecture
remains stable. The architecture life cycle is equivalent to the system life
cycle and transcends the life cycles of individual component subsystems.

The architecture process is not an egalitarian group process. A work of
fine art such as symphony composition or a museum painting are almost
always the work of an individual artist's vision. Good software architectures also are based substantially on a chief architect's vision and control
of the designs that implement the vision. The common notion that a group
of developers all "charge up the hill" as equals generally does not result in

effective software architectures. Good developers can always produce an effective demonstration, but ad hoc demonstrations rarely evolve into robust full life cycle architectures. Individual developers in a group will have different interpretations and concepts for a common architectural vision. It is a key architect's responsibility to communicate the system vision to developers and arbitrate between the differences of interpretation.

Software architecture design is a learning process. The design process is analogous to the incremental development concept from artificial intelligence. When the system is designed initially, the architect does not know many of the key facts and intuitions necessary to create an effective solution. The architect pursues an initial learning process through farming, mining, and composing to create a strawman architecture. The strawman architecture is evolved into the robust, finished architecture through a series of refinements, which involve new insights gained through the prototyping experience.

The Mining Process

The mining process involves the study of current technology and legacy systems. From these former designs, we hope to characterize the architecture-level support provided by these systems. In this step, we can also generalize the results so that a robust generalized component model emerges.

Figure 4.5 shows the set of models constructed during the mining process. This is a bottom-up process; the first step involves clarifying the models at the base of the diagram. The process proceeds to consolidate the models. In the last step, the architect refines the design for completeness and robustness.

The process begins by modeling the existing subsystems. These are models of specific concrete components. For example, if we are modeling database products, then we would create models for Sybase, Oracle, and other specific vendor products. In these models, we are seeking to represent an idealized API for each concrete component. These API models represent access to all of the functionality available, both that provided by the concrete API and that provided through the user interface. Often the functionality available through the concrete API is quite different from that offered through the user interfaces. The model API should capture a superset of both. OMG IDL is a suitable notation for describing the model APIs.

This first step serves to help the architect to understand a variety of alternative concrete subsystems in detail. In practice, we have found the artifacts of this step to be of minimal value. However, the learning process is invaluable, because the architect learns the commonality and differences between components. With this understanding, he or she can begin to create a robust architectural design that captures the commonality and abstracts the differences. Component interchangeability in the final architecture is a

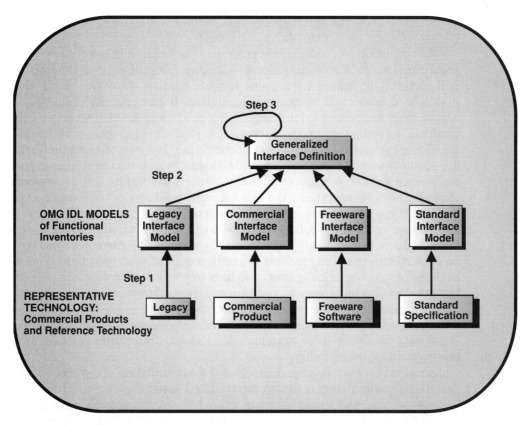

Figure 4.5. Mining process.

key goal of this exercise. To understand each component fully, the architect should consider taking developer training courses and conferring with expert developers in addition to reviewing the component's technical documentation in depth.

The second step is a process of generalization. With an understanding of the specialized components, the architect defines a common base class definition. The common base class (or generalized model) should represent a fully functional component API in its own right. It is possible to document the mapping from the concrete component models to the generalized model. In practice, we have not found much benefit in pursuing this exercise for more than one concrete model. The one documented mapping can be used as implementation guidance to the developer doing the integration.

The third step in the mining process involves the refinement of the design. Additional design concerns beyond capturing and abstracting the concrete subsytems need to be infused into the design. Whereas the first step in mining could be approached scientifically, the second and third steps increasingly involve the architect's artistic judgment, balancing cost concerns (i.e., complexity versus simplicity) with functionality concerns.

An important variable in this process is the breadth of selection of concrete components. If only one concrete component is studied, then the results will certainly be biased toward one implementation—in other words, the generalized model will be product dependent. If two concrete components are studied, component interchangeability is assured for at least those two products. In many technology markets, two products can represent a majority of market share, and this may be sufficient. If three or more products are studied, then the generalized model begins to capture the trends in the technology market. A large set of products represent current technology, but they also provide insight into the market niches and product differentiators. Some of these unique features will be adopted in the future by the market as a whole. In fact, we believe that most of the innovative features of future products can be found distributed throughout the current technology base, particularly in the products of small, technically advanced niche market vendors. As our mining study expands to cover these future component features, we can build very robust generalized models that can capture the visible market trends for the foreseeable future.

These concepts also apply to custom-software legacy systems. Two types of projects involving these systems might include migration systems and intersystem interoperability.

A migration system project involves the consolidation of several legacy systems providing similar functionality. The United States Department of Defense is currently pursuing more than 100 migration systems projects in order to downsize and save costs. The design process used to define the migration system architecture should include a mining study of the legacy systems. Such study can provide insights into the varieties of API interfaces and functionality needed to create a robust architecture. The mining study should consider external systems not directly involved in migration that can provide a more comprehensive model and provide for future contingencies. A major goal of migration systems should be to move to improved software architectures that will provide adaptability and reduce life-cycle costs.

Many organizations are pursuing interoperability projects involving legacy systems. In an interoperability project, the goal is to provide data and functionality interchange between independently developed systems. In general, this is a technically challenging and expensive proposition. A mining study of both systems can be used to define common architectural abstractions. Initially, the common abstraction can be used to provide interoperability by integrating each system to the common framework. In the long run, the common abstraction may define the architecture target for evolution of the independent systems toward a common architecture.

The Farming Process

Farming is the process of representing the system requirements at the software architecture level. Most requirements for systems focus on user interface characteristics. Software architectures deal with software-to-software boundaries. Good architectures are independent of user interfaces because user interfaces are some of the most dynamically changing parts of the system.

Formal requirements can provide an overall shopping list of the kinds of components that will be needed in the system, describe the general operation of the system, and give other useful characteristics. It is important to understand the requirements thoroughly, but it is unreasonable to expect to derive an architecture mechanically directly from requirements. Even if it was possible, we believe it would be a mistake. A requirements document is a snapshot of the user's current needs. A good software architecture should support these requirements at the system level and transcend them to provide enough adaptability to support all anticipated future needs and many unanticipated ones.

Consider the potential dramatic changes over a 10- to 15-year system life cycle. An important measure of the quality of the architecture will be how well it adapts to those dramatic unanticipated changes. If the architecture is heavily dependent on transient requirements, such as a particular commercial, off-the-shelf product API, then the architecture probably will become obsolete within three years, as soon as there is a major product upgrade. If the architecture is heavily dependent on the current business process, then it may become obsolete following a reengineering activity (perhaps within five years). The skilled software architect knows how to isolate these dependencies on transient requirements. We provide some strategies and techniques later.

Requirements-driven design does not result in effective architectures because the requirements are not written with an architectural perspective. Generally, written requirements documents do not contain enough architectural substance to impact architecture design choices substantively. While this gives the architect some freedom, requirements documents often neglect to specify the need for a software architecture. If a software architecture is not part of the system deliverable, the developer seldom makes an extra investment to create one. Lack of a deliverable software architecture is a serious requirements defect; most requirements will change substantially over the system life cycle, and the software architecture is the only deliverable facility that provides for overall system adaptability and stability.

In addition to the formal requirements, the architect also must perform some additional research on the problem domain. This can take the form of domain analysis, which allows the architect to formulate some new detailed requirements as well as to gain an intuitive understanding of the problem domain that may prove invaluable. Domain analysis allows the architect to view the system from the perspective of the end user. It can use formal methodologies and notations, including object-oriented analysis, object-oriented design, and business process reengineering.

Composing and Refinement

The composing process is an artistic process of creating the software architecture. It follows the background research processes, which may include farming and mining. Composition is a very individualized process. Some architects begin with a strawman design that they can refine. Some propose multiple design concepts and trade off the alternatives. For others it is a gestalt process where they create the architectural concept from knowledge of the problem domain, experience, and intuition. Most architects have some prior system success upon which they base their philosophy and concept for the new architecture. In the composing process, the architectural vision is first created and elaborated.

Informal design reviews play an important role in the creative process. After initial composition and some refinement, it is time to take the design to friendly audiences, including some other various experts, managers, and developers. Soliciting initial feedback is necessarily an informal process. As the design gains more exposure and feedback, the architect can refine the design to incorporate new ideas and test cases. In addition to developing the technical design, the architect is learning to sell the architectural vision. It is crucial for the architect to choose the right way of explaining the design so that people understand it and have confidence in it. Management can play a key role in supporting the architect's organizational charter to control the design and protect its integrity. Consulting with various technical experts is useful to refine specific portions of the design. For example, if the architect is proposing an innovative metadata scheme, he or she can gain confidence, knowledge, and credibility by consulting with a metadata expert to refine that portion of the design.

Ultimately the interaction with the developers is the most important of all, in that, through this relationship, the architect will gain necessary implementation feedback to determine the true effectiveness of the design. Participating in the development team is an added benefit that can provide the architect with hands-on knowledge of the prototyping issues and enhanced rapport with the development staff.

Communication of the architectural vision to the developers is a key factor to system success. As we have suggested, communication tools should include a tutoriallike architecture review. The tutorial should cover all the key design concepts, relevant new technologies, and standards. This is an important leveling step that is essential to communicating the vision. This type of design information has been very elusive in previous systems; we believe a videotape record of the architecture tutorial should be a mandatory part of every new developer's training.

Prototyping and Lessons Learned

The software architecture should be stabilized (or frozen) whenever it supports active development. After prototyping begins architectural changes should be considered very carefully, and the changes should be implemented in discrete updates, after which all the prototype software is upgraded to support the current version.

Architecture updates and prototyping should be synchronized carefully. The architecture updates should occur at natural transition points in the prototyping activity. Figure 4.6 shows an evolutionary development process that alternates architecture updates with prototyping activities. In this case, the design and development process is a series of iterative steps, which guar-

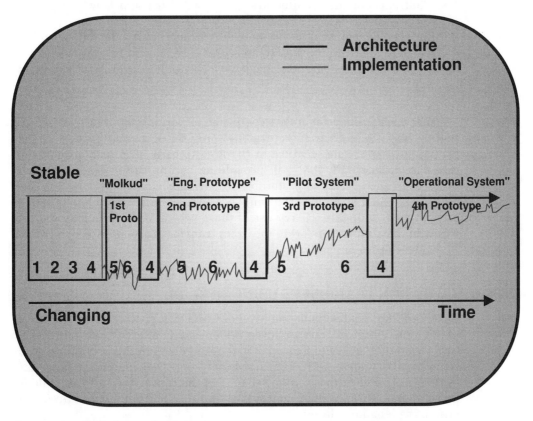

Figure 4.6. Evolutionary development.

antees architecture stability during development, and enhances architecture maturity (robustness) in each iteration.

Knowledge is gained at many levels during each architecture iteration. For example, there may be end-user deliverables that are driving the process. Through end-user and developer feedback, the architect gains insight into the architecture's strengths and weaknesses. The developer gains experience with the subsystems and component technologies as the system evolves.

Architecture updates should be driven primarily by real testbed experiences in implementing the design. Updates should be consistent with the architectural vision and avoid compromises for specific products, short-term performance needs, or component implementation dependencies. The lessons learned in the prototyping experience contain the detailed feedback that confirm or deny architecture choices and indicate the need for changes. In relating the lessons learned, key questions for the developer and architect to discuss include:

1. What parts of the architecture were used? Why and how? What parts were not used?
2. Does the developer understand the interoperability, flexibility, and extensibility features of the architecture? If so, how were these used?
3. Did the developer extend or need to work around the architecture in any way?

Wherever the developers are compelled to work around the architecture, there is likely to be an architectural flaw or a lack of communication. In fact, it is useful to put some feature in the architecture, such as a very flexible message-passing API, that will provide an escape valve to address these unforeseen needs. This is preferable to having the developers invent their own workaround strategies that may not be easily discovered or changed in an architecture update. Heavy use of these very flexible APIs may indicate a flaw in the architecture or an incorrect transfer of the architectural vision to the developers.

INTERFACE DESIGN TRADE-OFFS USING OMG IDL

Careful design trade-offs at the level of OMG IDL specifications are necessary to make the software architecture optimally effective. An idiom is an expression that is peculiar to a particular language. In this section we study some key IDL idioms. OMG IDL is distinct from other computing languages in its syntax and purpose. In order to give the reader the full rationale for these idioms, we introduce concepts from an important related area, programming language design.

Programming language design is a discipline closely associated with interface definition. It is a research area of computer science in which scientists define new high-level abstractions specifying the actions of computer systems. Whereas a software architect defines the programmer's interfaces to subsystem components, language designers define the programmer's interface to the machine. Some of the best languages are concisely specified, very easy to learn, and very flexible in their applicability. Good languages adhere to many of the architecture design principles that we are espousing in this book. Programming language design has more degrees of freedom than the practice of defining OMG IDL interfaces. Nevertheless, there are a number of important concepts from language design that are highly applicable to OMG IDL interfaces.

A key trade-off in programming language design involves the restriction of inefficient operations. A programming language defines a higher-level abstraction of the underlying machine. This abstraction must balance the convenience of specifying operations with the cost of the operations in terms of machine resources. In high-end systems, there has been an interesting shift in the underlying machine model toward vector and massively parallel processing. These changes are affecting new language definitions. For example, changes in FORTRAN from the 1960s to the 1990s show the increased importance of vector parallel processing.

An effective language design must restrict programmers from inadvertently invoking highly inefficient operations. For example, most languages restrict the passing of arrays and structures by value in function calls, an operation that might require memory allocation and copying of the structure.

These programming language restrictions actually make it more difficult for the programmer to do certain types of operations. To the software architecture designer this concept is very important. In many design choices, the architect controls the ease or difficulty of using an architectural feature. For example, if we want to guarantee certain properties in the architecture, such as interoperability or synchronization, we need to make it as difficult as possible for the programmers to work around our intentions. In other cases, we want to facilitate the ease of use. For example, we could include a powerful feature supporting extensibility that enables the developer to extend the architecture in useful ways. Generally it is a good idea to provide a range of restrictive and extensible operations in an architecture.

Data types provide some important idioms for controlling architecture restrictions using OMG IDL. The purpose of data types in OMG IDL is to allow the definition of the parameters of operations. There is a full range of available types, including scalar types and complex user defined types. Perhaps the most restrictive OMG IDL parameter type is the enumeration. The architect can define a fixed set of values that can be passed as a parameter. For example:

```
interface FruitBasket1 {
    enum  Fruit  { APPLE, ORANGE, PEAR };
    Fruit takeone(in Fruit preference);
    };
```

As a parameter, the Fruit enumeration will allow only the specification of apple, orange, or pear. Specifying a grapefruit or a watermelon would not be possible. Developers might try to work around this by specifying an illegal enumeration value. That would be a conscious subversion of an architectural restriction. The rationale for why an enumeration is used should be clearly defined in the architecture documentation and perhaps could be explained directly in the OMG IDL comments.

Other than modifying the specification, there is no legal way to extend an OMG IDL enumeration. Architects should use enumerations judiciously where they are necessary or where they are unlikely to change over the system life cycle.

An alternative approach that has much more extensibility is to substitute a string parameter for an enumeration, as in the following example:

```
interface FruitBasket2 {
    typedef string Fruit;
    Fruit takeone(in Fruit Preference);
    };
```

In this case, the choice of fruit preferences is unlimited. There also is no guidance to the developer as to what the potential choices are. (From the IDL, the developer does not know what fruit to ask for and has no way to anticipate of what fruit will be returned.) This dilemma can be solved in several ways. Without extending the interface, we could provide some constant definitions to establish a set of fruit terminology, for example:

```
//OMG IDL - Constant Definitions for Fruit Basket Interface
//Developers may define their own fruit types as new string
//literals.
const string APPLE   = "APPLE";
const string ORANGE = "ORANGE";
const string PEAR    = "PEAR";
```

We also could include comments such as the one just given explaining how developers can safely extend this interface by defining new string-valued fruit types. Architects want to resist creating new APIs whenever possible, because they add to system cost and complexity.

Note that the OMG IDL file containing the fruit types could be maintained separately from the OMG IDL file defining the APIs. In this way, we can extend the defined set of fruit without changing the base class definition file. This technique is discussed in the separation of Hierarchies section on page 86.

OMG IDL is a strongly typed language. It allows architects to define simple and complex types of many forms that are compile-time checked by the implementation language compilers. Strongly typed languages are great for defining type restrictions, and OMG IDL extends these benefits across many programming languages.

OMG IDL also supports dynamic typing through the type "any." Values of type "any" can be of an arbitrary OMG IDL type. A value of type "any" includes a typecode, which indicates the type. Typecode symbols generated by OMG IDL compilers, improve the convenience of the handling of type "any." Generally if the value of type "any" needs to be accessed, the typecode can be tested and the value recast to the appropriate predefined type.

Type "any" is very important to software architects interested in building extensible systems. For example, type "any" enables software to pass unforeseen types through a set of robust architecture APIs.

In some cases, the architect might avoid using type "any" because of its extreme extensbility. For example, type "any" should be avoided if we want to provide some set of restrictions on parameters that guarantee interoperability.

A more restricted alternative to type "any" is to use self-descriptive parameters. For example, the following is a very flexible type that can represent any file format, such as data formatted in TIFF or PostScript:

```
struct FormattedData {
    string          representation;
    sequence<octet> value;
    };
```

The structure for FormattedData contains a tag "representation" that identifies the format. Because this is a string-valued tag, it is user extensible. The "value" is any arbitrary sequence of bytes, which makes this a very general-purpose form of "flat-file" data.

The previous example uses a sequence type. The OMG IDL sequence type is like a variable-length array; the elements have homogeneous values (including type "any") and the length can be defined at run time. Sequences are very useful for passing lists of entities. The lists can be any runtime length, and they even can be object handles.

We have found OMG IDL to be an outstanding language for architectural specification. It allows a great range of control of architectural restrictions in interfaces, and these restrictions are enforced by compiler-time checks in multiple programming languages.

SOFTWARE ACHITECTURE DESIGN PRINCIPLES

As in programming language design, software architecture is more art than science. Nevertheless, there are many important architectural design principles (or design patterns) that can be useful in creating more effective software architectures. The following sections describe some of these key design principles and strategies.

Abstraction/Simplicity

Many organizations do not even consider abstraction or simplicity to be an important consideration in software design. We consider simplicity to be perhaps the most important architectural quality; that is why we are presenting it first among our architecture principles. Simplicity is the visible characteristic of a software architecture that has successfully managed system complexity.

Functionality and simplicity are often considered to be opposing goals. Functionality can be increased by adding new features to the design—by increasing the complexity. In a committee design process, it is usually more politically acceptable to add features than to remove them. In that way, everyone can contribute ideas to a design and no one's ideas get excluded. Without much difficulty, it is easy to create specifications that no one person understands because they are too large, too complex, and inconsistent. Unfortunately, most specifications that you will encounter in practice have these characteristics. Traditional, non-OMG standards have swelled to an almost unbelievable complexity. In one generation, Structured Query Language (SQL) has increased in complexity by an order of magnitude (from less than 100 pages to more than 500 pages). Technology suppliers are driven to excess complexity because having a lot of features is considered a marketing benefit. Understanding enough of one complex specification to provide some useful capability is a full-time challenge. To build a useful system, numerous specifications must be utilized and integrated. This is one of the key challenges of systems integration, and it is the software architecture's role to manage this complexity.

An important example of excess complexity is provided by EMACS, a text editor on UNIX systems. EMACS was developed in an academic setting, where multiple developers could contribute their software extensions. The user interface evolved into a classic committee design. EMACS commands comprise hundreds of unintuitive control sequences. For example, CONTROL-X+CONTROL-S and CONTROL-META-LINEFEED provide alternative ways to save the text file. EMACS is programmable, so that users may add their own control sequences. We know people who have spent major portions of their careers creating their personalized EMACS environments. We have used EMACS for many years but now find it quite anachronistic compared to today's mature editor technologies, which are quite intuitive and so simple that they can be learned and used easily without documentation.

EMACS provides an important analogy for software architectures. Like modern text editors, good software architectures are simple, elegant, and mature designs that are easy to understand. Ease of understanding can yield substantial cost savings. About half of all software development time involves "system discovery" (trying to understand how the system works).

A primary difference between software architects and programmers is that only the architect is concerned about the cost of the design. Architects deal with system-level issues where cost is a serious concern. A mistake or inefficiency in the architecture can have consequences in every subsystem, whereas a mistake in a subsystem is usually an isolated software defect.

There is a direct relationship between simplicity and cost. In computing, many phenomena occur in factors of 2. Let's consider doubling the size of an architecture specification, for example, providing twice as many APIs than a more simplified design for integrating legacy and COTS components. In an architecture, every new API adds development cost to every subsystem's integration code. Suppose several servers support each API as well as several clients. Doubling the number of APIs could more than double the cost of initial systems integration. Each time we add a new client or server, on average, we need to support twice as many APIs to provide interoperability; thus our system extension cost can double as well. System extension due to changing requirements involves about half of all software life-cycle costs. The new APIs can double the size of development documentation and can double the cost of interface design (both substantial cost factors). On average, testing and debugging will involve twice as many APIs, which will more than double the cost of these activities. Training of software developers can take double the investment and require double the replacement cost due to staff turnover. Overall, we pay a big price for complexity.

Only about one out of five software developers has the capability to create good abstractions [Coplien, 94]. Part of the problem is that abstraction is not a concept widely conveyed in computer science education. These one in five are different from the one in 20 developers who display exceptional programming productivity. In fact, abstraction abilities and exceptional programming abilities are somewhat incompatible because they represent two fundamentally different perspectives of computer systems, one desiring a simplified system model, the other thriving in the complexity of the details. In order to create good software systems, the people who have the abstraction ability should be recognized and promoted into positions of responsibility and authority as software architects.

Interoperability versus Extensibility

Interoperability and extensibility are also important properties of a software architecture. Here we define these properties and describe how they interact in an architecture design.

Interoperability is the ability to exchange functionality and interpretable data between two software entities. Interoperability can be defined in terms

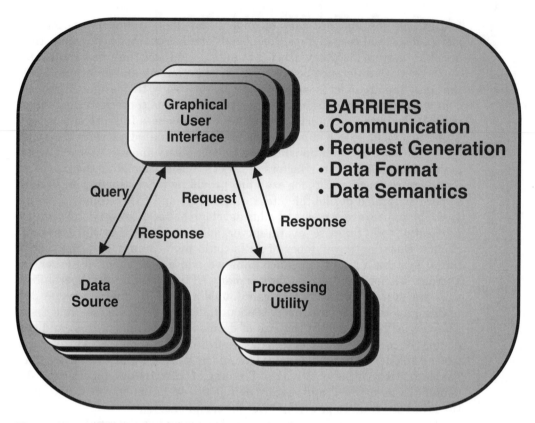

Figure 4.7. Definition of interoperability.

of four enabling requirements: communication, request generation, data format, and semantics. The software entities require a communication channel with a common communication protocol. Across this channel, the entities need to be able to formulate and transmit an interpretable request for functions or data. The result from the request must be returned to the recipient in a data interchange. Data interchange also implies a requirement for a data format that can be parsed syntactically by the recipient. The last requirement is that both entities understand the request and data through some form of semantic translation.

The interoperability problem in current software systems is that there are too many conflicting solutions for each of these requirements. There are many different communication protocols. Commercial and legacy software contain many different/conflicting protocols and levels. There are many standard and proprietary request generation languages and conflicting dialects of these languages, such as SQL, Wide Area Information Services (WAIS), scripting languages, and so on. There are numerous data formats; virtually every software package defines a new one. The semantic requirement is still primarily a research area, so the available solutions are divergent and immature.

CORBA simplifies the problem of interoperability somewhat. It provides a consistent, uniform service access mechanism that enables ubiquitous transparent communications. Through Object Service definitions such as the naming service and the query service, OMG standards provide standard ways to generate requests. Object Services such as the data interchange service will address data interchange issues. The OMG standards process can support the standardization and commercialization of new services covering semantic mediation and other areas of interoperability.

Extensibility is the characteristic of an architecture to support unforeseen uses and adapt to new developer requirements. Extensibility is a very important property for long life cycle architectures where many new requirements will be levied against the design. Built-in extensibility is necessary in order to support the needs of developers as they add new system improvements throughout the life cycle.

Interoperability and extensibility are sometimes conflicting goals in an architecture design. Interoperability requires a constrained relationship between software entities, which provides guarantees of mutual compatibility of request syntax and data formats. A flexible relationship is necessary for extensibility, which can easily extend into areas of incompatibility. In general, it is very easy to make two software entities incompatible; minor changes in data format or request syntax can easily prevent interoperability. It is no wonder that separately developed applications share so little software reuse and interoperability; lack of compatibility is the natural result of the brittleness of technology. Creating interoperability requires rigorous interchange conventions and extraordinary cooperation.

The architect can facilitate interoperability by designing some operations into the architecture that constrain the parameters to guarantee interoperability. The following is an example of a well-constrained interface for exchanging positional information. The "position" struct self-identifies its own unit value. It uses an enumeration to constrain the choice of units to two possibilities. It is a simple interface comprising send and receive operations. The exception values cover all of the reasonable cases, and provide good error traceability to the client. All of the data types are strongly typed. With this type of interface, interoperability is likely to be assured between a client and a server supporting it.

```
// OMG IDL
// Example Constrained for Interoperability
interface PositionInterchange1 {
      enum Units {INCHES, CENTIMETERS};
      struct Position {
            Units unitkind;
            double    x, y, z;
            };
```

```
exception X_OUT_OF_RANGE { Position position_parameter; };
exception Y_OUT_OF_RANGE { Position position_parameter; };
exception Z_OUT_OF_RANGE { Position position_parameter; };
void send_position(in Position current_position)
      raises(  X_OUT_OF_RANGE,
               Y_OUT_OF_RANGE,
               Z_OUT_OF_RANGE );
void retrieve_position(out Position current_position);
};
```

The architect can facilitate extensibility by designing some operations into the architecture that provide highly extensible parameters and request syntax. The extensible operations need to provide extra conventions in the IDL or documentation in order to encourage some level of interoperability. The following is an example of a more extensible version of PositionInterchange. Note that this example is an exaggeration of the changes that you might make to add extensibility. In this case, the Units type is an arbitrary string. We have established some units conventions using constants. The position structure contains a sequence of type "any" to specify the coordinates. This would allow for four-dimensional coordinates or virtually unlimited types of coordinate specifications. The operations now pass sequences of positions so that multiple entities can be monitored. Each position has a self-describing entity ID string that enables the association between entities and positions. The exception and the operations have an extra type "any" parameter, which would allow additional request or response information. The applications that use these interfaces can extend the uses of this interface widely. This interface also could be misused to convey messages unrelated to position interchange. Note also that this is a substantially more complicated interface to program than the restricted example; it requires more code to implement simple usages and a great deal of code to handle general cases of its usage.

```
// OMG IDL
// Example Unrestricted for Extensibility
interface PositionInterchange2 {
    typedef string Units;
    const string INCHUNITS = "inches";
    const string CENTIMETERUNITS = "centimeters";
    struct Position {
    string           entityid;
    Units            unitkind;
        sequence<any> coordinates;
        };
    typedef sequence<Position> PositionSeq;
    exception OUT_OF_RANGE { Position invalid_position;
                             any error_data };
```

```
exception BAD_REQUEST { any error_data };
void send_positions(    in any request,
                        in PositionSeq current_positions,
                        out any status )
                        raises(BAD_REQUEST, OUT_OF_RANGE );
void retrieve_position( in any request,
                        out PositionSeq current_positions,
                        out any status )
                        raises( BAD_REQUEST );
};
```

It is important to include a range of operation extensibility in software architectures. Some operations should guarantee interoperability, and some should provide for extensibility. It is unnecessary to go to the extremes of extensibility as shown in the previous example, but it is useful to have at least one highly extensible operation in the architecture as a last resort for developers to implement architecture workarounds. An analysis of the ways that developers utilize the extensible operation will reveal the need for improved communication of the architectural vision and provide important feedback to consider in architecture revisions.

Symmetry

Symmetry in the architecture design is a key property for achieving component interchange, code simplification, and reconfigurability. Symmetry is the practice of using a common interface for a wide range of software components. It can be realized as a common interface implemented by all subsystems or as a common base class with specializations for each subsystem. The common interface should embody the basic interoperability services provided by the architecture.

In a symmetric architecture, the clients are not hard-coded to specific services; instead they are coded to the common interface framework. Since all objects support the common interface, general interoperability is guaranteed. It is also possible to add, subtract, and interchange services without affecting the existing software.

In contrast, an asymmetric architecture is one in which every application provides a different software interface. In that case, the client code becomes dedicated to particular services. If a client uses multiple services, it must have separate code for each service. When a new application is added, new code must be written in every client using the service. Asymmetry leads to cascading costs, requiring architecture-wide code modifications whenever the system is extended or reconfigured.

Symmetric architectures have many advantages, and we believe that symmetry should be a principle behind most general-purpose architectures. If symmetry is implemented through a common base class, then the special-

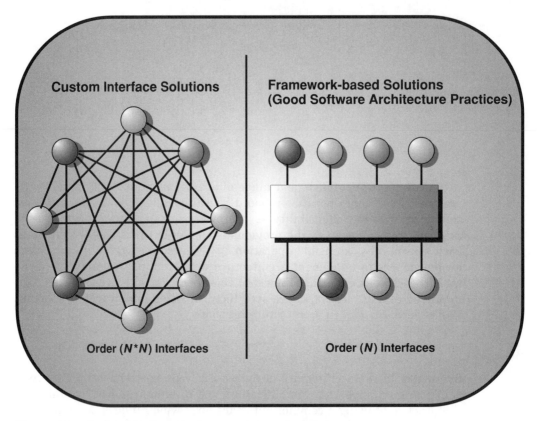

Figure 4.8.   Custom interfaces vs. framework-based solutions.

izations play the role of an asymmetric architecture overlying the symmetric architecture. There are many cases where this is reasonable. Two possible motives are for special performance and special functionality. Suppose an architecture needs general interoperability, but some subsystems need to interchange very large images. The image applications might need a specialized interface to support efficient image transfers. Another example is where there are special functionality needs, for example, between a back-end map database and a front-end mapping user interface. In this case, the mapping user interface could reasonably be dedicated to use a specialized back-end map service. If a standard is available supporting the special functionality, it is preferable to utilize the standard rather than a custom interface. Use of standards improves architecture stability, enables component interchange, and reduces risks.

Component Isolation

Component isolation is the architectural property that limits the scope of changes as the system evolves. Component isolation means that a change in one subsystem will not require changes in other subsystems. A good architecture limits the scope of changes within modules instead of across the system.

Object encapsulation is a basic concept behind component isolation. Encapsulation means that the users of an interface (clients) are isolated from the details of the implementation behind the interface. In other words, the implementation can be completely replaced or modified without impacting clients. OMG IDL is a useful tool for specifying good encapsulations. CORBA provides excellent isolation between clients and object implementations. Implementations can be replaced, modified, recompiled, in different languages, in different activation states, in different locations, and all these changes can be made without impacting client software at the OMG IDL level.

Conventions for handling parameter data also have an impact on component isolation. Different implementations can handle parameters differently, and the code that creates and utilizes this data may be impacted by changes in the implementation.

For example, if we have two SQL databases that support a common query service, and these databases use different dialects of SQL, then the interchange of these components could impact the client software that generates the dynamic queries. Wherever possible, the architect should anticipate the impact of changes at the parameter level and provide some approach to enhance component isolation. Possible approaches include: insertion of a mediator or middleware package that provides vendor-neutral SQL, use of self-identifying data to identify the SQL dialect, use of server metadata to provide some query templates, or the provision of some OMG IDL operations with constraints that guarantee interoperability. To elaborate this last point, we could include a special query operation that partitions the dynamic query into type-checked parameters that are independent of SQL dialect.

In the earlier description of the Mining Process, we discussed how to design generalized interfaces that provide a common abstraction of multiple commercial products and legacy systems. This is an important technique for isolating a system from component product dependencies.

Metadata

Metadata in an architecture is self-descriptive information. Metadata can describe both services and information. Service metadata describes the available services and functions that the reachable applications can provide. Information metadata describes the structure and access procedures for persistent information. An example of service metadata is the Macintosh chooser, which is an on-line directory of printers, file servers, and other services. An example of information metadata is the facilities within SQL92 that standardize how relational databases store and retrieve their schema data.

Metadata is essential for system reconfigurability. With metadata, new services can be added to a system and discovered at runtime. Metadata is the resource that allows client software to be written without hard-coding all calls to particular servers. This enables system reconfiguration, component interchange, and the possibility of multiple components providing similar services. For example, we could create an architecture that provides on-line metadata to identify the object handle of the database. In another installation of the software, we might have the clients access another database, which is at their location. In the future, we may want to add multiple databases to the system. The metadata supports the dynamic binding of the clients to the servers and enables the creation of multiple symmetric servers.

Metadata is most useful when it is provided in a consistent form across many services. Using metadata provides many benefits, but it does require additional software. The amount of software needed can be minimized if metadata is defined consistently and is accessed in the simplest possible manner to relay the essential information. Metadata's utility is maximized when it is used ubiquitously. The benefits of metadata greatly outweigh its cost and complexity.

Metadata does not have to be complicated to be useful. We have found that relatively simple forms of metadata that identify servers and provide a consistent denotation of schemas covers most of the metadata needs in an architecture. Metadata standards are very complex and expensive to implement. As an example, the Information Resource Dictionary system is a formal standard of nearly 1,000 pages of specification.

One simplifying technique for metadata involves consistent representation of schemas across many kinds of data sources. Figure 4.9 shows an example of a common scheme for representing schemas of relational databases, mapping databases, and object-oriented databases. This is a very high level of data abstraction, but it may be all the detail that is needed at the architecture level to provide interoperability. This particular approach will not meet all the needs of specialists in any of these fields, but it does provide an inexpensive common way for general-purpose clients and browsers to discover data across all types of data sources. Specialists can rely on much more complex vertical market standards for their needs, and they can do this without requiring every client to support the extra complexity.

The OMG has several current and future standards supporting metadata: the interface repository (IR), the naming service, and the trader service. The IR is an on-line source of interface descriptions. It is an integral part of

Data Model	Relational Table Analogy	Column Analogy	Retrieved Data
Relational database	Table	Column	A list of records
Map/GIS	Product	Overlay	A particular map
Image database	Image product	Overlay	An image with overlays
Object-Oriented Database	Class	Attribute	A set of instances

Figure 4.9. Consistent metadata abstraction.

the CORBA standard [OMG, 92a]. The IR supports runtime discovery and invocation of operations. The OMG IDL interface objects in the IR represent all the accessible object types. The naming service is an adopted specification, and part of the Common Object Services Specification [OMG, 94b]. The naming service provides a directory service analogous to the telephone book white pages. If the client knows the string-valued name of an object, the naming service retrieves the object handle. The trader service is currently a draft ISO standard, part of the ISO Open Distributed Process series of standards. When the ISO standard is stable, it will be submitted through the OMG Fast Track process for adoption. The trader service is a directory service analogous to the telephone book yellow pages. If the client knows the type of service, the trader can return a list of candidate services, including some key server characteristics.

The three OMG metadata services cover most architectural needs. Note that the naming service is supplied without a set of naming contexts, which should be specified by the architect. Similarly, the trader service is specified without a schema, which requires the architect to structure the service types and service characteristics.

Other types of metadata may be useful in an architecture. We have found that associating a metadata object with each server is a useful technique. The server metadata can provide more detailed information than stored in the trader. Since the server manages access to this data, it can be more sensitive in nature than information advertised in a public directory. It also can contain server-specific information, such as information about the schema, documentation, request syntax, sample requests, and request templates.

Separation of Hierarchies

Good software architecture provides a stable basis for component and systems integration. In a particular architecture problem, some aspects are more stable than others. By separating the problem into pieces, often we can enhance the stability of the whole.

Some parts of the architecture need to be very stable; other parts can be more flexible. The stability of the API designs is critical to architecture success. If the API designs are unstable, any changes can lead to systemwide software upgrades. Flexible elements can include virtually any domain-specific information. For example, the list of domain-specific properties might be relatively unknown at initial system design time and may even evolve while the system is operational. An important design strategy is to separate the uncertain or changing elements from the stable elements of the architecture. This separation can enhance the system's adaptability and provide a guideline for developers on how to extend the system.

In terms of OMG IDL, separation of hierarchies means creating separate IDL files. Perhaps the most critical OMG IDL files are sets of common base-class interfaces that provide the common set of operations for all components in the software architecture. Other OMG IDL files can contain the specialty API interfaces so that they can be included at the discretion of programmers. All of the API files need to be very stable, so they should contain the proper balance of interoperability guarantees and built-in extensibility. Other files in the flexible category include definitions of domain-specific object properties, specialty data types, domain-specific data types, and domain-specific constants. All of these specifications should be configured in a way so that individual developers can add extensions without changing the common definitions.

SOFTWARE ARCHITECTURE PATTERNS

The following sections describe a set of architectural patterns that present key tradeoffs in the design of effective software architectures. Since these are abstract architecture concepts, our intention is to provide enough information for you to understand the basic concept without investing excessive time. We present these patterns in particular because they highlight our architectural guidance.

The patterns are presented in three groups, the first focusing on the basic architecture concepts, the second explaining a particular family of advanced patterns, and the third looking at a wide range of architectural concepts to present these ideas within the more general context of commercial technologies.

Basic Architecture Patterns

The basic architecture patterns correspond to some general design perspectives. These patterns include custom, vertical, horizontal, and hybrid. The scope of these patterns relates to the specific architecture and the multiproject community context in which the design is formulated. This community scope is important because it represents the potential audience for reuse of

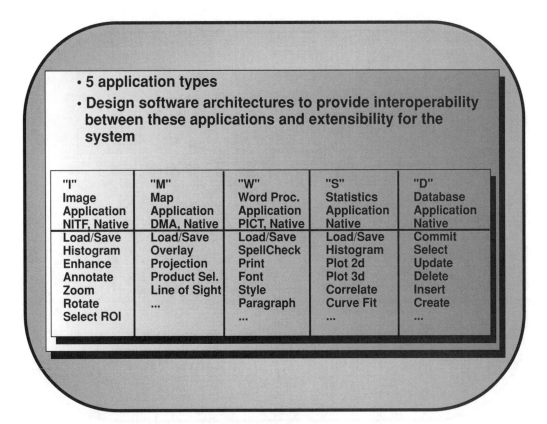

Figure 4.10. An example of an architecture design problem.

design and transfer of software. Our work differs from research on Design Patterns, which often has a focus on programming issues well below the architecture level. [Coplien, 94]

Here we compare the four basic patterns using a common design problem, the integration of five types of applications. A sixth application type is introduced when the system is extended.

In order to provide the community context, we consider the impact of the architecture pattern across two similar systems. The analysis includes a consideration of some common architectural changes: system extension, subsystem replacement, and system migration. In the latter case, we are considering the merger of the two similar systems into a common system. This corresponds to many current downsizing and migration projects. The analysis results define how the development costs scale with system size and provide some interesting quantitative arguments supporting our architectural guidance.

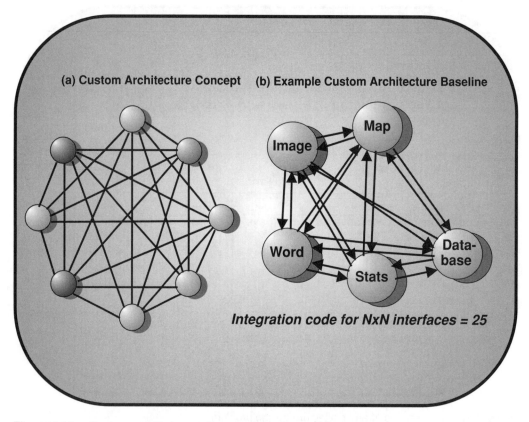

Figure 4.11.   Custom architecture pattern and baseline architecture.

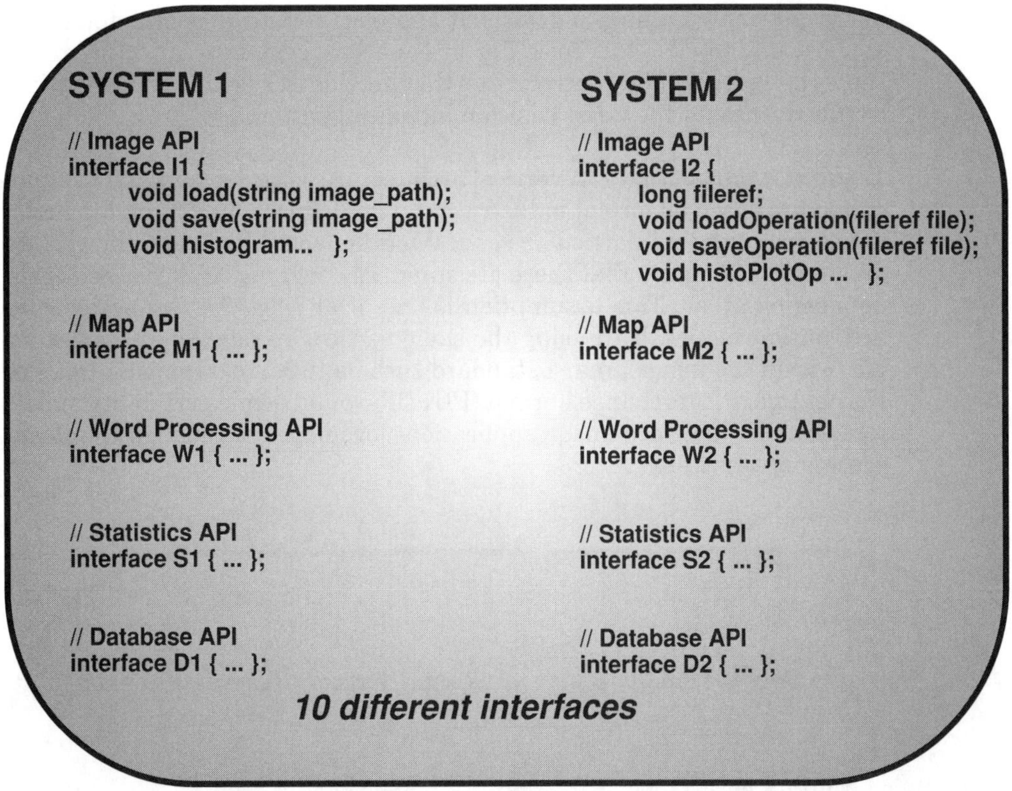

SYSTEM 1

```
// Image API
interface I1 {
        void load(string image_path);
        void save(string image_path);
        void histogram...   };


// Map API
interface M1 { ... };


// Word Processing API
interface W1 { ... };


// Statistics API
interface S1 { ... };


// Database API
interface D1 { ... };
```

SYSTEM 2

```
// Image API
interface I2 {
        long fileref;
        void loadOperation(fileref file);
        void saveOperation(fileref file);
        void histoPlotOp ...   };




// Map API
interface M2 { ... };


// Word Processing API
interface W2 { ... };


// Statistics API
interface S2 { ... };


// Database API
interface D2 { ... };
```

10 different interfaces

Figure 4.12.   Custom architecture PIDL.

Custom Architecture   A custom architecture is designed in terms of application-specific APIs. Each application has a unique API that is not based particularly on industry standards. A summary of the Pseudo IDL (PIDL) is provided in Figure 4.12. This IDL shows that two systems with five applications both designed as custom architectures will yield a set of ten unique APIs.

The custom APIs are utilized on an as-needed basis within the implementation. Our user model (based on two comprehensive surveys) indicates that there is a strong rationale for providing most or all of these connections; we would anticipate paying the development cost for fully populating these connections as system extensions over the system life cycle. In terms of our analysis, we shall assume that this is done as part of the initial development.

Custom architecture might be considered a negative example. Custom architectures are the natural result of design without architectural focus. In the integration capability model in Figure 4.3, the custom architecture is a typical product of organizations at levels 2 to 4. These are groups that are using distributed computing without applying architecture principles such as those presented in this book. For this analysis, custom architecture represents the experimental control group that provides a baseline for comparison of effectiveness of the other basic architectural patterns.

Vertical Architecture   A vertical architecture is the likely result of an architecture based on formal industry standards. Since many formal industry standards represent particular vertical market specialty areas, the vertical architecture assumes that there are standards defining APIs for each of the application areas. This assumption is true if at least the two systems we are considering are both using the same vertical specifications. For example, within the image area, a standard such as ISO Programmer's Imaging Kernel/Image Interchange Format (PIK/IIF) would define portability and interoperability between image applications for image interchange and image processing services.

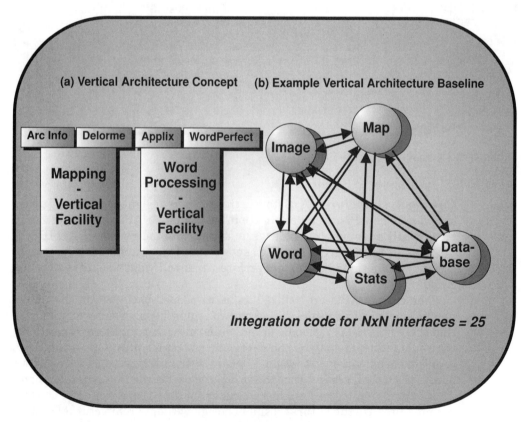

Figure 4.13.   Vertical architecture pattern and baseline architecture.

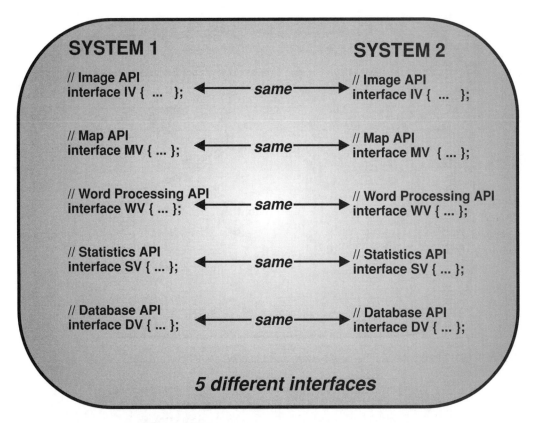

Figure 4.14. Vertical architecture PIDL.

The PIDL for the vertical architecture is shown in Figure 4.14. The vertical standards appear in the PIDL because the interfaces for each kind of application are identical across systems. Within each system, there are still five different API interfaces, one for each application. Between the two systems, there are five different software interfaces.

Horizontal Architecture   The horizontal architecture is an example of a fully symmetric architecture where the interfaces are common between applications. Integration of an application to a horizontal architecture requires only one interface to be constructed. Horizontal architectures are very extensible because of the low integration cost.

The PIDL for the horizontal architecture appears in Figure 4.16 on page 92. Since all interfaces are common, only one type of interface is needed for integrating all applications in both systems. DISCUS (see Chapter 7) and Object Linking and Embedding (OLE2)'s Uniform Data Transfer are real-world examples of horizontal architectures. The limitation of these architectures is

(a) Horizontal Architecture Concept
(b) Example Horizontal Architecture Baseline
Map
Image
Word
Stats
Data-
base
Integration code for 2N interfaces = 10

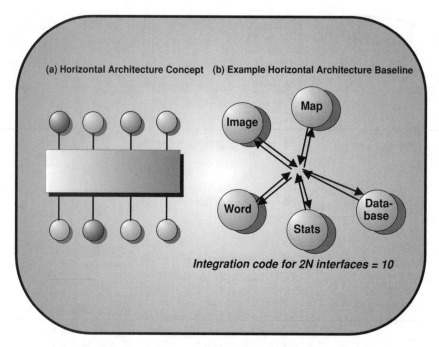

Figure 4.15. Horizontal architecture pattern and baseline architecture.

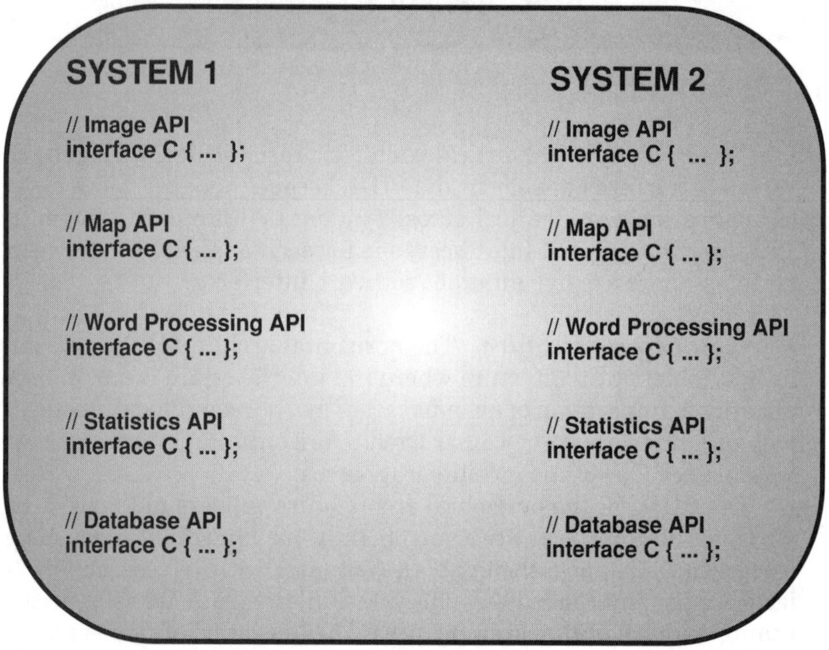

SYSTEM 1
// Image API
interface C { ... };
// Map API
interface C { ... };
// Word Processing API
interface C { ... };
// Statistics API
interface C { ... };
// Database API
interface C { ... };
SYSTEM 2
// Image API
interface C { ... };
// Map API
interface C { ... };
// Word Processing API
interface C { ... };
// Statistics API
interface C { ... };
// Database API
interface C { ... };

Figure 4.16. Horizontal architecture PIDL.

that they do not address specialized needs. They require an unprecedented level of consensus and coordination both within and between projects. With these limitations, pure horizontal architectures probably are not practical for large communities of developers. The next pattern, the hybrid architecture, uses both horizontal and vertical standards eclectically.

Hybrid Horizontal/Vertical Architecture   The hybrid architecture is a combination of both the horizontal and vertical concepts. The hybrid architecture uses a common horizontal interface as an inherited base class for each of the application interfaces. This guarantees a minimal acceptable level of interoperability between all applications. The hybrid also uses vertical standards where needed. The vertical standards are applied as specializations of the horizontal interface.

There is some latitude in the design of hybrid architectures. The horizontal and vertical standards represent a range of integration options. At a minimum, all applications should provide horizontal interoperability. Verti-

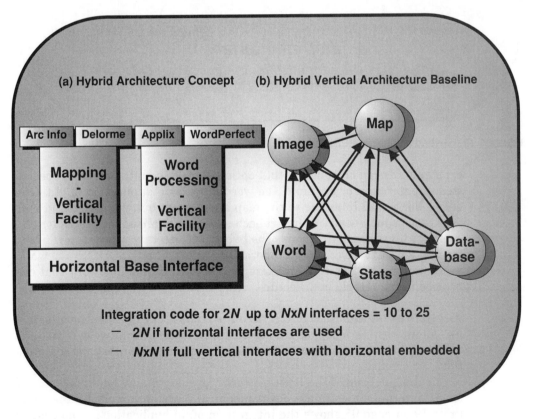

Figure 4.17.   Hybrid architecture pattern and baseline architecture.

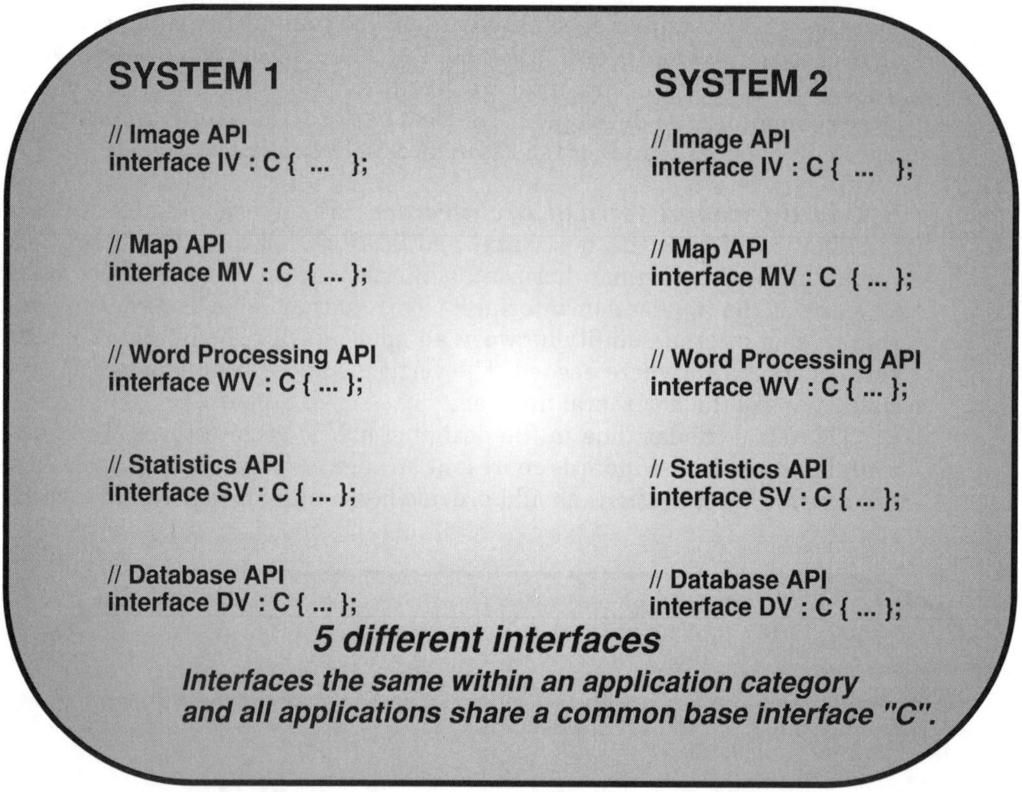

Figure 4.18.   Hybrid architecture PIDL.

cal standards can be added to that optionally, based on the need for specialized integration. For example, the word processing application might need
only a horizontal interface to the map application, but the image and map
applications may need to support each other's specialized interfaces for efficiency or functionality reasons. The hybrid architecture presents a range of
integration costs based on interoperability needs. The DISCUS Framework,
presented in Chapter 7, is an example of a horizontal framework that can
be used in the Hybrid architecture.

Analysis of the Basic Architecture Patterns   The basic patterns establish an interesting model of architecture development that we can compare
to different design practices and levels of community architecture coordination.

In this analysis of the basic patterns, we use the implementation code
for an interface to estimate development and system extension cost. Figure 4.19 on page 95 shows the integration of an application in the custom
architecture. The preexisting application is considered to be commercial or

legacy code that is supplied by an external technology source. To create the system, we add a layer of integration code providing support for the appropriate interfaces. In the case of the custom architecture, this integration code includes four client interfaces and support for one service interface.

Each piece of integration code must address many issues beyond basic support for the architecture APIs. The integration must address the mapping between the application's APIs and the architecture APIs. The integration must address the format mappings and required conversions. Security and error handling are also important issues that must be addressed in the integration code. In some cases there may also be a need for semantic translations of information. By bundling these issues into the integration code cost, we can total the number of interfaces to estimate the relative software cost of architecture development and modification for different architecture patterns.

Four development cost scenarios are evaluated for each of the architecture patterns, as follows. The first scenario is initial system development. The development cost reflects all of the initial integration code required to

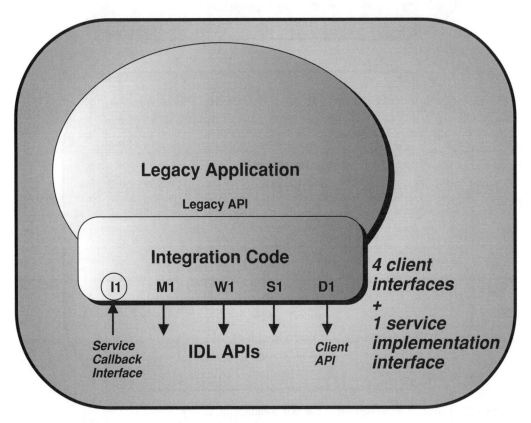

Figure 4.19.   Application code vs. integration code.

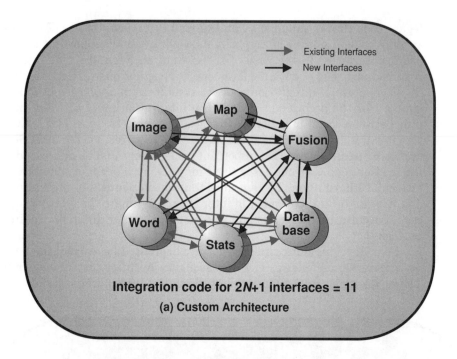

Integration code for 2*N*+1 interfaces = 11

(a) Custom Architecture

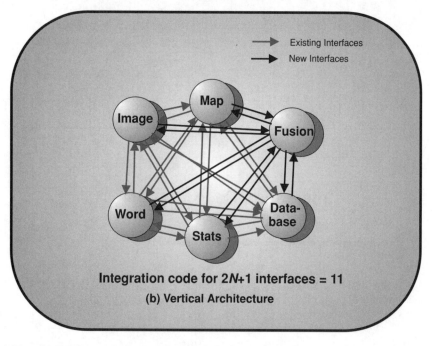

Integration code for 2*N*+1 interfaces = 11

(b) Vertical Architecture

Figure 4.20. System extension using the four architecture patterns.

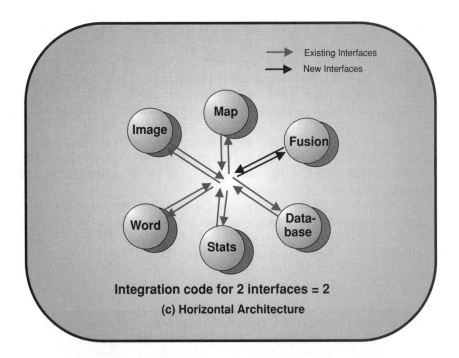

Integration code for 2 interfaces = 2

(c) Horizontal Architecture

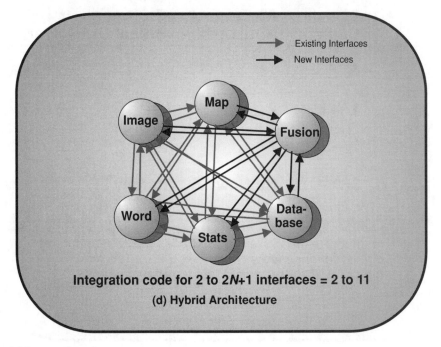

Integration code for 2 to 2N+1 interfaces = 2 to 11

(d) Hybrid Architecture

Figure 4.20. continued.

create the system. The second scenario is a system extension. In each case, a sixth application is added to the system. The new application obeys the same architecture pattern conventions. The third scenario is an application replacement. A new application is integrated in place of the one in the original architecture. In the fourth scenario, the two systems are merged to create a common interoperable system with twice as many applications.

In the analysis, the development cost is incurred for all of the integration code needed to implement the architecture-level interfaces. This includes both client and server codes for a particular application-to-application connection. If architecture standards allow the reuse of integration code, then this is reflected as a cost savings.

Figure 4.20 shows the results of the analysis for an arbitrary size system, where N is the number of applications. This model shows that the custom architecture requires high costs for initial system development and all forms of system modification. The vertical architecture provides no real cost benefits for initial development and system extension. It saves about half the cost of component replacement, and it is cost neutral to system

	#1 Custom	#2 Horizontal	#3 Vertical	#4 Hybrid
Baseline	$N \times N$	$2N$	$N \times N$	$2N$ to $N \times N$
Extend	$2N+1$	2	$2N+1$	2 to $2N+1$
Replace	$2N-1$	2	$N-1$	2 to $N-1$
Merge	$2N \times N + N$	No New I/F	No New I/F	No New I/F

Table entries show the number of interface implementations needed to integrate the system... multiplies the cost and complexity of the implemented system.
N = Number of Applications in Integrated System

Figure 4.21. Comparison of architecture patterns.

	#1 Custom	#2 Horizontal	#3 Vertical	#4 Hybrid
Baseline	-	71 %	0%	36 %
Extend	-	87 %	0%	44 %
Replace	-	86 %	57 %	71 %
Merge	-	95 %	95 %	95 %

Figure 4.22.   Example of cost savings $N = 7$

merger. This indicates that the vertical standards provide for intersystem interoperability (a capability also shared by the horizontal and hybrid architectures). The horizontal architecture provides the most ease of extensibility. The cost of system extension is constant regardless of the size of the system. As we stated earlier, the horizontal architecture provides many benefits, but it is not practical to assume that a community of developers will be strictly limited to common horizontal interfaces. The hybrid architecture includes a range of costs between the horizontal and vertical architecture examples.

System extension is likely to cost at the $2N + 1$ level of the custom architecture in three out of four cases. The key lesson is that architectural benefits are very sensitive to the way that the system is designed and extended. Potential benefits are significant, but they are likely to be jeopardized by subsequent system extensions which are not conformant to the architectural vision and detailed tradeoffs made by the architect.

Figure 4.22 shows the relative cost savings with respect to the custom architecture when $N = 7$, a typical system size. The hybrid can provide the cost benefits of the horizontal architecture with the specialized functionality benefits of the vertical architecture. Average cost savings for the hybrid architecture are substantial for development and all forms of system modification. In summary, the hybrid architecture is our recommended basic pattern for software architectures.

Advanced Architecture Pattern: Separation of Facilities

An advanced architecture strategy involves the separation of facilities. The Internet services have successfully demonstrated this approach. The Internet facilities are partitioned between the front-end tools (the user facilities) and the back-end information sources (the application facilities). The information sources are strictly back-end servers that can be shared by multiple clients. The user facilities are strictly front-end applications that serve one user. Some client applications can access multiple types of servers. The user has a choice of front-end styles for viewing data.

The Internet communication standards are defined in terms of lower-level communication layers, typically at the Internet Protocol (IP) level. Compared to CORBA, the IP level requires a substantial amount of client and server software in support of each interface. CORBA may have future impact on the Internet because it enables the rapid creation of many new services and customized interfaces.

The Internet provides an important example of how to structure an architecture in a distributed environment (see figure 4.23 on page 101). Shared data and services should be migrated toward the back-end application facilities. Customized user functionality should reside in separate user interface applications. Shared functions and data do not belong in the user facilities, and user interaction should not be associated with the shared services.

Beyond the Internet, there are many other reasons why architectures should be partitioned in this manner. In general, architectures should minimize the software investment in the user facilities and migrate as much functionality and data as possible to shared application facilities (see figure 4.24 on page 102). In the following paragraphs we make some of the key arguments why this strategy is necessary.

Shared services such as data repositories and search engines often require special processing resources. Repositories may have massive storage requirements and need high-speed disk interfaces. Computation-intensive services may need special processors to provide adequate response-time performance. For a shared service involving many users, it is usually cost effective to provide specialized processors, buses, and storage systems, tailored to the needs of these services. The cost of special hardware can be distributed among many users.

Most user interface facilities are platform-specific. Applications do not port easily between platforms unless some form of cross-platform development environment is being used. To take advantage of the best capabili-

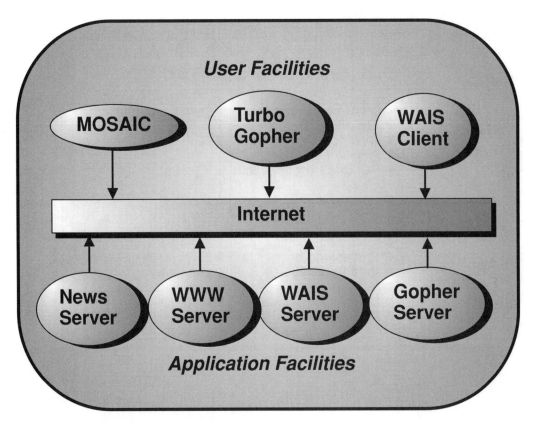

Figure 4.23. Partitioning of Internet.

ties of each platform, it is necessary to write the user interface code in a platform-dependent manner. Platform dependence will continue to be an issue with user interface software because the industry desktop market will continue to become increasingly fragmented. Emerging technologies such as COSE/CDE, OLE/COM, OpenDoc, OPENSTEP, Fresco, and Taligent are environments that will drive the need for partitioned software.

Architects should minimize software investments in platform-dependent software. This can be done by migrating as much functionality as possible to shared application facilities. Dependent software is expensive to port between platforms; the quantity of this type of software should be minimized. Any vendor-dependent software also is in danger of premature obsolescence and high operation and maintenance costs.

Simplifying the role of user facilities allows the creation of more customized user interfaces. It is very difficult or impossible to create a common user interface that is readily accepted by all user groups. The groupware software market is well aware of this issue. The failure of many group

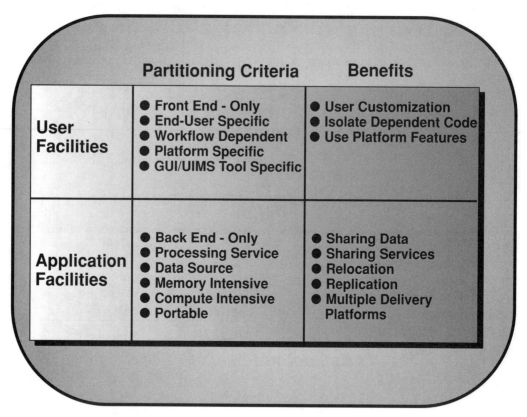

Figure 4.24.   Separation of user facilities from shared application facilities.

scheduling tools is an example of how user interfaces are closely tied to individual user preferences and group culture. By simplifying the role of user facilities, more customized user interfaces can be created to meet the needs of special-interest users' groups. Simplified user interface facilities require less code and are less expensive and faster to build and specialize. They also adapt to end-user needs and changing requirements.

The emerging market of user-interface rapid prototyping tools will enable dramatic reductions in the cost of user-interface development. Many of these tools will interface directly with CORBA. Independent software vendors such as Bluestone, Integrated Computer Solutions, Oberon, Netlinks, and others are developing or already have CORBA products on the market. It may soon be possible to implement a complete customized user interface within hours. This interface might provide all of the desired CORBA invocations without substantial development. As platforms and user needs change, new user interfaces can be created just as easily.

Some application domains may require an additional category of separated facilities. Workflow represents the organization's business process. An automated workflow supports the business process across multiple software packages. Workflow software can perform functions such as data transfer of results, automatic manipulation of data using multiple packages, and user notification.

In general, shared application facilities should be completely independent of workflow. The shared application facilities should be among the most stable subsystems in the architecture and should support flexibly many modes of utilization eliminating any hard-coded workflow from the access protocols. In some environments, workflow is naturally merged with the user-interface facilities. In others, the user interface facilities need to be workflow independent. This is often the case where there are multiple workflows in an organization that share common applications. Workflow can provide useful animation to a set of passive user facilities and shared application facilities. It is a good example of why good functionality through architecture-level APIs must be provided. A workflow process may need to control virtually any type of function that a software package provides. Workflow can be highly volatile, as an organization adapts to meet changing business needs. For this reason it is probably prudent to separate workflow in the architecture in order to localize the changes needed as workflow changes.

Other Architecture Patterns

There are a variety of other widely used architectural paradigms. In the following sections, we identify these paradigms and establish their relationship to the design of software architectures.

Ad Hoc Architecture   Ad hoc architectures are created whenever a system is integrated directly at the implementation level. These architectures contain a spontaneous mixture of communication levels and mechanisms; they are architectures without a vision. By choosing the most expedient ways to create interoperability, an ad hoc architecture can show some immediate interoperability benefits, but these benefits are short-lived and usually very dependent on particular software versions and the particular programmers who create the integration solution. These systems are very brittle; they seldom can adapt to any changes to the system, such as new software versions, new network configurations, porting to new platforms, and so forth. During the life cycle of such a system, programmers usually move on to new responsibilities, and new programmers find ad hoc systems impossible to maintain and extend.

For some organizations, such as small independent software vendors with a very stable programmer workforce, an ad hoc architecture may be reasonable, particularly if the product is undergoing frequent revisions that impact architecture-level issues. For most other organizations, ad hoc architectures are practical only for small-scale prototypes, such as user-interface mockups.

Software architecture designs should be initiated as early as possible in prototypes that are likely to migrate into operational systems. The process of creating a good architecture for a system is very closely related to prototyping experiences and should proceed in parallel. A key goal of any operational system prototype should be the creation of a robust software architecture that can adapt to the changing requirements of the users. Ad hoc architectures do not meet these needs, except in very special organizations.

Methodology-bound Architectures   Systems designed with rigorous software methodology can employ many architectural principles, such as component isolation and well-defined software boundaries. Occasionally, after we explain architectural principles to groups, someone responds: "We have all that, but we still cannot create a successful system." Obviously these projects are missing some ingredients.

The missing ingredients are more cultural than technical. Methodology-bound projects have a skewed value system, in which priorities in the methodology override the priorities of good architecture. For example, a commonplace methodology-driven question is: "Is that feature really object oriented?" This question may be very appropriate at an object-oriented programming level, but it has minimal relevance to software architecture. An architecture must use a wide range of concepts well beyond the scope of a single methodology. [Shaw, 93] The architecture must provide a stable solution over a decade-long system life cycle, well after the demise of today's popular methodologies. Other methodology-driven priorities include the mandatory creation of large quantities of design documentation that may be of little or no use to the developers and maintainers of the system. As the system evolves, the design documentation rapidly becomes obsolete.

In computing, we have seen many methodology trends come and go. Currently there are more than two dozen documented object-oriented methodologies. [Hutt, 94] The persistent trend is to move on to new methodology concepts.

To design good architectures, organizations must recognize that popular methodologies are transient. In fact, methodologies involve some of the most dynamic, rapidly evolving ideas in computing technology. The methodology business is also one of the most fragmented in the computing industry. There is little or no hope of standardization of methodologies; hence, there is no movement toward stability. Methodology practices will change dramatically over the course of a system life cycle. Good software architectures must provide much more stability than the methodologies that may be employed to create them.

There is probably no way to fix a methodology-bound architecture without fundamental cultural changes that allow software architects to design and implement their vision without the encumbrances of methodology-driven project culture.

Object-Oriented Architecture   Object orientation includes as one of its basic principles the modeling of natural real-world objects in the software system. This notion has roots in the semantic database modeling work of Dennis McLeod at the University of Southern California, where the computing object does not only represent the real-world object, "it is the object."

An important question for software architects is whether to include abstractions of domain objects at the system level. We have already said that it is not acceptable to publish unabstracted object models at the system level. Without abstractions, the architecture cannot manage system complexity effectively. There are two important considerations: (1) the stability of the domain models compared to the system life cycle and (2) whether hard-coding the domain models into the architecture provides significant system-level benefits.

Even in highly domain-dependent applications, such as simulation, the architect has a choice of whether to hard-code the domain objects into the core of the software architecture or to separate the domain-dependent hierarchies from the domain-independent hierarchies. For example, a domain-independent architecture can incorporate domain information in object method parameters as opposed to hard-coded attributes and API-level specifications.

Client-Server Architecture   Client-server is the precursor technology to distributed objects. Client-server technology is associated with remote procedure calls such as ONC and DCE, whereas distributed objects are associated with CORBA, which is the predominant industry standard for distributed objects. Distributed objects are peer to peer, whereas client-server is a constrained architecture with well-defined client and server subsystem roles.

Client-server technology contains some very useful concepts for the system architecture (as opposed to the software architecture), which includes hardware selection and physical allocation decisions. Client-server can be viewed as the antithesis to the migration of functionality from the mainframes to the desktop. In client-server, the focus is on creating high-performance centralized processing services. The centralized services run on high-performance systems with tightly integrated mass storage facilities. The capital resources are focused in the centralized server facilities and minimized on the desktop. When fully migrated to client-server, the desktops should be commodity terminals, such as personal computers or X Terminals. This model works because the cost of the centralized resources are shared among many users; sufficient savings usually can be obtained from the reduced costs of the commodity desktop systems. When properly configured, the client-server systems deliver better performance at lower cost than either mainframe-based systems or PC-LAN systems.

Client-server is not concerned with interoperability. Each application functions as a vertically integrated "stovepipe" system, self-contained and providing all levels to the user from user interface to back-end mass storage. In most client-sever systems, interoperability between applications is limited to desktop cut and paste—that is, exchange of text and bitmaps, not objects.

The second problem with client-server technology is that it is often vendor- and product-dependent. Since client-server products are vertically integrated, often there is no user-defined software architecture. We have heard people claim that "our architecture is <<place your favorite product here>>." In that case, the system is vulnerable to the commercial decisions of a single supplier, and there is a lack of control of the timing of product upgrades and associated maintenance costs. Users are forced to follow the vendor's lead or risk obsolescence. Many organizations have regretted this loss of control.

Most client-server vendors include API access to their products, so that they can be incorporated readily into user-defined software architectures. Techniques presented herein can be used with these products to create software architectures that provide vendor independence through component isolation. If a client-server product does not provide this level of API access, consider excluding it from the system. Lack of API access indicates the product has a closed, vendor-controlled architecture that could become a serious liability over the system life cycle. Even when an API is available, it should be mapped to *your own* IDL interface that *you* control.

Message-oriented Architecture   Message-Oriented Middleware (MOM) is designed to provide message model capabilities in a distributed environment. The networking world experience has shown that messaging can be quite beneficial. Message systems provide fault tolerance. Messages can be queued, routed, or stored until a system is available for reception. The system, therefore, does not have a single point of failure. Currently MOM can be based on the RPC model, on message queueing, or on models that attempt to utilize the best aspects of both. The main benefit of this architecture is its support of both the synchronous mode of communication as well as the asynchronous mode. However, it currently is immature. Thus, developers today face multiple nonstandard APIs and questions as to how MOM will interoperate with other architectures. MOM may require more code to utilize.

COMMENTS

The design of highly effective software architectures involves a great deal of intuitive judgment and experimentation. Rigorous methodologies that are executed mechanically can impede this creative process. The ability to create simplifying abstractions is a key innate talent of the software architect. Few individuals practicing in the software industry have this ability—perhaps as few as one in five software designers. [Coplien, 94] The next major trend in computing methodology, "design patterns" in part resulted from recognition of this fact. The Design Pattern practitioners are focused on project-centric solutions. Their concepts are synergistic with ours, in that we both are interested in techniques for creating better software architectures. Our approach goes beyond a project-centric focus to include the creation of standard reusable architectures that can fill important standards gaps and address interoperability needs for communities of developers. We have found that many recognized authorities minimize the importance of standards. In our opinion, without organizational interface standards there is minimal reusability and no leverageable technology progress from generation to generation of software systems.

A common misconception in object-oriented systems development involves the difference between object-oriented programming and architecture-based systems integration. Many developers have practiced integration by providing system-level exposure to their object classes and methods. This practice is problematic because it multiplies the complexity of the architecture by the complexity of the internal object models of each subsystem. When a typical program comprising 100 classes and 1,000 methods is integrated with ten other similar programs, a system complexity of 1,000 classes and 10,000 methods results. These methods would be used sparsely across program boundaries in a manner that is highly dependent on specific applications. In effect, the architecture becomes highly brittle because all the subsystems become intimately interdependent upon each other's detailed object schemas.

There is an interesting analogy here between software architecture and pop psychology. The discovery and definition of healthy boundaries is one of the fundamental principles of Gestalt psychology, the scientific basis for much of today's pop psychology movement. Highly interdependent, brittle software systems are analogous to codependent personalities. In both cases, there is a poor definition of boundaries between independent entities. This lack of good boundary definition leads to dysfunctional behavior. In computing, this behavior is exhibited by the fact that 50 percent of software cost is attributed to system discovery (where the programmer is trying to find out how the system works). In addition, so-called codependent systems lack adaptability. The systems are unable to grow to address new requirements and challenges without great expense. Difficulty in debugging and defect correction is another important result of poorly defined system boundaries.

Object-oriented programming and architecture-based systems integration are quite different practices with very different goals. The software architecture's role is to help control complexity and manage change in the system. Ideally, the software architecture provides a system-level abstraction that needs to contain only enough detail to provide the required system-level interoperability. Generally designers err on the side of too much complexity with insufficient abstraction. The most important and difficult decisions are not what details to put into the software architecture but what details to leave out [Brinch Hansen, 76].

The *Rule of Three Iterations* is another important analogy for the architecture process. This analogy was explained to the author by Professor Brinch Hansen at USC; it contains some important truths. Generally, three iterations of system implementation are needed to create a mature software architecture. We can illustrate this analogy with some well-known automobile models. The first prototype resembles a Ford Pinto. It is a fairly minimal design with some obvious weaknesses. The second prototype resembles a GM Cadillac. Success with the first prototype often leads developers to try to build an overly ambitious system. This system dramatically fails to meet expectations. The third prototype resembles a Volkswagon Beetle. Due to lessons learned, it is a simple, elegant design that provides the desired functionality, but with a very economical implementation. It is hoped that the third prototype becomes the operational system, because it can be developed and maintained at a very reasonable cost.

Using this analogy as a guideline, the architecture process should continually evolve the design towards a Beetle-like system, altogether avoiding the overly ambitious Cadillac-like system. The Beetle-like system carries many benefits:

- Cost effective in declining budget times
- More versatile
- More adaptable
- More migratable
- More efficient

5

Security

With the advent of open systems and networking we have seen accompanying social by-products, such as viruses, Trojan horses, unauthorized accesses, and damage by disgruntled employees. Security is an essential capability needed by the public and private sectors, in government, finance, medicine, and general business. These industries need to protect information from unauthorized access and modification, to protect privacy, to guard trade secrets, and to protect data.

Extensive research has been performed on computer security, such as secure operating systems and secure databases. In the past, not many implementations were commercially available, particularly in the challenging multilevel-security (MLS) arena. MLS security enables the interoperation of systems operating at different levels and supports multiple levels on the same system. While the number of available products and technologies that address this area is increasing, these implementations are not prevalent. MLS is still a difficult issue; without it users may not attain all of the desired benefits that distributed object management can provide while answering all of their security needs.

Because computer security historically has been viewed as a small specialty market, the commercial success of security technologies has been disappointing. Available security technologies are limited to specialized versions of platforms and products. These specialized versions are typically generations behind the state of the art in terms of cost, features, performance, robustness, and usability. In order for security to be effective it must be ubiquitous, but security is unlikely to achieve pervasive support if suppliers do not bundle it with mainstream platforms. One necessary change is a fundamental recognition by suppliers that virtually all end users need security, not just selected narrow markets.

Some end users believe that the only available course of action is to wait until MLS security is commercially available—they ignore security or opt for physical isolation. We believe that this sort of argument should not be accepted anymore. Security must be taken into consideration, especially during system architecture design. Even though security may not be available in some of the newer emerging technologies, architects should plan on integrating and phasing it in.

Architects and developers sometimes view security as too difficult and defer it rather than build it into the architecture from the start. Often they believe that security complicates a system, imposes restrictive policies and procedures, and may impact performance. Mainframes and PCs had colocated disk packs or hard drives that were physically secure. Local area networks, remote access, and global internetworking have made security a complex challenge. Distributed systems introduce new problems, such as applications that run across several systems. When we add object-oriented technology to the equation, we find that conventional security mechanisms and architectures are woefully insufficient. The CORBA architecture attempts to provide transparent object location and activation, while the security policy may require a client to know it is communicating with a trusted object.

Security has many diverse aspects, examples of which include physical security, personnel security, information security, prevention of electromagnetic emanations and their interception, operations security, computer security, and network security (software and hardware). In this chapter we concentrate on the technology related issues.

We look further into advanced security issues that arise when using an object request broker (ORB) in a distributed system. We review several important security standards and research projects that apply to multiple levels of security architecture. In addition, in Chapter 7 we present the security support as implemented in the DISCUS framework.

The Need for Security

A common misconception is that only governments are interested in security. Often software vendors or systems integrators argue that they are not concerned with security because they target the commercial world. Interestingly, while their requirements are somewhat different, security needs in the commercial world are just as prevalent as in the government.

Governments are interested mainly in protecting information (often military) from enemies. As such, they are interested both in preventing unauthorized disclosure and in maintaining data integrity. Limits are imposed on who can access information for updating and modification and also on who can access the information for reading. The private sector is driven mainly by business decisions and their cost effectiveness. In the banking industry, protecting someone's account balance total from being read is not as important as protecting it from being modified. The private sector is therefore more interested in protecting information from being changed (i.e., restricting write access). Sometimes, although not as often as in the government or military, companies are interested in restricting *any* access to information, especially trade secrets from competitors [Chalmers, 90].

Nowadays, the needs of the government and the private sector seem to be converging. Viruses, Trojan horses, worms, and wide use of the Internet have raised the user community's awareness for security, possibly with varied emphasis. For example, the military may be concerned with data integrity in the case of data that affects nuclear weapons launches. The private sector also is concerned with the integrity of the data and wishes to protect it from unauthorized modification. This takes the form of well-formed transactions and separation of duties in the workplace. Separation of duties provides security, for example, by requiring several signatures in order to validate some operation (e.g., purchase order, release of funds, etc.). Similarly, in the military it may require several people to authorize a nuclear launch.

Security Issues

At some level both camps are interested in authentication, auditing, monitoring, and of course good performance. Because of these requirements, care must be taken when designing a security system. Here are a few things to consider, especially when introducing security into a distributed, heterogeneous environment [Fairthorne, 94—also known as the OMG Security White Paper]:

- The security model must be independent from specific security algorithms. It must enable access to and selection of, the algorithms and support more than one security policy. This is important because different platforms and domains may have different security policies. (See section titled Security Policies on page 114.) Governments also may regulate some of the mechanisms (e.g., cryptographic algorithms), therefore, different installations of a system may need to use different algorithms. The model also should be *extensible*.
- The model must *support small* systems *and very large* distributed *systems*. This means that the mechanisms must support control and access of few users or whole groups of users. Different security policies between domains must be dealt with.
- The security policy enforced by the system *must not be bypassed* in any way. Different levels of trust have been defined by government and international criteria documents (see section titled Survey of Related

Standards on page 115). For example, if a system is being built for users who use the Trusted Computer System Evaluation Criteria (TCSEC) (see Section titled TCSEC on page 115) policies, the security model should stand an evaluation at the appropriate level of trust defined in that set of criteria.

- The White Paper notes that if an object is not responsible itself for a particular security policy, that it should be *portable* to a system that may be controlled under a different security policy. If an object is responsible for part of a policy, portability may depend on the compatibility of policies between different systems. In reality, portability of an object (even if it does not participate in any security policy) also depends on how it is implemented. An object may contain code that would introduce loopholes if it were run on a system supporting some security policies.

- The system must support object *interoperability* with other objects that may reside in different domains, that are implemented by different vendors and/or using different ORBs, and that may or may not contain security.

- Because of the wide range of security needs between different types of organizations (both within the commercial world and government), and the cost associated with various options, the system should be *flexible* to allow for a variety of choices and configurations.

- Simplicity is the key to the introduction of any system. In order for users and developers to *use* security, it should be *simple* for developers to implement it, for users to use it, and for administrators to manage it.

- Often the introduction of security can have a *performance* impact, either positive or negative. Some TCSEC evaluations have actually shown that when source code review is part of an evaluation, the improved bug detection and methods of computing actually may yield increased performance.

BASIC SECURITY TERMINOLOGY

Security provides access to the information system for authorized users and is supposed to prevent unauthorized use of the system, its resources, data, or operation. The important objective of data protection is supported by various security services, functions, and mechanisms. To understand these better we define some of the most commonly used terms:

Data Confidentiality

Data confidentiality is concerned with the disclosure and protection of data. Information (the data itself or the information about it) is not made available or disclosed to users (people or processes) that are not authorized to access it.

Data Integrity

Data integrity is concerned with the protection of the data itself from unauthorized modification. When resident in the file system or memory, or sent via communication lines, data must be protected from unauthorized alteration or destruction.

Identification and Authentication

The user ID identifies the particular user. In the authentication process, rights are granted to users. The authentication validates to the system that the user is indeed who he or she claims to be.

In a distributed system, identification and authentication may be required to be repeated many times. It is complicated by applications acting on behalf of other applications and the user.

Access Control

Access control is designed to allow controlled access to information resources. It also means that the resource should not be used in an "unauthorized manner." Discretionary Access Control (DAC) is judgment-based and depends on users granting access to objects. Often it is implemented by using Access Control Lists (ACLs). These lists of authorized users may be set up by a system administrator, for example, for system resources, or by individual users to limit (or provide) access to their own resources and files. Mandatory Access Control (MAC) is another form of access control. It enforces rules regarding which subjects may access which objects. MAC often is implemented using labels [EOSC, 92].

Auditing

Auditing is the process of data collection of significant security-related events to ensure that the security policy and procedures are being complied with. Data is collected in the form of system records and user activities and available for review in order to detect security breaches and unauthorized use.

Communication Security

Communication security is concerned mainly with data protection during transmissions. Data integrity and confidentiality may need to be enforced, and protection may need to be provided against the capture and replaying of data and messages.

Security Administration

Security administration has two aspects. One is concerned with access control over adminstrative operations. The other relates to the system policy configuration and maintenance.

Non-Repudiation

Non-repudiation ensures that an action originator cannot deny that it performed the action. For example, a message originator cannot deny that it sent the message and the recipients of the information also cannot deny that they received it. Digital signatures or public key encryption mechanisms are useful for implementing non-repudiation [Shaffer, 94].

Assurance

Assurance represents the level of trust that an element of the security architecture (software or hardware), a service, or the whole system enforces the security policy and performs its function as expected. Assurance can be gained via NSA evaluations and certification, and via testing (such as penetration testing, modelling, and simulation) [Shaffer, 94].

SECURITY POLICIES

A security policy comprises a set of rules and practices designed to counter some threat. Security policies allow different organizations to impose security in a manner that is consistent with each organization's mission and goals. Authorization, or identity-based policies, filter access to resources depending on the user's identity and need to know. A rule-based policy may use object labeling to determine the sensitivity of information. Often organizations that truly require a very secure environment simply impose a policy within their systems and disconnect themselves from the rest of the networked world. Such isolation may provide the required security; however, it obviously detracts from open and distributed systems. History tells us that isolation limits advancement.

Different security policies between different organizations introduce new challenges and complicates distributed environments. Guards or gateways may be needed to translate between different security policies. Furthermore, some systems may be required to support more than one policy.

Dealing with security in the architecture requires very careful farming and mining (see Chapter 4). One could design a distributed architecture that is technically sound and enables distributed communication between various applications and objects. It may be discovered later that a certain security policy prevents key information from travelling from one segment of the network or system to another.

SURVEY OF RELATED STANDARDS

In this section we briefly survey some of the well-known standards and some of the important initiatives under way that may shape security criteria for the next several years. These are some of the key standards and technology that we feel are important, or could play a role, in systems integration using distributed objects.

ISO 7498-2 Security Architecture

This standard defines the general security-related architecture elements that can be used to provide secure communication between open systems [ISO, 92].

The document defines the standard security services: Authentication, Access Control, Data confidentiality, Data integrity, and Non-repudiation. Security services are invoked at the proper ISO layers and in proper combinations to support certain policies and user requirements. The document also defines security mechanisms that are used to implement the basic services. These include encipherment, which is the cryptographic transformation of data to produce cyphertext; digital signature mechanisms, which are appended data that provide data integrity; access control that may involve using security labels; traffic padding, to protect against traffic analysis; routing control, to allow use of specific physically secure parts of the network; and notarization, which is the use of a third party for authorization.

The standard also defines "pervasive security mechanisms" that are defined as the Trusted functionality to establish effectiveness of other security mechanisms. As part of the Trusted Computing Base (TCB), these components are expected to be trustworthy. The document also defines security labels, event detection, audit trail, and security recovery.

The standard presents a view of the placement of different types of security as they relate to the ISO 7 layer model. It should be noted that layer 7, the application layer (which is also the layer of CORBA application integration), presents all security services.

TCSEC

In 1985 the Department of Defense (DoD) published the Trusted Computer System Evaluation Criteria, also known as the Orange Book [DoD, 85]. The document defines a secure computer system and identifies six requirements that a Trusted Computing Base must satisfy in order to be considered a secure system. According to the TCSEC, a secure system is one that, through the use of security features, controls access to information such that only properly authorized individuals, or processes operating on their behalf, can have access to this information.

The TCSEC defines six requirements that a "secure" system must satisfy. Four deal with what the system must provide in order to control access to the information it manages; two deal with how assurances can be obtained so that the first four requirements may be accomplished.

- *Security policy.* The system must enforce an explicit, well-defined policy. Given subjects and objects, there must be a set of rules that the system can use to determine whether a given user can have access to a specific object.
- *Marking.* Objects must be marked with sensitivity levels (classification).
- *Identification.* The system must require individuals to identify themselves. It must control access to information based on this user id.
- *Accountability.* The system must collect audit information and protect it, so that actions can be traced back to users.
- *Assurance.* This includes hardware and software mechanisms that can be evaluated independently to provide assurance that the system is enforcing the preceding four steps.
- *Continuous protection.* Hardware and software mechanisms must be protected against unauthorized changes.

Divisions and Classes   TCSEC defines a set of standards for computing systems having different levels of security requirements. Security criteria is divided into four categories, A, B, C, and D. Category A represents systems with the most comprehensive security. Each division may be subdivided into classes with numeric suffixes; higher numbers represent a higher level of security. For example, B level represents higher security than C level, and B3 represents a higher level of security than B1. Most vendors today have systems with at least a C level of certification.

The Orange Book is considered somewhat outdated. It relates mainly to mainframe operating systems and is too inflexible for nonmilitary uses. TCSEC-based systems do not necessarily interoperate [Shaffer, 94].

Other Criteria Initiatives

The Trusted Network Interpretation of the Trusted Computer System Evaluation Criteria (TNI) was created because of the difficulties in extending the TCSEC as a criteria for networks. The TNI covers network partitioning into components of different ratings to support components that perform functions requiring varied degrees of assurance. Each distributed part of the network trusted computing base (NTCB) can have a separate set of objects, subjects, and security policy [EOSC, 92].

The European Community (EC) has published its own evaluation criteria known as the Information Technology Security Evaluation Criteria (ITSEC).

Canada also has its own Canadian Trusted Computer Product Evaluation Criteria (CTCPEC). These two standards and the Orange Book need to address broader functionality and assurance.

The Common Criteria (CC) is a multinational effort that began in 1993. Its main objectives are to develop open and flexible frameworks for defining new requirements for Information Technology security; to gain international recognition for evaluation results and through modernization of the process to reduce cost; to modernize security criteria to address open distributed systems and integrated computer and communications security; and to protect previous investment in security products while reducing trade barriers. While we expect that in the long term there will be international standards and a revision made to the Orange Book, currently the CC is still in development and somewhat immature. Products with new function and assurance combinations are still several years away.

SURVEY OF RELATED TECHNOLOGIES

Much research has been performed in the areas of security architectures. In this section we investigate some of the more relevant technologies that may be used in distributed systems and in conjunction with object management technology. There are other technologies that are potentially relevant, but are beyond the scope of this book.

Kerberos

Kerberos is a distributed authentication service developed at the Massachusetts Institute of Technology (MIT). It is a symmetric security system where a client and server share a key for encrypting and decrypting data [IETF, 93; Malamud, 92].

Kerberos simply delivers credentials, which are made of a "ticket" that contains information authenticating a user to the server and a session key required to use the ticket in the authentication transaction. Kerberos does not impose any rules on how tickets are used by clients and servers. In a normal exchange, a client requests access or "credentials" to a specific server from an Authentication Server. The Authentication Server has access to a database of client and server keys. The server sends a packet back to the client encrypted with the client's key that includes a ticket for the requested server and a session key. The client then sends the information to the server encrypted in the server key.

Tickets may be temporary and clients may need to request new tickets intermittently. The ticket is the authenticator and is encrypted by the server key so that the client can use it but not modify it. Once authentication is complete, the client and server may not require further authentication, or they may continue to encrypt further communication. More keys, called subsession keys, also may be exchanged.

While kerberos can be used between organizations, it does not scale well to large networks [Malamud, 92; Shaffer, 94]. This is especially true in the case when some organizations use kerberos and others use other authentication mechanisms.

Trusted Computing

Trusted Computing Base   In order for a system to function as a Multi-Level Secure (MLS) system using sensitivity labels, it must have a Trusted Computing Base [Fellows, 88]. The TCB components must be dependable in the sense that they cannot be modified by unauthorized users or processes, and they always must function correctly in performing their security-related task.

A distributed TCB must perform all of the functions that a normal TCB does, but verification is much more difficult. A TCB on a domain that encompasses many systems faces a number of problems. These problems may be straightforward (although not necessarily simple), such as different policies across different domains, and they also can be more subtle. For example, timing across components can cause inconsistencies in the security contexts and their states. This can result in states that are not ordered, especially if components are replicated across the system to provide fault tolerance.

As part of TCBs in systems that use TCSEC level B2 criteria or higher, a trusted path must exist to ensure to users and programs that they are indeed communicating with the TCB.

If a system requires complete security at each level of the ISO model (seven layers), Trusted Protocols are needed at each level. Often security is added to existing standard protocols rather than new protocols being created. As such, it is likely that security will have to be added also to the Object Management layer to guarantee end-to-end security between applications.

Distributed TCB   It is possible to provide a Trusted Computing Base in distributed environments by using a distributed hierarchical TCB [Fellows, 88]. Such a TCB makes use of other TCBs. If each local TCB enforces its policy, the distributed TCB is ensured that its policy is enforced. This sort of structure, though, can be complicated by various state transitions.

The consistency of states and security contexts is very important to maintaining secure systems. Even if a part of the system is down or not available, security and data must not be compromised; rather services should be denied. The states must be synchronized intermittently between the local and distributed system TCB. Marshalling of data, as is often done with the ORB, can cause replication of data. It is necessary to have vertical security between layers and horizontal security between different ORBs.

Compartmented Mode Workstation   In 1985 the Defense Intelligence Agency (DIA) started the CMW (Compartmented Mode Workstation) program to define the security requirements for workstations that handle compartmented mode information. A compartment is a designation applied to a type of sensitive information. It indicates the special handling procedure to be used for the information and the general class of people who may have access to the information. In 1991 the CMW requirements were defined in the CMW Evaluation Criteria using the TCSEC baseline with the addition of deltas [CMW, 91]. Several vendors were contracted to produce commercial off-the-shelf workstations based on the CMW requirements, which include TCSEC B1-level features plus some B2- and B3-level features; they are referred to as a B1+ system.

By definition, CMWs restrict information sharing, flow, and exchange between processes, users, the file system, other systems, and a combination of these. To support these requirements, the window system must be able to display security labels and the window manager must control information flow between windows. A Trusted X server had to be developed to provide secure communication between X window components. The Trusted X server labels windows and other X objects as well as user input. The window manager is part of the TCB and intercepts certain events, such as cut-and-paste, between windows. If the user attempts to move information between windows with different security labels, the window manager might prompt the user to downgrade the classification of the information, if the user is appropriately authorized to do so.

This sort of small granularity event interception can cause a large performance overhead, especially in distributed object-oriented environments. It is clear that security in the ORB environment can get complicated quickly if, as in the Trusted X system, each object access, embedding, and linking may have to be checked.

Trusted Mach B3   The developers of the trusted Mach operating system have found that using object-oriented techniques in secure systems assisted in meeting the assurance and security policy defined by the TCSEC [Gupta, 93]. The designers found that using an object-oriented language, such as C++, with the TMach kernel allowed them to implement a multilevel secure operating system utilizing the client-server model. The kernel provides process security using task IDs and isolation and intertask communications utilizing messages. The use of an object-oriented language in general provides for modularity, inheritance, and the exchange of messages. Other benefits are abstraction and data hiding. The data hiding can be provided through restricted interfaces, such as the public and private access in C++.

CORBA-compliant Security in Synergy   Realizing that existing security models and architectures will not meet the needs of distributed systems, the

National Security Agency (NSA) embarked on a research project called Synergy to develop a portable, microkernel-based security architecture [Saydjari, 93]. Synergy plans to provide flexible support for multiple security policies, including commercial and government policies.

Synergy is an ongoing prototyping effort, and some changes to the information presented here are expected. Its architecture is planned to support networked MLS systems that use trusted gateways to access untrusted machines. The gateways label the data. At present, Synergy is concentrating on a homogeneous environment. In Synergy, separate servers exist for auditing, authentication, cryptography, and security. The servers are accessed via the microkernel, which provides a common machine-independent interface. The microkernel is based on the Mach 3.0 microkernel from Carnegie-Mellon University [Saydjari, 93].

- *Security server.* Provides access control. Policy decisions and enforcement are separate. This server controls access control only; the microkernel and other servers perform the enforcement.
- *Audit server.* Provides a centralized auditing facility that can receive messages from all parts of the system.
- *Cryptographic server.* Available to applications, this subsystem can provide access to various mechanisms and algorithms.
- *Network server.* Uses the X-kernel protocol and provides secure multi-level communication across unprotected networks.
- *Authentication server.* Provides user authentication and system authentication.
- *O/S server.* Currently built on BSD 4.3 UNIX. It should be able to support other operating systems in the future.

In Synergy, UNIX processes are single-threaded microkernel tasks. Memory objects that correspond to address space segments are mapped into the task's address space. All memory objects have security attributes, and it is up to the microkernel to enforce the security policy.

An example of how the microkernel does this is when an application uses the fork system call to fork a process. The child inherits the parent data and labels. If the child changes the label, the microkernel checks all memory buffers and resources and may prevent access to certain parent information. The microkernel uses emulators that look like standard system calls or file system calls, but performs certain additional security checks. Files are mapped onto memory objects. Memory objects have security attributes. Pipes and sockets are mapped to microkernel ports and therefore also can be checked using the microkernel mechanisms.

At the networking level, only multiple single-level connections are supported. This is because multilevel connections will require changes to networking protocols. The MLS local area network (LAN) assumes that con-

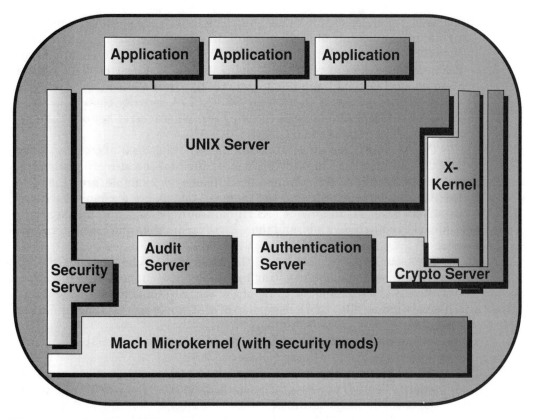

Figure 5.1.   Synergy architecture.

nections are connection-oriented and performs access control only at connection establishment. This part of the system was developed as a proof of concept and does not support Connectionless data [Saydjari, 93].

X-kernel is a network protocol from the University of Arizona to support secure communications and is used in the workstation to provide network support. It supports decomposition of complex networking protocols into "microprotocols" allowing more flexibility and building blocks to build other protocols. The breakdown provides the same functionality but easier insertion of security mechanisms at each level.

The authentication server makes use of the Generic Security Service Application Program Interface (GSS-API), as do the Crypto and security servers.

GSS-API

The Generic Security Service Application Programming Interface is intended to provide generic security services independent of the underlying mechanisms or technologies [McMahon, 93]. The user of the GSS-API may be an application, or simply another protocol. In either case, the communications between entities needs to be protected. The user may be interested in authentication, data integrity, and confidentiality. The user receives a token from its local GSS-API and exchanges it with a peer application or protocol, which in turn passes it to its local GSS-API. A security context is established by the GSS-API between the two peers where secret-key or public-key cryptographic systems can be used.

The GSS-API uses structures called Credentials that allow peers to establish security contexts. Data elements called tokens also are transferred between GSS-API callers. Context-level tokens, for example, are used to establish and manage contexts. Per-message tokens are exchanged with an established context to provide security for data messages. Contexts are established using credentials, and there can be more than one context between peers.

The security mechanism type is the underlying mechanism the GSS-API uses for encrypting and decrypting that both peers support. Naming also is provided to allow for the handling of the security context as opaque octets. Channel binding allows for the binding of contexts to specific communication channels.

Here is an example of a typical GSS-API session [Wray, 93].

1. An application or process acquires credentials so that it can prove its identity to other processes. The application must not reveal the name of the user who is executing it.
2. Using the credentials, two applications can establish a joint security context. Usually the application that initiates the communication must be authenticated to the receiver; however, authentication also may be requested from the receiver to the initiator. An important feature of the GSS-API is that it allows delegation of rights to a peer and the ability to apply security services, such as confidentiality and integrity, on per-message basis. The receiver may then create more contexts on the initiator's behalf, using credentials similar to those of the initiating application. Some GSS-API calls use an opaque data structure called a token. The token must be passed from the caller to the peer, who must pass it to its local GSS-API to be decoded and extracted.
3. Some services may be invoked on a per-message basis to provide data confidentiality and integrity. The peer application may verify the data it receives, or "unseal" it.
4. At the end of the communication, the context is deleted.

The GSS-API has been very well received by many standards organizations [McMahon, 93; Wray, 93]. A list of the various organizations that have adopted the GSS-API standard follows.

- Internet Engineering Task Force Request for Comments (IETF-RFC) for base GSS-API.
- X/Open and POSIX investigating adoption of GSS-API.
- OSF DCE 1.1 to include GSS-API for non-RPC applications to access DCE services.
- ISO SC21WG6 Upper Layer Security Rapporteur's group based on input derived from GSS-API.
- European Computer Manufacturers Association Technical Committee, ECMA TC36/TG9 "Security in Open/Systems" group to develop standard to support GSS-API.
- SESAME project proposes extensions to GSS-API.

The proposed extensions for the GSS-API may be very important to the ORB environment because they have to do with the delegation of control. In the ORB environment, servers also may act as clients for other applications. For example, a map query tool may be activated on behalf of a word processor to query map databases for data. It is essential that the query map tool, working on behalf of the originating application and user, relays the correct credentials to the map servers to ensure that the user does not gain access to data he or she is not supposed to receive.

The base GSS-API does not fully support an access control security service, and the controls on delegation are not fully specified. For example, it is not possible to support selective delegation. The extensions define mechanisms that allow for the control of who can use credentials for access control or for delegation [McMahon, 93].

SECURITY IN THE CORBA ENVIRONMENT

The requirements for security in the CORBA environment applies to objects in addition to users. Instead of controlling only user access, we must now ensure that object access also is controlled. At the same time, we must recognize that the ORB developers and OMG wish to limit the effect of security on the ORB software. Complexity can be detrimental to any standard. Simplicity, in the form of implementation hiding, minimal TCB implementation, and fewer requirements on clients and object implementations, are key to a successful security architecture in the CORBA environment.

Here is an example of how security may be used in the CORBA environment [Fairthorne, 94].

1. User logs on and is authenticated on the local system.
2. The user then activates a client application that attempts to invoke an object.
   - The user's credentials are made available to the client.
   - The client calls an object.

- The client and object need to establish mutual trust.
- The client and object may select to have data integrity turned on.
- The client and object establish a security context.
- The user must be verified for the requested method execution.
- The method invocation may be audited.
- The object is activated.

3. The object implementation may perform its own access control against the user's credentials.

4. If the object implementation calls another object on behalf of the client and user, it may need to use its own credentials, or the user's credentials, through delegation.

Security will be required at almost every level of the CORBA specification. For example, object creation may depend on a user's credentials and security level. Object services also will be affected. The trader service, for ex-

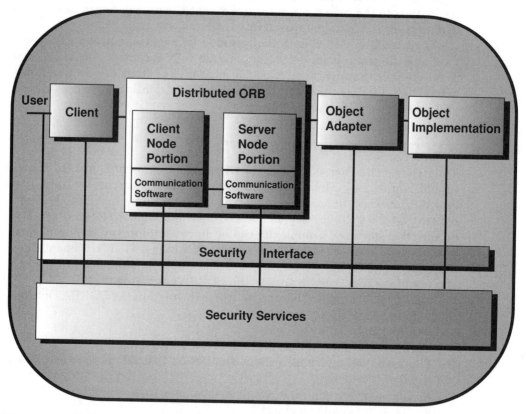

Figure 5.2. OMG white paper security architecture.

ample, may have to return to callers only information that they are allowed to "see" or access.

The GSS-API may fit the CORBA architecture very well because it provides some of the features that are required by an object-oriented system and desirable simplicity. The security mechanism used in the GSS-API may be hidden from clients. Neither the client nor the server needs to understand the security token or the mechanism in order to use it.

The placement of the calls to the security interface still needs to be determined by OMG; no doubt there will be various implementation suggestions in the responses to the request for proposals (RFPs).

The architecture provides a wide range of implementations on the server skeleton side. Access control can be performed by the ORB itself, by the Object Adapter (OA), by the object itself, or by a combination of these. Both access control and auditing should be performed by the ORB and/or OA, especially if support is required for objects that are not aware of security. This way, security can be supported across all objects, not just the ones that have implemented security themselves [Fairthorne, 94]. This is also important in isolating Trojan horse objects that can otherwise masquerade and connect to an unsecure ORB or OA.

In order to complete the secure architecture, the ORB and Object implementations should run under a secure operating system. Such a system is a key to providing a complete secure environment with file system security, auditing, and access control.

The ORB, the operating system, some communication channels, the Object Adapter, and secure mechanisms (e.g., GSS-API) may be part of the trusted computing base (TCB). The TCB also may include object services that are called by these components as well as object services that perform other security functions on behalf of other objects and clients.

The OMG White Paper identifies four possible levels of interfaces needed for the various security functions.

- *Application level.* Security parameters could be added to the Interface Definition Language (IDL) specifications to allow for the selection of security algorithms, quality of service, and so on.
- *Security aware but mechanism independent.* This is intended to be a GSS-API–like interface that the ORB can use to set up and manage security context using various security mechanisms.
- *Security services.* This interface is specific to each security mechanism and service that the software can use. It should be hidden by the security context.
- *Security service provider.* This interface should be standardized if possible because it is used to support the visible portion of the interfaces just discussed. It is used to select different mechanisms and services. This interface probably will not be standardized in response to the first security RFP [Fairthorne, 94].

The ORB introduces many complex issues. Security used to be much simpler, because we dealt only with single desktop machines or isolated mainframes. Local area networks complicated the issue, but the problem was still contained to a room, floor, building, or company. The access the Internet provides and the myriad of hardware and software protocols brought on spies, Internet worms, viruses, password cracking, and back-doors. Access to machines is easier, and holes in some communication protocols enabled security breaches and break-ins. Even today, in order to create a secure UNIX environment while still connected to the Internet, certain features must be turned off (for example tftp without -s) and other well-known bugs must be patched.

The ORB environment only adds to the complexity of the problem. In a distributed environment no longer can we simply isolate a workstation or a process. Processes may run on various machines, and a process may divide its tasks among machines. CORBA security requirements must ensure that all standard security requirements, such as auditing and authorization, are maintained and that users and objects cannot modify or have access to parts that they are not supposed to.

COMMENTS

Security entails many interesting and controversial issues. We would like for ubiquitous security services to become available and commercially successful within our lifetimes. A fundamental problem, not unique to security, is the lack of common infrastructure and common service access mechanisms that characterize computing technology. Without commonality on these levels, security solutions are unlikely to be very effective. End-user pursuit of a fragmented set of low-level distributed computing technologies, such as Open Network Computing (ONC), Tooltalk, and Distributed Computing Environment (DCE) is just exacerbating the problem. Further fragmentation of the available distributed computing market can delay the availability of commercially successful computer security technologies indefinitely. We believe that many of the technical barriers are artificial and can be overcome by market convergence on a common infrastructure, as represented by CORBA. For example, a relatively new, immature distributed object technology, such as the Common Object Model (COM), could readily evolve toward support of OMG IDL. This logical move would unify the distributed object market for suppliers and consumers, thus enabling globally applicable security technologies to emerge.

Many key security issues are unresolved by existing standards and available technology. We enumerate some of these key issues in the list that follows. Some issues are unique to distributed objects. Others are common to both distributed objects and legacy environments. In either case, architects and developers need to plan how to resolve these issues early in the software architecture process. Retrofit of security capabilities involves pervasive, expensive, and risky software modifications.

Security is also a very sensitive and politically charged topic for many individuals and organizations. With this caveat, here are some of the key issues (in our humble opinion):

- *Heterogeneity.* Heterogeneity of software and hardware will be pervasive in distributed object environments. In virtually all environments, there will be multiple kinds of ORBs, operating systems, integration techniques, and application packages. There are potential security issues at every boundary between these types of components. For example, consider the security implications of CORBA 2.0 interoperability. Security is an important issue at ORB-to-ORB interfaces and at other levels of the system.

- *Public metadata.* The CORBA Interface Repository and Object Trader Service make their data generally available to application software. These services may be revealing information that should be restricted by security. This is an example of general issues involving trade-offs between interoperability and security.

- *Transparent activation.* CORBA's ability to activate objects transparently leads to a new form of the Trojan horse scenario. Because the ORB can activate objects automatically, it might be tricked into transparently activating a Trojan horse object instead of the intended object. Due to CORBA's inherent transparency, this event may be difficult to detect. Since CORBA has not standardized the Implementation Repository, controlling this problem across multiple ORBs will be difficult.

- *Security and embedded objects.* Object references that are embedded in application data may lead to some interesting security issues. For example, what if there is an embedded reference to an object that should be hidden from a user? In general, how would these types of object references be detected and controlled?

- *Delegation of credentials.* Many CORBA-based application architectures will utilize multiple levels of nested invocation (such as when a client calls an implementation that calls another implementation and so forth). How and when should security credentials be delegated, and how are servers that can work on behalf of many users handled? Since it is not realistic to delegate credentials to untrusted software, delegation has important architectural implications. On one extreme it is possible that the application architecture eliminates nested invocations; this would be a severe architectural restriction. On the other extreme is the possibility that the TCB expands to encompass more of the system, such as all object services, all common facilities, and some application software; this has significant cost and schedule risk implications.

- *Security retrofitting.* Migration to a secure environment probably will involve substantial modifications to software. Applications that utilize secure facilities also require modification to support security interface protocols. In our opinion, security retrofitting is difficult if possible; security should be designed into the system from inception. Commitments to secure capabilities must be made early in the architecture process to avoid the substantial risks and costs of retrofitting. Architects should plan for evolution of the system and the security facilities as commercial technology and standards evolve.

THE PRACTICE
OF SYSTEMS
INTEGRATION

Framework
Examples

Frameworks represent reusable architectures, and there are many examples available to study. In the following sections, we examine some widely used commercial frameworks, including: Microsoft's Object Linking and Embedding (OLE), the X Consortium's Fresco, and CI Labs' OpenDoc. We also describe an important historical framework project, the Autonomous Land Vehicle, which shows the complexity of heterogeneous computing prior to CORBA.

At the time of this writing, the commercial frameworks were in initial releases, but they were being actively used by programmers. Whereas OLE represents a de facto standard from a dominant industry vendor, Fresco and OpenDoc represent future voluntary industry standards from an influential nonprofit consortium. All three frameworks address the area of in-place graphical embedding, a complex interaction between software components. OLE is defined through language-specific bindings to C++ and will support CORBA interoperability through alliance products (from DEC and Candle Corp.) and potential future Object Management Group (OMG) standards. Fresco was designed from the start to be a CORBA-compliant facility. At the time of writing, Fresco was in the X11R6 adoption process at the X Consortium. Both Fresco and OpenDoc were proposed for the Common Facilities RFP1 Compound Document specification. OpenDoc is a CORBA-compliant compound document facility from CI Labs, a consortium whose members include Apple, Novell, IBM, SunSoft, and others.

FRESCO

Fresco is a user interface framework that supports graphics, widgets, and embedded applications [Linton, 94]. It is CORBA compliant, in the sense that all application program interfaces (APIs) are specified in OMG Interface Definition Language (IDL). The reference implementation for Fresco is written in C++ and uses a library-based object request broker (ORB). OMG IDL enables Fresco to support multiple languages (current and future bindings of OMG IDL) as well as straightforward transition of software to distributed computing.

Fresco adds many new capabilities to the X Consortium's X-Windows technologies. Its new technologies include a standard object model, distributed objects, multithreading, resolution independence, and graphical embedding. These technologies are explained in more detail later.

Fresco's standard object model is the OMG's object model. Fresco's CORBA compliance is based on its use of standard OMG IDL to define all APIs for the framework. This enables the distribution of functionality across a network; however, it also allows the use of Fresco functions within the same address space that is the default implementation. In a CORBA-based environment, the applications software is identical regardless of distribution. Most ORB products support local and remote processing, including clients and server objects in the same address space. Fresco's is implemented using a library ORB (same address space), so that the ORB overhead is comparable to function calls. The use of OMG IDL enables the later distribution of client and service functionality.

Fresco provides an OMG IDL-enabled C++ programming environment by providing a reference compiler for IDL to C++ called Ix. To demonstrate how OMG IDL can enhance the utilization of C++, Fresco provides a facility for specifying object encapsulations free from implementation. Using C++ alone to specify encapsulations often involves the subtle incorporation of implementation dependencies. For example, C++ constructor functions imply a local implementation of object creation; an object factory (local or distributed) is the appropriate facility to create location transparent objects, as specified in the COSS Life Cycle service. Fresco also eliminates the multiple redefinitions of operation prototypes typically required when programming with C++ virtual functions.

Multithreading (MT) is a capability in operating systems for supporting multiple concurrent processes within a single program. Fresco supports both MT and non-MT operating systems. Many current windowing libraries are not compatible with MT (so-called MT unsafe code); the programmer needs to stop all concurrent threads before entering MT unsafe code. MT safety is also a significant issue in the integration of legacy software of all types. Since Fresco is an MT safe library, it can be used with MT programs without modification. Fresco uses multithreading optionally, if it is available on the platform operating system. Using multithreading, Fresco can respond flexibly to windows events while a separate thread concurrently performs the screen refresh.

Fresco's graphics model provides resolution independence. The primary change is an abstraction of device-dependent pixel-based coordinates. Fresco uses floating point coordinates exclusively (except if the programmer insists on access to pixel coordinates). This enables the support of multiple screens and output devices from the same application software. Thus the application software is effectively independent of output device. This feature has substantial portability benefits and also is useful for groupware applications that support heterogeneous displays. Fresco supports both 2X3 and 4X4 transformation matrices so that the framework can be used for both 2-D and 3-D applications. This is in contrast to many current graphics standards (i.e., the Graphics Kernel System [GKS] and the Portable Hierarchical Image Graphics System[PHIGS]), which are decidedly either 2-D or 3-D and require the programmer to learn two separate specifications.

In this section, embedding means combining multiple component objects into a container object to form a compound document. On the screen, most systems with embedding restrict the embedded object to a 2-D rectangular area, and the area is assumed to be opaque. Fresco's graphical embedding extends the concept by allowing objects to be arbitrary shapes (including shapes with holes); the objects may be graphically transformed (such as rotated, translated, and zoomed); and they can be visually transparent. These advanced capabilities enable many new uses of embedding, such as advanced user environments, 3-D visual simulations, and virtual reality.

The Fresco framework comprises about 40 OMG IDL interface definitions. These 40 object interfaces, an encapsulation of 150 underlying Fresco implementation classes, form a very flat hierarchy with most interfaces inheriting from a few common base classes.

The Fresco framework has four key object types: Viewer, Glyph, Style, and Inset. Viewer objects provide a user interface to data. They control input handling, focus management, menus, and color palettes. Glyph objects are graphical objects. Glyphs also control geometry management and screen updates. The style objects provide resource attributes, which can be modified at runtime. Inset objects store the data that is displayed by other objects. Conceptually, the Fresco framework is not unlike the well-known Model-View-Controller (MVC) framework from Smalltalk [Goldberg, 83]. Inset plays the role of the MVC Model, and the Fresco Viewer and Glyph play the roles of MVC View and Controller with a different partitioning of responsibilities. Fresco supports more flexible and extensible relationships between multiple instances of each object type than found in MVC.

The following program provides some OMG IDL specifications from the Fresco sample release in May 1994, including the interfaces for Glyph and Viewer. At the time of writing, sufficient documentation to describe these interfaces in detail was not available; however, the sample programs in the release do provide several examples of how these interfaces are used. We look forward to the X Consortium and OMG standardization of Fresco and subsequent commercialization as X11R6 becomes the dominant release of X Windows.

```
interface Glyph : FrescoObject {
  struct Requirement {
    boolean defined;
    Coord natural, maximum, minimum;
    Alignment alignment;  };
  struct Requisition {
    Requirement x, y, z;
    boolean preserve_aspect; };
  struct AllocationInfo {
    Region allocation;
    TransformObj transform;
    DamageObj damage;
    };
  typedef sequence<AllocationInfo> AllocationInfoList;
  attribute StyleObj style;
  TransformObj transform();
  void request(out Glyph::Requisition r);
  void extension(
    in Glyph::AllocateInfo a, in Region r);
  void shape(in Region r);
  void traverse(in GlyphTraversal t);
  void draw(in GlyphTraversal t);
  attribute Glyph body;
  GlyphOffset append(in Glyph g);
  GlyphOffset prepend(in Glyph g);
  Tag add_parent(in GlyphOffset parent_offset);
  void remove_parent(in Tag add_tag);
  void visit_children(in GlyphVisitor v);
  void visit_children_reversed(in GlyphVisitor v);
  void visit_parents(in Glyphvisitor v);
  // screen update
  void allocations(out Glyph::AllocationInfoList a);
  void need redraw();
  void need_redraw_region(in Region r);
  void need_resize();
};

interface Viewer: Glyph {
  Viewer parent_viewer();
  Viewer next_viewer();
  Viewer prev_viewer();
  void insert_next_viewer(in Viewer v);
  void insert_prev_viewer(in Viewer v);
```

```
      void insert_first_viewer(in Viewer v);
      void insert_last_viewer(in Viewer v);
      void link_next(in Viewer v);
      void link_prev(in Viewer v);
      void remove();
      void insertion(in Viewer v);
      void removal(in Viewer v);
      Focus request_focus(
        in Viewer v, in boolean temporary);
      boolean receive_focus(
        in Viewer v, in boolean primary);
      void lose_focus(in boolean temporary);
      boolean first_focus();
      boolean last_focus();
      boolean next_focus();
      boolean prev_focus();
      boolean handle(in GlyphTraversal t, in Event e);
      void close();
    };
```

OBJECT LINKING AND EMBEDDING (OLE2)

Object Linking and Embedding, Version2 (OLE2), is an object-based framework for desktop application interoperability. It is one of the two foundational APIs (WIN32 is the other) that are supported by Microsoft Windows 3.1, Windows NT, and future systems from Microsoft, such as Windows 95 and Cairo. Current Windows 3.1 supports the legacy DOS and Windows APIs as well as OLE2 and WIN32 APIs. Windows 95 is a transitional step in Microsoft's strategy to migrate the software vendors and platform base toward Cairo, which is a follow-on to Windows NT.

A key feature of the OLE2 framework is its support for application embedding. This provides seamless application integration at the user interface. Similar to Fresco, OLE2 supports application embedding, although in Microsoft's terminology it is called in-place activation. In-place activation allows a container application to display component objects from multiple applications. When the user selects a component object, the container's menus change to allow the user to edit the object using the component application's operations. In practice, Microsoft has found intuitive user acceptance for this form of interoperability.

Microsoft is supporting OLE2 on Windows, Windows NT, and Apple Macintosh platforms, which are the target platforms for the Microsoft Office products. Since OLE2 has many implementation restrictions that limit it to a single machine, distributed extensions will support only a subset of the OLE2 framework. In particular, the DEC/Microsoft Common Object Model will distribute only persistence, monikers (naming), and data transfers, but not compound documents. The Common Object Model is a future distributed version of the nondistributed OLE2 Component Object Model, to be discussed.

Technical Description of OLE2

OLE2 is a complex collection of related technologies. It is organized so that developers can implement application support for OLE2 incrementally. Figure 6.1 provides an overview of the technologies of OLE2. The communication infrastructure of OLE2 is the Component Object Model. It defines the basic interface mechanisms for invoking OLE2 objects. Compound files is an object persistence facility that replace normal file-based storage with a more sophisticated facility for storing the data from multiple applications within a single file. This is a key enabler of object embedding, the capability to store multiple objects within a container object. Embedding supports OLE2's in-place activation, which is the capability to edit objects

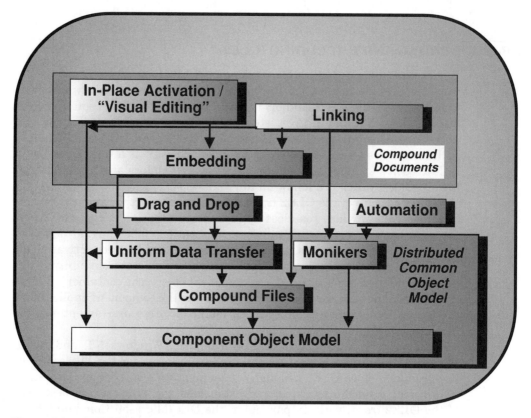

Figure 6.1.   OLE/COM technology overview. Reproduced by permission of Microsoft Press. All rights reserved.

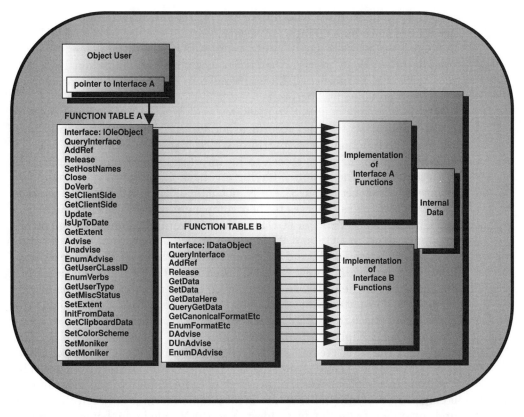

Figure 6.2.   Component object model. Reproduced by permission of Microsoft Press. All rights reserved.

within a container object without creating a separate application window. Uniform data transfer is an upgrade to the Windows clipboard facility that adds OLE2 data objects to the clipboard. OLE2 drag and drop is a finer-grain extension of Windows file-based drag and drop. In OLE2, subsets of documents may be dragged and dropped between similarly enabled OLE2 applications. Whereas OLE2 embedding results in a separate copy of the source data, OLE2 linking supports the display of common data in multiple documents with updates. The moniker facility provides a naming capability. The implementation of monikers is server-specific; names make sense only to the application that creates them. Monikers also support linking using file pathnames. OLE2 Automation is the capability to control applications electronically through a dispatch function that is similar to a nondistributed version of CORBA's Dynamic Invocation Interface (DII).

OLE2 Component Objects are invoked through function tables. Object invocations are equivalent to calls to dynamically linked libraries (DLLs). Each function table contains three or more function pointers, since all objects must support three base functions from the interface IUnknown. OLE2 predefines more than 60 interfaces, each containing a number of APIs. User-defined interfaces are possible but require the user to implement custom marshalling code, a process that is not documented comprehensively. For most practical purposes, OLE2 is intended to be used with the predefined interfaces provided by Microsoft.

Each component object implements one or more OLE2 interfaces. A client application with an interface pointer can request other interfaces through the function QueryInterface, which is present in all interfaces. An object can grant or deny access to its interfaces based on its response to QueryInterface. The notion of having an object identifier as a complete reference to an object is purposefully not supported in OLE2. This enables OLE2 objects to grant access to their component interfaces selectively.

Uniform Data Transfer (UDT) replaces several data interchange mechanisms present in DOS and Windows, such as file drag and drop, dynamic data interchange (DDE), and OLE Version 1. UDT reuses the existing Windows clipboard with a new protocol based upon OLE2 Data Objects. Data Objects support the interface IDataObject, which provides a new facility for transfer of formatted data. Data objects may be transferred through the clipboard or through OLE2 drag and drop.

The OLE2 clipboard framework operates as follows (Figure 6.3). The source for the data creates a data object and posts its IDataObject interface pointer to the clipboard using the DLL function OleSetClipboard. The data source can post several alternative data formats to the clipboard to increase the probability of transferring a common format between the source and consumer. Once the data object is on the Windows clipboard, its implementation is provided by the OLE2 DLL and delegated back to the original object. The consumer can obtain the DLL's Data Object interface pointer using the function OleGetClipboard; then the consumer can retrieve data using Data Object functions such as EnumFormatEtc (to obtain a list of potential formats), QueryData (to determine if request for a specific format would succeed), and GetData (to retrieve the data) [Microsoft, 94a].

Secondary storage mechanisms in OLE2 are defined as a specification called structured storage. OLE2 provides an implementation of this specification called compound files. Compound files enable the storage and partitioning of complex data from multiple embedded objects into a common file. Compound files replace the need for ad hoc approaches such as multiple separate files or complex storage schemes. An example of a compound file is shown in Figure 6.4 on page 140. Compound files are created and managed by OLE2 container objects. Container objects allocate storage in the compound file for embedded objects that perform their own input/output functions using OLE2 persistence APIs. When an embedded object is activated, it is passed a pointer to its compound file storage. Compound files comprises 9 interfaces with more than 70 API functions to support these capabilities [Microsoft, 94a].

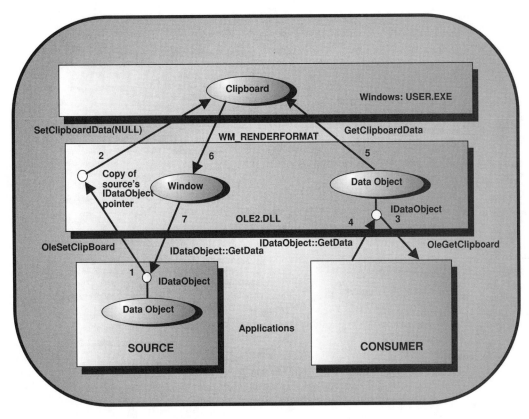

Figure 6.3.   Clipboard framework. Reproduced by permission of Microsoft Press. All rights reserved.

Comparison of OLE/COM and CORBA

In this section, we compare and contrast the features of OLE/Common Object Model with CORBA. OLE/COM is the next generation of OLE2 with some distributed capabilities for persistence, naming, and data transfer. In this discussion, we refer to OLE2 as needed, because it represents the currently available technology. Our perspective is in terms of a software architect evaluating the two mechanisms as the basis for an end-user system.

Object-oriented system developers must choose between OLE/COM and the Object Management Group's CORBA. This choice is an important one, because these two mechanisms comprise the future technology direction of the volume platform vendor and the balance of the computing industry, represented by the 500+ members of OMG.

Both OLE/COM and CORBA provide general capabilities for application integration. CORBA is a general-purpose communications infrastructure for object-oriented software. It is an industry standard supported by multiple platform vendors and independent software vendors. OLE/COM provides an

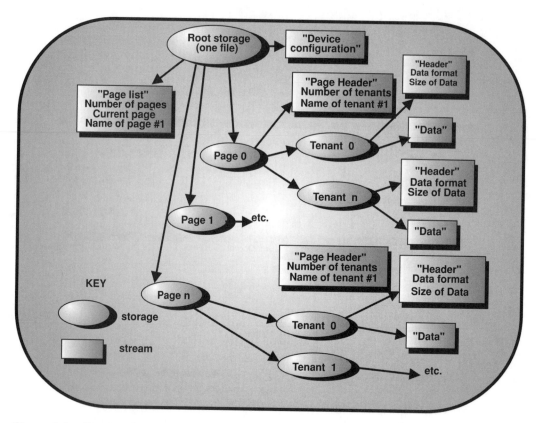

Figure 6.4. Structured storage. Reproduced by permission of Microsoft Press. All rights reserved.

object-based software infrastructure, but it is better known for its compound document framework.

This discussion examines the relative trade-offs between OLE/COM and CORBA. Suppose we are reengineering an end-user application system, a commonplace activity in today's computing environment. The end-user system includes a combination of custom software and commercial off-the-shelf software. A mixture of computing platforms is present, since no one type of computer meets all needs. The goal of the reengineering activity is to provide data sharing and interchange between all units of the organization to foster increased productivity and flexible redefinition of end-user roles. The resulting system should be adaptable to new requirements during its life cycle and should minimize costs for development, operations, and maintenance.

For the system developer, some key criteria defining the choice between the OLE/COM and CORBA include: (1) the generality of the mechanism and its adaptability to the integration problem; (2) the mechanism's support for extensibility; (3) the cost implications of each mechanism; and the (4) stability of the mechanism's technology over the system life cycle.

Generality of OLE/COM vs. CORBA   A first consideration in the comparison of CORBA and OLE/COM is the generality of the mechanism and its adaptability to the software integration problem. Some key factors include support for distributed processing, multiple platforms, and integration with other communication mechanisms.

Distributed Processing   Distributed processing is a key requirement for today's increasingly networked systems. A challenging activity for programmers, distributed processing is costly due to its inherent difficulty. When software is communicating across a distributed system, there are many possibilities for errors, failures, and unpredictable events. The distributed software must be configured correctly, in the appropriate running state, and issues such as the machine-level data representation between the machines and the network must be resolved for software to execute as desired. CORBA is a distributed processing standard defined to simplify these issues for the programmer. It automatically handles data conversions, server activation, and reliable handling of errors. The major object request broker products all support these distributed processing advantages through the CORBA standard.

In contrast, current OLE2 technology does not support distributed computing. The current OLE2 product and supporting frameworks are designed for single-user, single-machine applications. Distributed computing in the OLE/COM environment will be supported by a new mechanism based on proprietary extensions to Open Software Foundation Distributed Computing Environment (OSF DCE).

Heterogeneous Platforms   Integration across multiple operating system platforms is a key requirement in many end-user environments. A mixture of different platforms is an unavoidable fact of life in most organizations, because many jobs require the specialized functions of several computing systems. The ability to interchange data between different platforms would offer a significant productivity boost in these environments.

Current CORBA ORB products support software integration across multiple platforms. Using today's ORB products, each product bridges multiple platforms, providing a consistent set of application software interfaces on any platform. In the future, CORBA products will be bundled with many platforms, and these ORBs will interoperate with other CORBA implementations. The developer will have the choice of using a single ORB across multiple platforms or multiple interoperating ORBs. Some products, such as DEC ObjectBroker, IBM System Object Model (SOM), and IONA's Orbix, are targeting the current and future multiplatform markets. While products such as Hewlett-Packard ORB+ and SunSoft DOE are focused on a single platform, these vendors have recruited allies to provide mutual ORB interoperability solutions.

OLE2 offers platforms for Windows and Macintosh. The Windows platform is supported more because it is described in the published OLE2 documentation [Brockschmidt, 94; Microsoft, 94a; Microsoft, 94b]. Coincidentally, these are the platforms where Microsoft's Office products are deployed. DEC's alliance agreement with Microsoft for the OLE2/CORBA Common Object Model gives DEC the charter to cover other platforms, and other vendors are planning to supply CORBA products for this niche. Available OLE2 technologies do not address multiplatform interoperability since it does not support distributed communication between Windows and Macintosh. OLE2 is not a multiplatform technology, but it may migrate that direction through third-party CORBA support, such as through OpenDoc.

Multiple Communication Mechanisms   Integration with multiple communication mechanisms is an important capability to support software integration. Because so many mechanisms (sockets, Open Network Computing [ONC], DCE, TOOLTALK, etc.) are available, any given assortment of legacy and commercial software will utilize a variety of them. A key role of object-oriented software architecture is to encapsulate the differences between these mechanisms and provide a consistent system integration solution. The technology chosen to resolve these issues must offer support for encapsulation that hides underlying implementation differences.

The CORBA specification is explicitly defined to be independent of underlying communication mechanism. Any given communication mechanism can be encapsulated behind an OMG IDL application program interface, and this encapsulation is devoid of implementation detail. ORB developers and CORBA users frequently apply this concept, encapsulating many levels of communication mechanisms behind OMG IDL APIs.

OLE/COM does not have any explicit support for the integration of multiple communication mechanisms. Its underlying communications mechanisms are provided by Microsoft and are not suitable for replacement by developers or multiple suppliers.

Example Object Identification in CORBA and OLE/COM   Object identification is one of the fundamental concepts in object orientation. CORBA provides a unique object identifier for each object instance. Its object identifiers (OIDs) are opaque to the programmers. CORBA makes issues such as differences in location, language, and operating systems transparent to clients. The object identification mechanism is supported by the COSS naming service, and the trader object service that provides white pages and yellow pages directory services.

OLE/COM does not have a comparable concept of object identity. OLE/COM discourages the notion that anyone can have a pointer to an entire object [Brockschmidt, 94]. Instead clients can have transient pointers to particular interfaces of an object. OLE/COM also has an object naming facility called a moniker. File monikers store absolute and relative file pathnames to provide two ways to find a file. The absolute pathname is tried first; then the relative pathname is sometimes successful if an entire directory structure has moved. This is an incremental improvement upon OLE1, which lost its file links whenever files were renamed and moved. Item monikers are used by an object to define its own namespace. OLE2's lack of object identifiers is an impediment to distributed processing, in which location-dependent names do not translate across machine boundaries.

Extensibility of OLE/COM vs. CORBA   Developers of object-oriented software architectures require mechanisms that support user-defined objects. The extensibility of the mechanisms to support new standards and alternative implementations of predefined specifications is also important for the tailoring of the mechanism to meet application needs. CORBA and OLE/COM differ dramatically with respect to these criteria.

User-Defined Interfaces   Support for user-defined interfaces is fundamental to the implementation of application software architectures. User-defined interfaces are also essential to object orientation, which is based on a concept of domain objects that represent real-world entities or concepts. User definition of these objects is an essential requirement, since these domain-specific objects cannot be encapsulated adequately with vendor-predefined data types and interfaces. Features to be supported in the user definitions include all details of object encapsulations. For example, encapsulations should include declarations of object types, specifications of method signatures, definitions of parameter data types, declarations of attributes, and relationships between object types.

CORBA supports user-defined interfaces through the OMG's Interface Definition Language. OMG IDL is a comprehensive specification language supporting all the just-mentioned features of object encapsulations. OMG IDL interfaces are independent of programming language, so that one specification applies to multiple language bindings. OMG IDL specifications can be compiled into language-specific header files and stub functions. These files support static compile-time checked-method invocations in a form that is natural to the programming language. Dynamic binding to objects is implemented by the ORB mechanisms, and there exists a dynamic invocation interface to support runtime-constructed invocations. Early ORB products (1991–1992 timeframe) were based entirely on the DII without support for static invocation stubs. In practice, the OMG IDL–generated static stubs are a much preferable interface approach. Static stubs allow a seamless programming language interface to objects, which supports encapsulation through compile time parameter checking, efficiency, and ease of use.

OLE2 supports user-defined interfaces through two approaches. Users can write their own marshalling code to support new OLE2 interfaces [Brockschmidt, 94]. Writing marshalling code is analogous to rewriting the internals of an object request broker; this process is not comprehensively documented for OLE2 [Microsoft, 94a].

The second approach is supported through OLE2's interface IDispatch [Microsoft, 94b]. The IDispatch interface is similar to CORBA's DII as utilized in early CORBA products. The user defines an object's interface in the Object Description Language. ODL is compiled into a type library description for use at runtime. In order to send the message, user code must assemble a dynamic parameter structure using OLE2 APIs and call the IDispatch function invoke. A parameter structure is returned from the invocation with any exception information. IDispatch is the central interface of OLE2's automation facilities, in which OLE2 provides mechanisms for multiapplication controls.

In the future, COM will support user-defined interfaces through a proprietary extension to OSF DCE's interface definition language, called Microsoft IDL. This mechanism supports language-level and binary-level APIs that are unique to Microsoft's OLE/COM implementation.

Extensibility of Predefined Services   In addition to the user-defined objects, any predefined interfaces must be adaptable to the needs of applications. For example, an event notification facility should be general purpose enough support application events in addition to the predefined events provided by the vendors.

CORBA-related standards for predefined services includes the Common Object Services Specifications (COSS) and the Common Facilities Specifications. The COSS services are fundamental object service specifications that are intended to be globally applicable solutions that can be specialized for particular domains. COSS and the Common Facilities Specifications are the consensus standards of the multivendor supported industry, and many adopted specifications are already available. For example, the COSS event notification service is a generic reusable event service that provides a comprehensive selection of event supplier and consumer integration approaches [OMG, 94b]. The ORB vendors will supply the implementations of COSS services, and the users can readily reimplement the services to tailor the implementation behavior for their own purposes. The OMG standards do not predefine the domain content of these services, so users can define them as needed.

In its 60+ interfaces and nearly 400 APIs, OLE2's service definitions are specialized to particular OLE2 framework needs, such as uniform data transfer or structured storage. These framework interfaces support specific forms of interoperability that are predetermined by OLE2. It is clear from their design that the interfaces are not intended to be global solutions that are tailorable to application requirements. For example, the interface IAdviceSink provides the OLE event notification service. IAdviceSink is a special-purpose interface for OLE2 container objects to receive notifications of specific types of events [Microsoft, 94a]. It has method definitions, including OnDataChange, OnViewChange, OnRename, OnSave, and OnClose. The method signatures predefine the specific change indicated in the event, such as a change to a new clipboard data format in method OnDataChange. These particular events would not support arbitrary uses of an event service; the OLE2 service would not be extensible to support application-specific needs.

Cost Implications of OLE/COM vs. CORBA   OLE/COM and CORBA are new technologies that may have substantial impacts on end-user systems; it is important to examine the potential impacts of these technologies on life cycle cost. Some key cost factors include: savings from use of commercial off-the-shelf products, costs related to the complexity of the mechanisms, support for reuse, and support for portability. The portability issue can impact cost when a system must be deployed and maintained on multiple platforms. An important related issue is the need for multiple system builds to support different configurations, programming languages, memory models, and so forth.

Commercial Off-the-Shelf vs. Custom   A key argument for adopting technologies like OLE/COM is the potential for no-cost integration with shrink-wrap commercial applications. Life cycle experiences indicate that cost advantages of using commercial applications are not always clear. It is well known that operations and maintenance consumes 70 percent of life cycle costs. Hidden maintenance costs are associated with the lack of control end users experience when choosing off-the-shelf over custom software. Commercial vendors control the features in the product; they also control when new versions are released and the APIs that any end-user software may depend on for interoperability. When many off-the-shelf products are involved, reintegration of upgraded software is a continual maintenance activity. In some cases, maintenance agreements and licenses can lapse, such that repurchasing the software becomes necessary. Reintegration costs can be substantial when a product upgrade of two or more versions is required after repurchase.

The potential for shrinkwrap off-the-shelf integration through CORBA can be supported in several ways: directly through OMG standards, indirectly through gateways, and directly through end user–sponsored specifications.

Future CORBA-based standards based on technologies such as OpenDoc can provide direct shrinkwrap integration. Because OpenDoc is defined and controlled by multiple vendors, suppliers and consumers view these specifications as a much lower risk than a single-vendor, competitor-controlled technology like OLE/COM.

Integration with non-CORBA mechanisms (OLE2, ToolTalk, etc.) can be supported through gateways to end-user software architectures. In this approach, no-cost shrinkwrap integration is supported through the gateway, and the software architecture isolates the application code from direct dependence on the external mechanism. If the external mechanism changes, operating and maintenance costs are limited to the gateway code. Multiple external mechanisms (OLE2 and OpenDoc) could be supported through this approach. As complete industry convergence is unlikely at the level of compound document architectures, this is likely to be an important approach.

The third approach for CORBA/commercial off-the-shelf integration using CORBA is through end user–sponsored standards. End users pursuing system development frequently produce quality interface specifications. In many cases, these specifications are years ahead of comparable standards activities in the commercial market. Through coordination with others, groups of end users can form new markets by adopting common specifications. Involving vendors in an open specification process is also effective in achieving commercial buy-in. Sufficient market development can prepare a standard for formal adoption by standards groups.

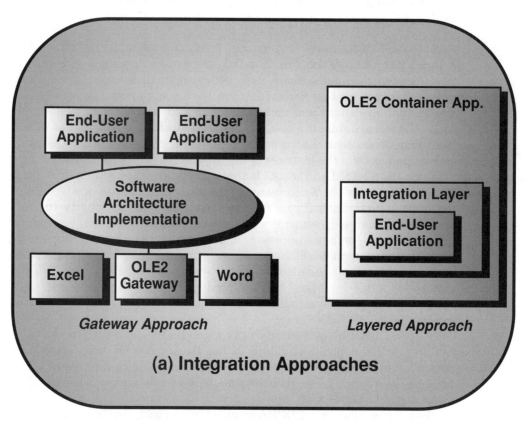

Figure 6.5.   Gateway integration of software architecture and OLE2.

Complexity of Mechanism   An important cost factor involves the integration of custom software with OLE/COM and CORBA. The complexity of the APIs, the documentation, and the available training are indicators of how costly each mechanism will be to learn and utilize.

OLE2 is one of the most complex technologies ever to be released by Microsoft [Brockschmidt, 94]. Brockschmidt, author of *Inside OLE2*, characterizes OLE2 as being significantly more complex than the Windows operating system [Brockschmidt, 94]. The documentation for OLE2 consists of the *Inside OLE2* developer's guide (925 pages), the API Reference (650 pages), and the OLE Automation Reference (400 pages) [Brockschmidt, 94; Microsoft, 94a; Microsoft, 94b]. Even at 925 pages, *Inside OLE2* does not cover significant parts of OLE2, such as OLE Automation. To use OLE2, a detailed understanding of the operating system's API (WIN32) is also required [Brockschmidt, 94]. Developer's experiences indicate that OLE2 requires a very steep learning curve. There are some development tools, such as visual basic, which simplify OLE2 integration.

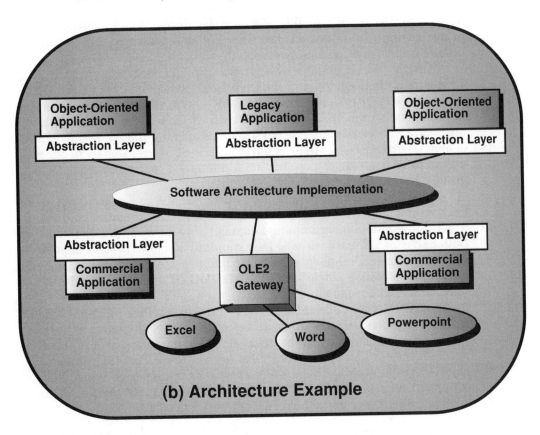

Figure 6.5.   (continued)

In contrast, the CORBA specification is defined in 178 pages. Most CORBA products provide their complete documentation in another 200 to 300 pages. Training is widely available; virtually every CORBA vendor has a one-week hands-on training course, and at least four independent training companies offer general training on CORBA. With appropriate training, user experiences are very positive: CORBA is easy to learn and apply. Quite a few independent software vendors, including Bluestone, Forte Systems, Tivoli, Oberon, and Netlinks, have released CORBA-based products.

One interesting aspect of CORBA is that the system developer can control the complexity of the APIs in the application system. Using OMG IDL, developers can define an application-specific software architecture. The architecture can be tailored for the appropriate integration cost. OMG IDL is a good tool for defining software architectures and delivering the resulting APIs to large software projects that involve multiple development organizations. This concept has been applied with success in the DISCUS Framework. (See Chapter 7.)

Support for Reuse   Reusability of code and of design is an important source of cost savings. Inheritance is the principal object-oriented mechanism for code reuse and design specialization.

CORBA directly provides inheritance through subtyping in OMG IDL. This is inheritance at the interface level only, which enables design reuse. A number of CORBA products (IBM SOM and others) are also supporting implementation inheritance, which is a direct form of code reuse. With implementation inheritance, it is easy to reuse existing objects, redefine parts of objects, and specialize their behaviors. IBM SOM uses this in an effective way to provide a reusable replication framework to support development of group applications. (See Appendix.)

OMG IDL also has significant potential for design reuse. It is a specification language that is devoid of implementation information and can be applied to multiple programming languages, operating systems, and distribution schemes. Some have called it a standard for defining other standards, because it is a general-purpose notation that provides multiple implementation bindings from a single specification. OMG IDL allows the architecture to be product independent.

OLE/COM does not support inheritance but another related construct called delegation. In delegation, to reuse code, the programmer provides method implementation that contains a call to the reused code supplied by another object. This is a less controlled form of reuse than that provided by object-oriented systems. It is really programmer-supported reuse, instead of support for reuse by OLE/COM. Microsoft believes that there is minimal need for inheritance in its third-party software market.

Portability and Multiple Builds   Portability is an important cost issue because many applications need to support multiple target platforms, such as different variations of UNIX, DOS/Windows, Macintosh, and other operating systems. A related issue is the need for multiple builds of software to support interoperability with other languages, memory models, and other factors.

One of the key advantages of CORBA is that the APIs are consistent between all platforms. When standardized, the OMG IDL language bindings are consistent for that language across all platforms. In general, CORBA will not be a cause of platform dependency; other factors such as the operating system APIs and windowing system APIs are potential sources of portability problems. These are addressed through other standards, such as POSIX and MOTIF, with significant success. CORBA eliminates the need for multiple software builds when client and server are implemented in different languages. Products such as IBM SOM also isolate clients and servers from differences in memory models and other implementation factors.

OLE2 is best supported on Windows platforms. It is available, but not as well documented, on the Macintosh. Third-party vendors (such as DEC) will support a subset of distributed COM functionality on other platforms. The OLE2 APIs as supplied by Microsoft are a significant source of platform dependency now and in the future. Since OLE2 defines explicit bindings to Microsoft C++, OLE2 is also language dependent and will require significant developer effort to provide alternative language bindings and code reuse between languages.

Stability of OLE2 vs. CORBA   End-user system life cycles involving custom software development typically range from 10 to 15 years. This range defines the practical life span of a technology. Commercial software technology works on a more compressed timeline; new products and major upgrades are introduced to the market at six- to 12-month intervals. The commercial viability of a major technology can be as short as one to three years before a new wave of innovation changes the market. In order to remain competitive, commercial vendors must begin development well in advance of the current state of the art. In markets undergoing revolutionary changes (such as CORBA and OLE/COM), marketing staff must recruit an enthusiastic group of early adopters to ensure independent software vendor and end-user support. The marketing staff must also educate independent vendors and users in the mainstream market about the revolutionary benefits of the new technologies, lobbying mainstream organizations to align their strategic plans to adopt their technologies as they are delivered to market in productized form.

OLE/COM is an excellent example of this process in action. There is an increasing number of OLE2-compliant commercial software due to the 80%+ desktop market share controlled by Microsoft. Microsoft is preparing its market for a revolutionary shift to new operating system technology, through the transition platform of Windows 95 and then to Cairo. Microsoft is a major independent software vendor in its own right and has used its internal products as the early adopter group to support OLE2 with the Microsoft Office products. Through conferences Microsoft has been working to educate external developers about the new technology. It also has issued press releases and worked with magazines and other publications to reach the mainstream market with its message.

Given that competing technologies, such as OpenDoc, Taligent, and Fresco, are being released to the market with technology advantages over OLE2, Microsoft must advance its strategy to a new generation of technology within the next two years. A key problem for developers is that rapid innovation causes API obsolescence. An end-user system that adopts OLE2 with a 10- to 15-year life cycle would be assuming an extreme risk. If as is likely, Microsoft upgrades or replaces this API in two years, there will be significant operating and management costs to pay in end-user systems in order to continue to keep pace with Microsoft's rate of innovations. Upgrading all independent vendors' software may be necessary as well. Microsoft is attempting to provide transition support with backward compatibility from Windows 3.1 to Windows 95.

An important factor that moderates the pace of commercial innovation and technology obsolescence is standardization. Standards are a widely used marketing strategy; the cost of most standards activities is an investment provided by for-profit companies. Standards reduce risk for both suppliers and consumers and bestow credibility and acceptance on new technologies. Standards allow common infrastructure to be established that vendors and end users can leverage to support more platforms and more functionality. Formal standards creation through national and international bodies takes at least four years. Voluntary industry groups (such as OMG) can establish major standards much faster.

Once standards are established, the standard extends the life cycle viability of a technology (Figure 6.6). In the case of layered technologies (such as networking), standards can extend the viability of a technology indefinitely. The OMG has established a hierarchy of technologies that are layered upwardly in its Object Management Architecture [OMG, 93]. In the OMG model, the Object Services are layered on CORBA, and the Common Facilities are built on the Object Services.

Due to its multivendor support, standards basis, and layered architecture, CORBA has all the indications of being a technology with a long life cycle. Its life cycle continues to extend as other standards bodies increasingly utilize CORBA as the basis for standards (such as the International Standards Organization's Open Distributed Processing, X/Consortium, X/Open, etc.).

THE OPENDOC FRAMEWORK

OpenDoc is a framework supporting innovations for the end user (compound documents) and the developer (component software). OpenDoc is a multivendor technology destined for standards support. For the user and developer,

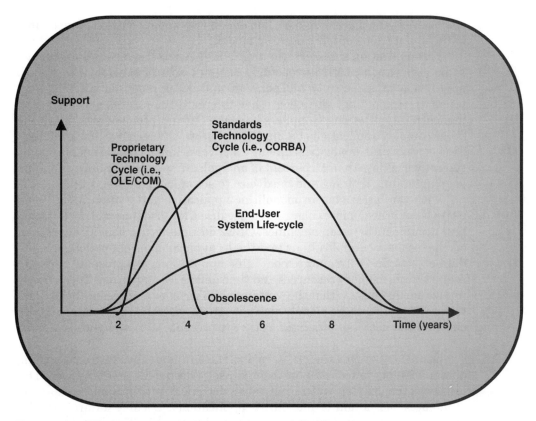

Figure 6.6. Standards and technology cycles vs. system life cycles.

OpenDoc offers some fundamental innovations in technology, representing the next generation of the end-user desktop and the application development environment. We begin our examination of OpenDoc by explaining the user interface model and how it differs from previous technologies.

OpenDoc User Interface

Today's application-based desktops force end users to work in restricted modes. Each application has a unique data format and a unique set of commands for manipulating that format. The command set is restrictive in terms of manipulating external data formats. In order to manipulate information in another format, the end user must move to another application, with similar restrictions. Most end-user document products involve more than one form of data. If data is combined through a clipboard data exchange, then data fidelity or the ability to edit the data may be lost. If data is combined through linking, applications still have to be switched to manipulate linked data. Linking is very brittle in today's desktop technologies such as OLE2.

End users spend a great deal of time and energy coping with the constraints of the application-centered desktop model.

For application suppliers, the trend has been to create very large monolithic applications with increasingly complex sets of controls. Since each application must be fully independent and do as much as possible, suppliers are competing with each other to create the largest, most complex monolithic applications. Suppliers have the difficult problem of maintaining these complex applications on multiple platforms (which are also evolving). This increasing complexity is having an adverse impact on the end user, who typically uses less than 15 percent of an application's functionality and must keep upgrading training and hardware to accommodate these trends.

With the latest step in monolithic application integration, OLE2, end users become even more constrained because they lose their ability to transport documents between machines. OLE2 documents are heavily dependent on the local set of applications and the local pathnames of applications and data objects. In OLE2, large monolithic applications are present; they still require large memory resources and time delays for activation. The primary innovation in OLE2 is that the container application can present the user interface of another large monolithic application. OLE2 has not fundamentally changed the desktop paradigm; rather it presents it in a slightly different way.

OpenDoc changes the end-user interface fundamentally, from focusing on applications to focusing on the end-user's document products. OpenDoc refocuses the desktop on the end user's document products and completely eliminates the notion of monolithic applications. Documents are containers that can contain any types of content (Figure 6.7). The container itself is content neutral, and global functions, such as Undo, are transparently coordinated among the parts.

Each type of content can be manipulated by associated software called a part. Parts have sample documents called stationery. To insert a new type of content, the end user drags the stationery into a document. The user can drag and drop content between documents, creating a new copy or a linked copy under user control.

OpenDoc containers support a standard pair of menus: Document and Edit (Figure 6.8). The Document menu replaces the traditional File menu. Because OpenDoc eliminates the concept of separate applications, there is no quit command; documents are opened and closed instead of applications being launched and quitted. The Drafts command supports a version control capability built in to OpenDoc. Users can create multiple drafts of a document, which can be retrieved and edited later. The Mail command indicates that all OpenDoc documents will be mail-enabled. A parts bin is available, similar to the scrapbook, which contains reference objects.

The Edit menu is similar to conventional Edit menus (Figure 6.8). The Undo command applies globally across all parts within the document. This

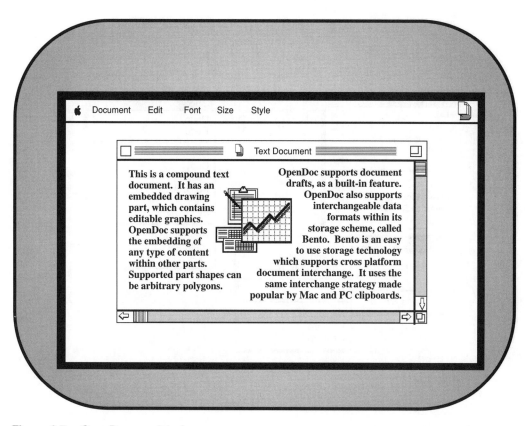

Figure 6.7.   OpenDoc user interface.

is a powerful capability for undoing actions, regardless of the responsible part editor. The Cut, Copy, and Paste commands manipulate the clipboard. The end user may utilize drag-and-drop operations to perform these functions. The Paste As command supports active linking. The View as Window command allows any part to be instantiated within a separate window. This is convenient for some end-user editing operations.

OpenDoc documents are stored in interchange formats, similar to today's PC clipboards. Stored formats are platform independent and identified with registered format descriptors. This allows documents to be easily relocated, viewed, and edited by alternative software, depending on the platform. OpenDoc links, implemented through CORBA objects, can be translated across machine boundaries in a distributed network. These features allow compound document relocation, an important capability not found in other technologies, such as OLE2.

OpenDoc will be fully interoperable with OLE2. OpenDoc parts can be embedded in OLE2 documents, and OLE2 components can be embedded

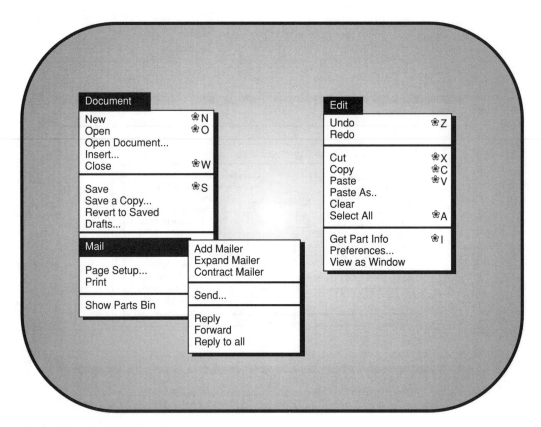

Figure 6.8. OpenDoc menus.

in OpenDoc containers. OpenDoc offers a simpler way to integrate OLE2 capabilities than direct OLE2 integration. It also offers other advantages, such as a more flexible embedding model and distributed support through CORBA.

Parts also have part viewers, which suppliers generally give away. Part editors and part viewers are much smaller and simpler than today's mono- lithic applications. Parts can provide specialized functionality without hav- ing to provide a complete stand-alone application around it. Suppliers can focus their resources on part editors that manipulate specialized content, instead of competing with all other monolithic applications that replicate a great deal of each other's functionality.

OpenDoc Technology and CI Labs

OpenDoc is a technology administrated by a nonprofit consortium, the Com- ponent Integration Labs (CI Labs). Sponsor members of the CI Labs include Apple, Borland, IBM, Lotus, Novell, Oracle, Sun, Taligent, WordPerfect, and

Xerox. Several sponsors have made substantial corporate commitments: Apple contributed foundation technologies; IBM contributed CORBA implementation; and Novell is developing the Microsoft Windows implementation and the OLE2 interoperability solution to OpenDoc. Other sponsors are committed to providing OpenDoc integrated with their products and available for development on their platforms.

CI Labs ensures that the OpenDoc technology is vendor independent. It maintains the OpenDoc source code, disseminates development kits, and documentation. It also pursues testing, registry, and standards activities.

One of CI Labs' key roles is OpenDoc parts testing, called the validation service. For a fee, CI Labs will validate that a supplier or end user's OpenDoc part is compliant with the OpenDoc specifications. Compliance will assure cross-platform portability. CI Labs will maintain a hardware suite of all the available OpenDoc platforms and special versions of the OpenDoc implementation to assure independence from underlying platform implementations.

CI Labs maintains a registry of OpenDoc usage conventions that will assure interoperability between parts implementations. One of the registries is a list of categories of OpenDoc content types. Example categories may include text, tables, and graphics. These categories organize the registry for other registered items, such as storage data formats and predefined scripting events. System software can use content types to associate locally available parts editors with parts data. Registered data formats will be transportable across platforms and viewable/editable by a wide range of software.

CI Labs coordinates OpenDoc standards activities. CI Labs and OMG are developing a standard compound document framework based on OpenDoc. The adopted specification will be a language- and platform-independent compound document standard that enjoys strong international support.

Technologies underlying OpenDoc include the System Object Model, Bento, and the Open Scripting Architecture (OSA). These technologies are licensed to CI Labs for redistribution.

SOM is a CORBA-compliant object request broker. It is available across a widening range of PC, UNIX, and mainframe platforms. Originally developed for the PC-class OS/2 operating system, it supports the low-overhead efficiency needed for PC desktops. SOM enables transparent use of multiple programming languages with OpenDoc (initially C, C++, and SmallTalk). With additional CORBA language mappings, virtually any language can be integrated to OpenDoc transparently. SOM interoperability with other request brokers will allow OpenDoc to operate transparently across a network, supporting functions such as distributed linking (Mosaic-like hypermedia), remote part editors, and multiuser collaboration. SOM and OpenDoc will be integral elements of Copeland, Apple's next-generation operating system.

Bento is a compound document storage specification. It is a very flexible and simple technology that supports storage of any content type and is platform and media independent. Bento handlers, which perform the low-level storage manipulation, can implement device specific buffering, packing, and encryption. The device handlers are transparent to the part editor code.

The OSA supports interpart communication in OpenDoc. OSA will enable groups of OpenDoc parts to work together in documents. For example, a group of parts may want to choreograph an animated display of information in a document. OSA combines a high-level messaging facility with a common scripting language and a common event format. OSA supports the consolidation and abstraction of events by the operating system, called semantic events. For example, instead of reporting a low-level mouse action (MouseUp, pixelX, pixelY), OpenDoc's semantic events might report: ("Copy" Command, Cell D10, "July 94 Report" Spreadsheet).

OSA supports three forms of interoperability with scripts. *Scriptable* parts are those that can receive commands via OSA scripts and events. *Recordable* parts are ones that can create reusable scripts by recording end-user actions. *Tinkerable* parts are parts whose behavior can be modified through the attachment of scripts by external applications. CI Labs envisions a large third-party market for script-authoring packages and intelligent agents that can create and execute multiapplication scripts.

The OpenDoc Architecture

Using the OpenDoc architecture, the developer is involved in creating the *grand illusion* of direct manipulation. To the end user, it appears as if the mouse is hard-wired to the on-screen sprite, and the user can drag and drop desktop objects as if manipulating real-world objects. Behind the scenes, direct manipulation is implemented entirely using software. OpenDoc and the operating system implement the lower-level details of the grand illusion. OpenDoc presents a much-simplified abstract programming interface for the application-level software developer. Its developers can create new direct manipulation applications with less software than previous technologies required. OpenDoc has made it easier for developers to implement the compound document model, where the granularity of direct manipulation is at the embedded part level instead of the file level. In addition, OpenDoc software is a portable cross platform, is interoperable with multiple languages, will automatically support OLE2, and supports distributed processing. The potential advantages for the developer and end user are substantial.

OpenDoc is a sophisticated compound document architecture, comprising several dozen object types. Most of this complexity is transparent to the developer. Almost all of these object types are already implemented by OpenDoc. Fortunately, OpenDoc part developers are concerned only with the implementation of one object: their own part. Simple parts might interact with a handful of OpenDoc objects. Complex parts might interact with a dozen or so other OpenDoc objects. It's all a matter of how much of OpenDoc functionality a part supports. Functionality can start out simple

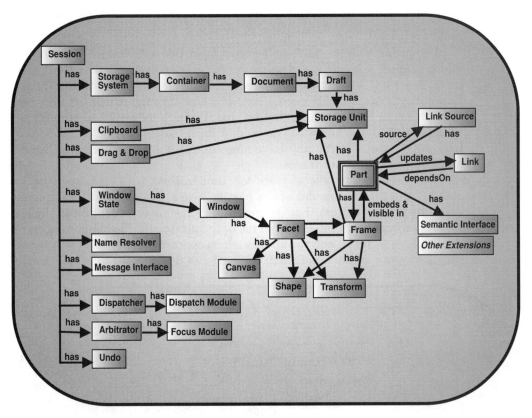

Figure 6.9. OpenDoc object relationships.

and grow incrementally with the part. Initially, storage, controls, and display are the most basic functions. More advanced capabilities include the clipboard, linking, and drag and drop. Advanced capabilities include embedding and scripting. Implementation of object embedding within a part is an advanced function that not every part will support.

OpenDoc provides support for creating a comprehensive template for the part software, through a point-and-click application called PartMaker. PartMaker creates a complete set of source files, header files, and makefiles. These files support default OpenDoc functionality, and the templates contain the entry points for every potential capability of an OpenDoc part.

One of the key objects in the OpenDoc architecture is the Session object. There is one session object for each OpenDoc document. Parts use the session object to locate other OpenDoc objects. For example, a part needs to interact with other OpenDoc objects that manage desktop resources and provide other OpenDoc functionality. The Session object implements messages such as GetClipboard and GetLinkManager to retrieve the object reference of the requested object.

The primary presentation objects in OpenDoc are Frames and Facets, which support printing and display. A Frame is an area of a document allocated to a part. A Facet corresponds to any displayable area in the frame. Conceptually, we can think of a Facet as a lens through which the user can view a Frame. Facets are created by OpenDoc automatically when a frame becomes viewable. The part is notified of these events through various callback entry points. Parts may have more than one frame; there also can be more than one facet per frame.

The presentation objects work together in the OpenDoc framework to simplify the drawing model of the part software. Frames and Facets have associated shape objects that define their geometric extents. Shape objects are used to constrain the frame shape of the document, the clipped shape of the displayable facet, and the shapes of objects embedded in the part. When the part's draw method is called, the part can draw to the allocated frame

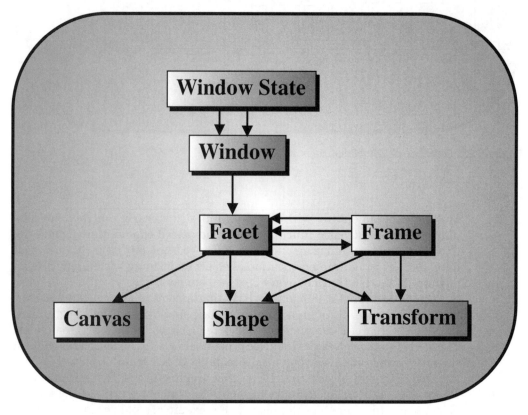

Figure 6.10. OpenDoc windowing objects.

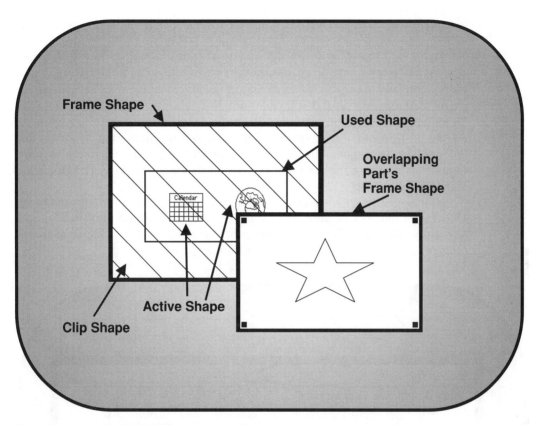

Figure 6.11. OpenDoc clipping.

shape, and the displayable clip shape can be applied transparently. The part can then invoke the draw method on embedded parts to redraw contained areas. Transform objects are used to indicate the location of a frame or facet within a containing part and the amount scrolled for scrollable parts.

Events are a key feature of OpenDoc available for use by developers. An OpenDoc part receives events through a HandleEvent method invoked by the Dispatcher object. Events identify the Frame, Facet, and self-descriptive event information, such as the event type, time, location, and option keys. The Dispatcher object filters platform-dependent events, so that parts perceive that events are handled in a platform-independent manner.

OpenDoc has a set of event focuses (i.e., keyboard, mouse) that must be allocated by parts in order to receive events. Ownership of event foci determines the distribution of an event. The Arbitrator object manages the allocation of foci. Some examples of event foci include the keyboard, the mouse, and the menus. For example, a part may obtain the keyboard focus from the Arbitrator and then receive subsequent keyboard events. Parts generally request a complete set of foci when they are activated. OpenDoc provides a complete protocol for focus acquisition, preemption, and relinquishment.

Parts that obtain menu focus may modify the menubar to reflect part-specific commands. This straightforward procedure includes adding new menus and commands to the base menubar. The new menu structure can be assembled offscreen and displayed immediately after obtaining menu focus. To make the menu commands localized (for internationalization), the menu command titles should be retrieved from stored resource files. The part developer also is responsible for enabling and disabling menu items. A part is notified to adjust the menus just prior to menu selection by the OpenDoc WindowState object.

Storage units are the basis for persistence and data interchange in Open-Doc. Every part uses a storage unit to save and retrieve its persistent state. The same storage APIs are the basis for all forms of OpenDoc data interchange, including the clipboard, drag and drop, and linking.

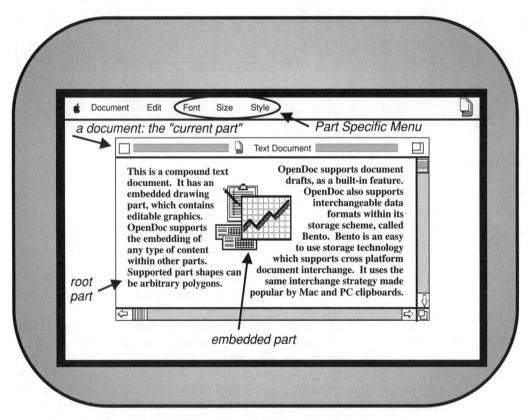

Figure 6.12.   OpenDoc user interface parts, containers, and menus.

OpenDoc storage units are based on the Bento storage specification. Technically, Bento provides a simple API and storage structure that replaces conventional file input/output. Bento containers are a sequence of named properties. Each property can have multiple named representations. The data representations are byte sequences. In order to store structured data or pointers, the part must convert the data to a byte sequence before writing to the storage unit. This data structure flattening operation is called externalization. Conversely, the part must internalize the data to reconstitute the information when initialized from the stored state. OpenDoc calls the part's Externalize and InitPartFromStorage methods to request these actions.

Bento containers typically are implemented as files. Each container can store a complex compound document, comprising data from multiple part editors. This replaces the need for multiple files, created by separate applications.

OpenDoc parts typically store information in multiple exchange formats, similar to a clipboard. The part can store its highest-fidelity data format, followed by one or more common exchange formats. This feature of OpenDoc greatly increases portability of documents; other compound document technologies (i.e., OLE2) have limited ability to move documents between machines.

OpenDoc parts must keep track of lists of several important items, including the frames it supports, the objects it embeds, and active links with other parts. These lists should be stored in the object's persistent state so that they can be retrieved upon activation. A reusable collection class for iterating through these lists is useful for managing this process.

The OpenDoc Clipboard is an object created by the Session object. The Clipboard is used to interchange data, as on PC desktops. Before the Clipboard is accessed, it must be locked for exclusive access. The data on the Clipboard is in an OpenDoc Storage Unit. Parts can monitor changes to the Clipboard through the retrieval of a Clipboard version key.

The Clipboard supports data interchange in multiple fidelities. This is the same strategy used by current PC and Macintosh clipboards. The parts write their highest-fidelity native format, followed by other interchange formats. For example, a word processor part might write native format, Apple-styled text (a popular interchange format), plain text, and a link specification. This last piece of information would support active linking if the end user creates a link while pasting the information. Link objects also use Storage Units to transfer information.

The final use of Storage Units is in support of Drag and Drop. Drag and Drop is one of the most complex protocols for desktop objects. OpenDoc has abstracted the process to its essentials. The following is a brief synopsis of a typical Drag and Drop operation.

To initiate a drag within a part, the part receives a mouse event and must determine if it refers to a specific selected object (i.e., a drag is initiating); otherwise the mouse event is indicating some other operation. The part can then write to data to the DragAndDrop object's Storage Unit. The part then calls the StartDrag method of the DragAndDrop object. The balance of the Drag and Drop protocol involves the recipient of the Drag and Drop.

If a part is the recipient of a Drag & Drop (indicated by an OpenDoc call to the part's DragEnter method), then the part can determine if the appropriate format resides in the DragAndDrop object's Storage Unit. If so, the part can highlight itself (indicating potential acceptance); otherwise it can ignore the drag operation. The part can receive one or more DragWithin method calls during this process. The part receives a call to its Drop method if the user releases the mouse button; then the part reads the data, as if reading the Clipboard's Storage Unit.

Embedding is the most complex aspect of OpenDoc programming. Embedding is the ability of a part to contain other parts. OLE2 uses a single-layer embedding model with nonoverlapping rectangular frames. An OLE2 application implements either a container or an embedded component, but not both. OpenDoc embedding capabilities are much more flexible. Embedded shapes can be arbitrary polygons; embedded objects can overlap. Objects can embed within other objects to any level of nesting.

This complexity is hidden from the part developer who does not support embedding of other parts. The container object must deal with the unusual shapes of embedded objects and these other issues. When an individual part supports embedding, it must also contend with these issues.

AUTONOMOUS LAND VEHICLE

An interesting example of a framework-based development occurred on an Advanced Research Projects Agency (ARPA) project called the Autonomous Land Vehicle (ALV). The research was conducted at the Martin Marietta Corporation (MMC) from 1985 through 1989. The design of the architecture predated CORBA but utilized many of the architectural principles presented in this book. Follow-on projects to ALV are being actively pursued at MMC and at many universities and contractors.

The ALV technical challenge was to develop a rapid prototyping testbed for intelligent mobile robotics research. The testbed supported the rapid integration of technologies from four research fields: image understanding, artificial intelligence route planning, sensors, and experimental parallel processors. These technologies were supplied by external research groups at universities and contractor organizations, evolving their research prototypes in parallel.

To prove the testbed capabilities and provide a general integration framework, MMC first developed and demonstrated its own set of algorithms. The first experiment included continuous-motion road following. This demonstration was beyond the state of the art of what had ever been done in the research community; each run of the vehicle over its track included processing of over 700 video images. Prior to this experiment, the image understanding research community had focused on a small number of test images and had not demonstrated continuous-motion robotics. By processing so large an image set, ALV fundamentally changed the nature of the research problems.

Early ALV experiments focused on this continuous-motion road following. Later experiments demonstrated increases in road following speed using ARPA's advanced parallel processors. Other advanced experiments shows obstable avoidance with continuous motion and off-road cross-country navigation.

A key function of the testbed was the hosting of external research software. Each research group had a particular focus, such as the vision or route-planning aspects of the mobile robotics problem. It also had particular hardware and operating system dependencies; some ran on VAX/VMS, on VICOM VDP, on Sun workstations, on Symbolics, on ARPA/CMU/GE Warp Machines, and so on. The ALV testbed supports a highly heterogeneous environment, including, in addition to the preceding machines, Multibus I chassis, VME chassis, the ARPA/BBN Butterfly Machine, and potentially any other commercial or research platform. In addition, programming language support requirements ranged from assembly languages, to Pascal, FORTRAN, Lisp, and C. ALV needed to support all these heterogeneous requirements in a distributed laboratory, where different parts of the processing could occur potentially on any of the platforms. The ALV laboratory was distributed between the onboard processors and the laboratory facility, a conventional computer room environment. The vehicle and computer room were interconnected through a private FCC-licensed radio and TV station, which provided two-way digital data transfer and video transmission back to the laboratory.

ALV would be a challenging system to implement today; in the mid-1980s it required an extraordinary architectural vision and discipline to create a system flexible enough to cover all of these platforms, languages, and distribution options.

The ALV solution was to create a flexible integration framework that provided a consistent access mechanism for communication between distributed processes, called Real-Net. For the application programmers, Real-Net included a simple messaging API that provided transparency of location, platform, and language. Individual components of the ALV software could be replaced and/or relocated without impacting other elements of the system.

Real-Net was implemented primarily over an Ethernet LAN connection, with Real-Net software communicating at the UDP level. Because of the mobile distributed environment, the Ethernet protocols also ran over the digital radio link. Real-Net supported other hardware connections, such as real-time direct memory access (DMA) transfers between VME chassis. The choice of networking hardware and protocols was made transparent to the application software.

Application software communicated through a simple set of send-and-receive APIs. It provided the application-level parameters and abstract destinations. The parameter formats and network addresses of the messages were stored in tables that were initialized at system boot time. The details of the network addresses were hidden from the application programmers. This allowed the processes to be replaced and migrated without changing application software. The Real-Net architecture provided native language and operating system APIs on each of the heterogeneous platforms. Part of the system was implemented in the native languages of the platforms involved. The commonality occurred at the network packet level, which could be marshalled and unmarshalled according to the platform and language-specific requirements.

With today's CORBA-based technology, ORB vendors provide a great deal of the Real-Net functionality as specified by OMG standards. CORBA provides transparent heterogeneous processing that is location, platform, and language independent. CORBA actually provides more flexibility, in that it binds processes at runtime and can establish new process allocations and relationships dynamically. Flexibility in the CORBA standard allows different kinds of underlying ORB implementations, including real-time and non–real-time products.

COMMENTS

There is certainly no way to guarantee CORBA's continuing viability. Developers can approach CORBA in two alternative ways, and their choice will greatly influence the magnitude of the opportunity cost. The two approaches are: (1) use CORBA in a product-dependent manner for its ORB-dependent benefits, or (2) use CORBA in a technology-independent manner to define better software architectures.

If CORBA is used in a way that is heavily dependent on product-specific extensions to the standard, then CORBA failure will have a catastrophic impact. Some dramatic examples of this type of mistake became evident when HyperDesk withdrew its non-compliant ORB product from the market. A similar error might be made if an application system were developed to be highly dependent on OLE2, DCE RPC, or ToolTalk, since these technologies also might have short life spans.

Migration to CORBA should be approached with technology independence in mind. A primary goal of the migration should be the creation of an effective software architecture. The software architecture (specified in OMG IDL) should be designed to provide functionality in a cost-effective manner.

This can be achieved by selectively hiding, exposing, and abstracting the complexities of the subsystems. The software architecture should isolate the subsystems from each other and provide overall product independence so that subsystems can be replaced readily. It should support system extensibility by providing sufficient metadata and symmetry of representation to allow the addition of new subsystems without the need to modify existing subsystems. All of these features should be captured in the system's OMG IDL specifications. If one ORB product fails, the system can be ported to another ORB with minimum impact. If no ORBs are available, the OMG IDL APIs can be layered on top of an alternative mechanism, such as Remote Procedure Call (RPC). If this technology-independent approach is taken, the opportunity cost of using CORBA will be a net benefit, regardless of the success or failure of the CORBA standard.

In-Depth Example: The DISCUS Framework

The Data Interchange and Synergistic Collateral Usage Study (DISCUS) developed the U.S. government's first CORBA-based application system. DISCUS has been recognized by technologists and the media as one of the best examples of the benefits of distributed object technology. For example, it was a finalist in the Computerworld Object Application Awards. DISCUS has been presented and demonstrated at more than a dozen national conferences. For software architects and developers, DISCUS is an important case study, demonstrating many successful strategies for systems integration using CORBA.

The DISCUS framework (without the demonstration system) was the primary technology product of the project. The framework comprises less than 150 lines of Object Management Group Interface Definition Language specifications (OMG IDL). For such a small amount of specification, it has been shown to yield some interesting and important results. The two key results include substantial interoperability benefits and low integration cost. The interoperability provided by DISCUS includes universal data interchange, data format conversions, universal data source access, and scriptable application control. This is achievable with a very minimal amount of integration code, averaging about 500 lines for each application. Compared to traditional integration projects, this represents more than an order of magnitude reduction in integration cost and complexity. Some of this gain was due to CORBA, but most of the benefits are due to good software architecture design coupled with a strong architectural vision shared by developers and program managers. CORBA and the OMG played a key role in DISCUS by clarifying the importance of good software architecture and the need for interface standards.

The DISCUS framework is unique in its simplicity. Only four operations form the core set for understanding the framework. DISCUS can be considered as the software analogy of Reduced Instruction Set Computer (RISC) microprocessor architectures. The DISCUS framework is simple and therefore easy for developers and organizations to learn and to use. Simplicity also reduces the integration complexity; less specification results in fewer application program interfaces (APIs) and less integration code.

DISCUS represents an architecture design point that balances integration cost and provides modest levels of generality and functionality. This design point might not be appropriate for all applications, but it seems to be a very good one for government software integration; we believe that it is applicable to the needs of many end-user organizations. The DISCUS framework presented here can be used readily by commercial and end-user organizations for integration projects.

In the following sections, we define the concepts, operations, and key services comprising DISCUS. The section on Framework Concepts presents the basic concepts of the architectural vision. Sections titled Application Objects, Data and Table Objects, and Factory Objects define the basic classes of the framework, their operations, and key design rationale. Framework Services describes some of the fundamental services supporting conversions, interchange, and metadata. Section, DISCUS Implementation covers important implmentation approaches. The last section, DISCUS Issues and Futures, describes the key issues and futures for the DISCUS framework.

FRAMEWORK CONCEPTS

DISCUS's architectural vision is to provide interoperability using a small set of common interfaces defined in OMG IDL. In general, interoperability is guaranteed if all subsystems in an integrated system share common interface and operations, as in a hybrid architecture. (See section titled "Software Architecture".) DISCUS is the minimal set of such operations that can be supported by different types of applications. The system is then extensible because new applications can be added (plugged in) without requiring changes to existing software.

Today custom interfaces are required to integrate most subsystems. Each subsystem usually requires a separate interface to each other subsystem. This is called the $n \times n$ order interface solution (Figure 7.1).

If a single IDL interface is defined across the applications, the client can communicate with both implementations using a single set of operations (Figure 7.2).

The common interface solution allows more clients and object implementations to be added and to communicate with all existing and future applications (Figure 7.3). CORBA also supports the application-specific interfaces that may be published. Using OMG IDL subtyping, it is possible to define the application-specific interfaces as specializations of the common interfaces.

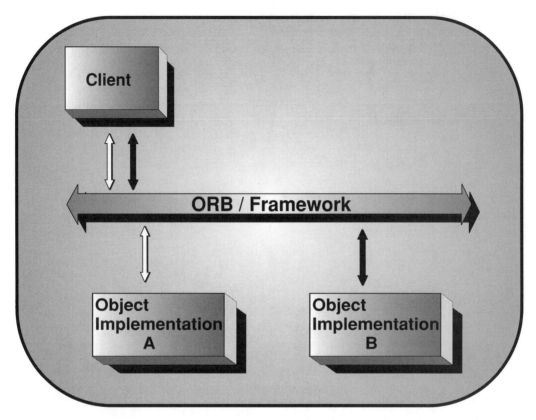

Figure 7.1. Client communicating with two object implementations with different IDL interfaces.

In order to facilitate interoperability between applications and between applications and data sources, the framework defines a set of operations for data interchange, query, data conversion, object wrapping, and encapsulation. The framework is made up of only the interfaces and a factory object; it does not define the implementation of the applications or the operations themselves. Different types of software applications can use these general-purpose operations. The operators can be defined as object-oriented specializations of a general application class. An application class can extend on the interfaces for communication with other members of the same class (e.g., Geographic Information System [GIS] mapping applications and data sources). However, the framework provides the minimal set of common operations that allow for interoperation with other types of applications without custom interface programming. In addition to the OMG IDL and factory, we also have implemented a set of framework services, such as the trader service and a conversion service. The infrastructure requires an underlying communication facility, such as a CORBA-compliant commercial object re-

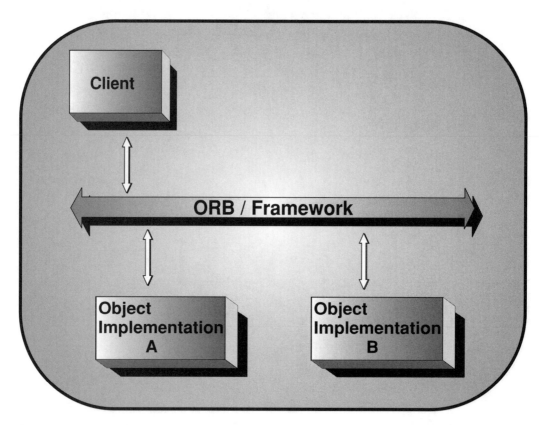

Figure 7.2. Client communicating with two object implementations with same framework IDL interface.

quest broker. Alternatively, it is possible to utilize an RPC mechanism as the underlying facility. However, if an RPC or other mechanism is used, there is a corresponding sacrifice in implementation flexibility and added coding.

At the highest level, the DISCUS framework comprises both application and data objects. The application objects are encapsulations of legacy applications, commercial applications, or new software. The data objects are generic containers for transfer of information. All of the applications, regardless of type, are encapsulated consistently with a common set of operations and consistent conventions for metadata. Communication between applications is in terms of the core framework operations that are used to transfer information encapsulated in data objects.

Four core framework operations provide the key benefits: interoperability, simplicity, ease of use, flexibility, and extensiblity. These operations are:

- Convert
- Exchange
- Query
- Execute

These four operations provide the functionality of a whole host of complex specifications, from standards and proprietary sources. DISCUS is an application architecture that abstracts the interoperability solution to a very simple form. DISCUS is easy to learn and inexpensive to utilize due to its simplicity.

Extending from this simple core are a variety of design and implementation elements that complete the framework. Some of the key elements include table objects, factory objects, trader service, and object implementation metadata (described in the subsequent sections). The table objects are

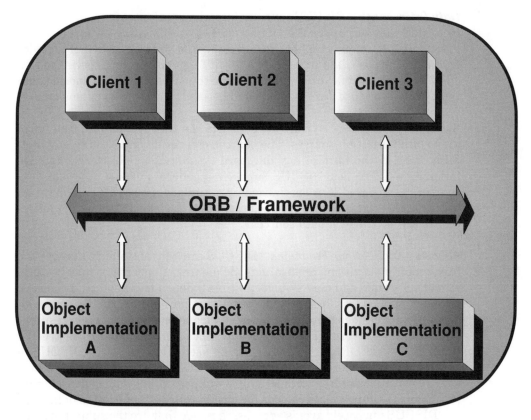

Figure 7.3. More clients and object implementations can be added without modification to existing software.

generic containers for tabular data. A tabular representation is very useful for interchanging metadata, query results, and other information. The factory objects manage the creation, copying, and deletion of data objects and table objects. The trader service manages systemwide metadata, including the location and basic capabilities of all services. The object implementation metadata comprises a more detailed form of object implementation-specific metadata, such as the object implementation's information schema.

APPLICATION OBJECTS

The Core Framework Operations

DISCUS supports interfaces for basic interoperability through the use of the four core operations. The forms of interoperability supported include data interchange, access to data sources, and access to application functions.

Data Interchange   DISCUS supports interchange of most types of data used in a wide range of application domains. For example, the data can be images, maps, bitmaps, graphics, text, binary, and so forth. DISCUS provides a general-purpose data interchange facility, as opposed to a specialized facility. A specialized facility might optimize the interchange of a specific data type, such as a video stream, and could become a compatible extension.

Access to Data Sources   DISCUS supports the retrieval of data from most kinds of information sources. The sources can reside on virtually any platform or be in the form of any database type, such as object oriented, relational, and flat files. DISCUS supports a general-purpose access to data sources, as opposed to a specialized or optimized access. By making data source access consistent, DISCUS simplifies the client programming for access to a wide range of data sources.

Access to Applications Functions   DISCUS provides the ability to reuse the functionality of existing applications. Sequences of operations may be automated via scripts and may involve multiple independent application objects. DISCUS applies this form of application automation consistently across all kinds of applications using data objects to transfer arguments and results.

DISCUS is a working example of an application architecture constructed using CORBA. CORBA's flexibility can be used effectively with DISCUS to build highly interoperable systems. The DISCUS framework provides necessary structure to assure interoperability while providing sufficient flexibility to support the functionality needs for a wide range of application domains.

DISCUS purposely avoids addressing issues that are the subject of near-term standards from the OMG. Issues such as linking and embedding were delegated to the standards activities. DISCUS allows for the transitioning to and leveraging of these technologies when they become available. The framework is flexible enough, though, to provide for similar capabilities now via other means.

DISCUS provides a fundamental level of guaranteed software interoperability. It is designed to be a reusable open architecture that does not define new standards but instead allows for use and leveraging of existing and future information systems standards. The framework defines two generic classes of objects: application objects and data objects.

Application objects include any type of applications, such as desktop applications, back-end servers, legacy subsystems, commercial software packages, and the like. Interoperability is guaranteed when these application objects implement the four basic DISCUS operations.

Data objects are used as containers for data interchange and results passing. Data objects can contain virtually any type of information. As simplicity for developers was a key goal of DISCUS, values are stored and retrieved using string-valued names with the simple set() and get() operations. The DISCUS factory controls the life cycle of data objects, their creation and destruction. The factory design is implementation dependent. The data objects may be passed between application objects, or the object references only may be passed and used as pointers to a data object stored possibly within a factory application object using a database.

Convert Operation   The convert operation is a general-purpose facility to convert data between various formats. The data formats may be imagery formats, document formats, spreadsheet formats, and others. The client provides the data with the current format and specifies the desired format. The implementation returns the data in the desired format, or an exception if the conversion failed. The generality of the operation enables each application (or vendor) to provide its own conversion(s). The trader service's metadata table for the convert operation allows each client to search for the availability of certain conversions and conversions may be added dynamically at any time. The client, or a smart conversion broker, may search the table for a series of conversions from format A to B. If no direct conversion is available, the conversion may be performed in multiple steps, from A to C and from C to B.

Exchange Operation   The exchange operation provides a simple general-purpose data interchange capability. Basic interoperability can be achieved if each application, at a minimum, implements the exchange operation. Applications can use the exchange operation to interchange data objects of any type and specify the type of exchange using a small number of enumerated options. The exchange may be used to transmit or receive data or to signal a request to open a front-end application on a data object. Clients also may use the exchange to request object implementation metadata. (See the section titled "The Trader Service and Metadata Objects" on page 206). The object implementation metadata is a DISCUS data object that contains information regarding the object implementation data models and schema as well as operations and sample scripts that it may perform. Using DISCUS convenience functions, the client is able to utilize scripts without depending directly on the scripting language used by the object implementation.

Query Operation   The query operation should be used to retrieve data when the desired data is not known ahead of time. The query server creates a new data object as the result of a query-driven search. A client may access an arbitrary data source using the query operation. It passes a script for the query server to perform, and the server returns a new data object if the query is successful, or an exception if it is not successful. The script is self-describing because a tag is attached identifying the query language (i.e., SQL89 Level 2). The script may be dynamically created, or it can be a predefined script retrieved with the server metadata. The server metadata object allows dynamic description of data sources, data types, and schemas. These facilities in combination can support almost any type of query accessing almost any kind of data source. New data sources and their query languages can be registered with the trader service to announce their availability. Each data source should be able to return a server metadata object in response to an exchange operation.

Execute Operation   The execute operation is an automation facility that combines the features of the exchange and query operations for encapsulation of applications, such as legacy systems. The operation allows the passing of a script and a sequence of data objects to be operated upon. The object implementation modifies the data objects or creates new ones and can return a sequence of output data objects.

The following example best describes the possible use of the execute operation. Let's consider a legacy application that takes only command-line arguments and options and that can read two image files, register them (perform algorithmic operations that overlay the images and rotates them if necessary), and produce the output as a single new image file. The execute operation can be used to pass the commands in the script and the images within two image objects. The object implementation then can create the two image files from the display representations found within the data objects and execute the registration program using the script and file pathnames. Upon successful completion of the execution, the object implementation can create a new image object and encapsulate the resulting file into its display representation. The execute operation then returns to the client a sequence containing the single newly created data object.

The execute operation provides a structured way to access applications and utilities through scripts. It should be contrasted with the CORBA-defined Dynamic Invocation Interface (DII), which provides dynamic access to applications via their available interface in the interface repository.

OMG IDL Specifications for Application Objects

All of the DISCUS objects inherit from an abstract class CommonObject. Its role is a mix-in class—a class that promulgates common definitions. CommonObject's operations include open, close, and destroy.

All objects in the DISCUS framework implement the operations open, close, and destroy. The open operation is used to establish a client-to-object implementation session. Open allows the object implementation to set up any necessary resources. The close operation terminates a client-to-object implementation session. The destroy operation indicates that the object implementation should remove all associated resources for the session with that client.

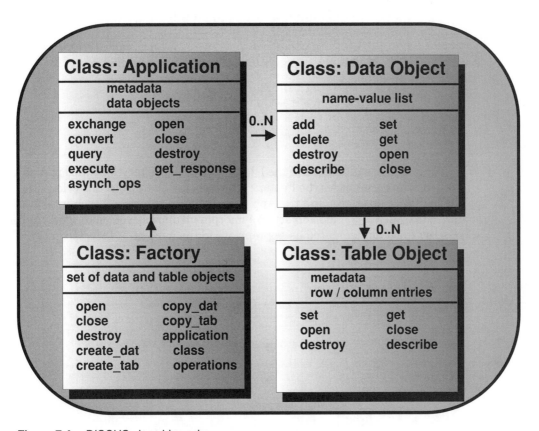

Figure 7.4. DISCUS class hierarchy.

```
// o---------------------------------------------------------o
// |                   -- interface CommonObject --          |
// |                                                         |
// | Abstract Class defining Common exceptions and           |
// | operations                                              |
// o---------------------------------------------------------o
   interface CommonObject {

     //common exceptions
       exception ALREADY_OPEN DS_exception_body;
       exception NOT_OPEN DS_exception_body;

     // Delete all associated resources
     void destroy()
         context ( DS_context_attributes );

     // Establish Client to Object implementation Object Session
     void open()
         raises( ALREADY_OPEN )
         context ( DS_context_attributes );

     // Terminate Client to Object implementation Object Session
     void close()
         raises( NOT_OPEN )
         context ( DS_context_attributes );

   }; /* end interface CommonObject */
```

The concrete interfaces of the DISCUS framework are contained in module DS, which comprises the Factory interface, the Data Object interface, the Table Object interface, and the Application Object interface. Each interface inherits from the common object. Polymorphism allows each open, close, and destroy to be implemented as appropriate to the particular interface.

```
module DS {
interface CommonObject {
......
}; /* end interface CommonObject */

interface ap:DS::CommonObject {
.........
}; /* end interface ap */

interface dt:DS::CommonObject {
.......
}; /* end interface dt */
```

```
        interface ft:DS::ap {
        ......
        }; /* end interface ft */

        interface tb:DS::CommonObject {
        .......
        }; /* end interface tb */

        }; /* end module DS */
```

The OMG IDL C mapping for the ft interface open is:

```
DS_ft_open();
```

Each interface represents a CLASS. Class application has a 0-to-N relationship with CLASS data object. Each application may reference zero or more data objects. Data objects, in turn, may reference zero or more table objects. The factory is a specialized application and inherits from the application class. It manages the life cycle of data and table objects.

The DISCUS operations are methods that should be implemented by each and all object implementations. Even if a specific operation is not supported, the method must return an ex_DS_ap_UNSUPPORTED_EXTENSIONS exception. The application object inherits the DS_ap_open(), DS_ap_close(), and DS_ap_destroy() from the Common object.

```
// o-------------------------------------------------------------o
// |                      -- interface ap --                     |
// |                                                             |
// | The DISCUS application Object.  All DISCUS application       |
// | interfaces inherit from this.                               |
// o-------------------------------------------------------------o
   interface ap: DS::CommonObject {

   // DATA EXCHANGE OPERATION
   // This service should be supported by all applications.
   enum Operation    {  GETDATA,
                        PUTDATA,
                        OPENFRONTEND,
                        GETMETADATA };
   exception INVALID_EXCHANGE_TYPE DS_exception_body;

   void exchange (      in    Operation exchangetype,
                        inout dt          dataobject )
                        raises ( NOT_OPEN, INVALID_EXCHANGE_TYPE )
                        context ( DS_context_attributes );
```

```
// FORMAT CONVERSION OPERATION
// Convert data from one format to another
exception INPUT_FORMAT_UNKNOWN DS_exception_body;
exception OUTPUT_FORMAT_UNKNOWN DS_exception_body;
void convert (
        in    string  format, // desired data format representation
        in    string  propertyname,  // property containing input data
        inout dt      data object ) // object containing formatted data
        raises ( NOT_OPEN, INPUT_FORMAT_UNKNOWN,
                    OUTPUT_FORMAT_UNKNOWN )
        context ( DS_context_attributes );


// QUERY/RETRIEVAL OPERATION
// Retrieve data from an application object based on some query
struct Script    {
        string language;       // query or script language
        string statements;  }; // query or script statements
exception UNSUPPORTED_LANGUAGE
  DS_exception_body;
exception SCRIPT_SYNTAX DS_exception_body;
exception UNSUPPORTED_QUERY DS_exception_body;
exception UNKNOWN_OPERAND DS_exception_body;
exception INCOMPLETE_QUERY DS_exception_body;
void query (
        in  Script   query,
        out dt       responsedataobject )
        raises (    NOT_OPEN, UNKNOWN_OPERAND,
                    UNSUPPORTED_QUERY,
                    INCOMPLETE_QUERY,
                    UNSUPPORTED_LANGUAGE,
                    SCRIPT_SYNTAX )
        context ( DS_context_attributes );


// EXECUTE OPERATION
// This operation should be supported by all scriptable applications
// and processing services, i.e. any service not appropriate for
// Convert() and Query(). The processing is controlled with a
// script.
// Example "script"s:
//  "sh", "csh", "perl", "AML", "CSL", "Tcl"
typedef sequence<dt> SeqObject;
void execute (
        in    Script      commandlist,
        in    SeqObject   inputdataobjects,
        out   SeqObject   outputdataobjects )
```

```
raises ( NOT_OPEN, UNSUPPORTED_LANGUAGE,
         SCRIPT_SYNTAX, UNKNOWN_OPERAND )
context ( DS_context_attributes );

}; /* end interface ap */
```

Open   The application open operation should be called prior to the invocation of any other operation. The call establishes a connection with a particular object implementation and may be used by server implementations to set up any required resources.

The open is the first operation in which an object implementation receives the client's CORBA invocation context. The context may play a very important role in how communication and resources are set up for the rest of the session. In the context, the client may provide some information regarding the user's window system preference, communication-line capabilities, security information, and so on. Object implementations also may need to

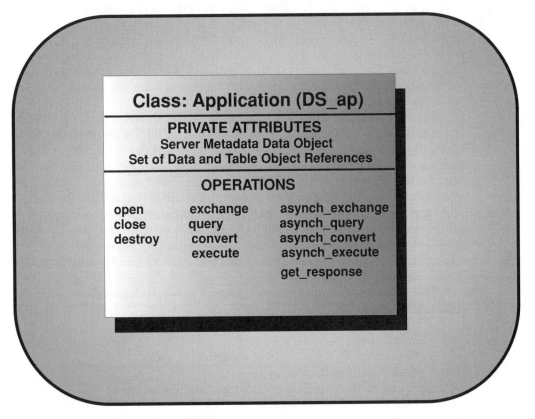

Figure 7.5.   Application class definition.

retain certain client information if they are capable of supporting several clients at the same time.

Close and Destroy   The application close operation is intended to signal to the object implementation that a session or logical set of operations have been completed. In some cases object implementations may choose to release certain resources at this point. The application destroy operation destroys all resources associated with a particular connection to an object implementation and signals the ORB that the connection with the particular object implementation should be terminated. The destroy should be called only after a **DS_ap_close** has been called. In other cases, where object implementations have some knowledge or understanding of the type of clients that they serve, resources may be released only using the destroy operation. The combination of close and destroy allows a client to signal the session status and give object implementations more flexibility to manage their resources. Otherwise, object implementations may have to wait until a time-out has occurred prior to releasing the resources. Use of time-outs to release resources can lead to problems, such as the unexpected invalidation of a bound object handle.

Exchange   The exchange operation is provided to allow for the interchange of data objects when the data is known ahead of time, for example, as the result of a user selection.

In order to guarantee data interchange interoperability, the Exchange operation is the simplest and most restrictive of all the framework operations. By convention, all applications should provide client and object implementation support for the **exchange()** operation. An enumerated parameter defines the type of the interchange. The data object exchange can be from the client to object implementation only, from the object implementation to the client only, or from the client to object implementation and back. One of the enumerated types also supports the exchange of object implementation metadata information. This area should be supported to guarantee that clients can "discover" new object implementation capabilities dynamically and communicate with them.

The following example shows a typical invocation sequence using the exchange() operation.

- A client opens the framework factory.
- A client creates a data object of a particular type.
- A client opens the data object.
- A client sets the values of a data object as needed.
- A client closes the data object.
- A client opens a connection to an object implementation using open operation.

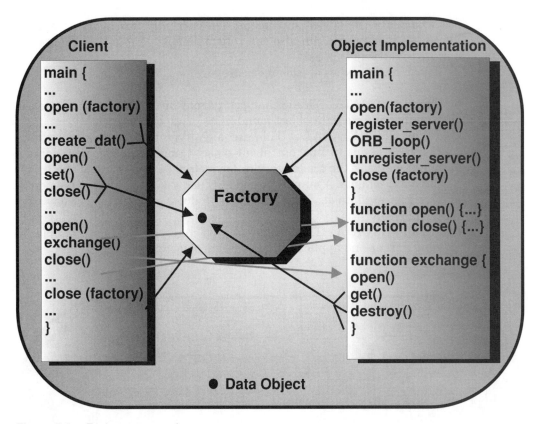

Figure 7.6. Exchange scenario.

- A client invokes an operation (exchange, convert, query, or execute).
- If the operation carries a data object reference, the object implementation may open the data object, get and set properties, and then close or destroy the data object.
- A client checks the returned exception status.
- Upon success, the client gets returned values from the same or new data object.
- The data object may be destroyed or stored persistently.
- The client can close and destroy the connection to the object implementation.

While CORBA clients and object implementations can use the OMG IDL repository to "discover" new services and learn about their interfaces, the object implementation metadata exchange provides much more detail as to the type of data that clients can exchange with the object implementation and what data the object implementation currently has in its databases. The object implementation also can return sample scripts that clients can execute to retrieve this data.

The following types of exchanges are legal.

- DS_ap_GETDATA   This exchange type may be used, for example, to ask a clipboard for a data object found in its paste buffer.
- DS_ap_GETMETADATA   This exchange type may be used, for example, by a client to find out about object implementation metadata. A client may ask the trader service for metadata consisting of the trader database schema. A map front-end may ask the map object implementation for metadata describing the map products and overlays it may have available.
- DS_ap_PUTDATA   This exchange type may be used, for example, to send a front-end application an existing object for editing.

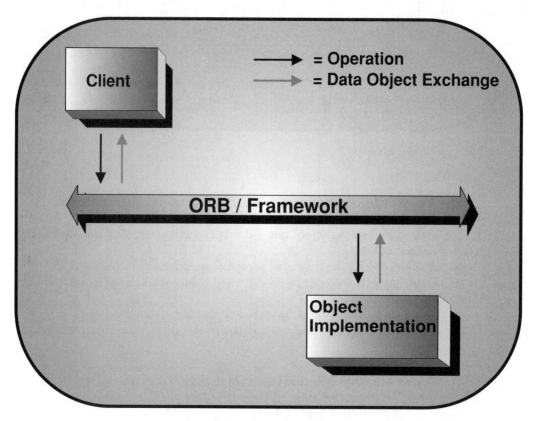

Figure 7.7.   GET_DATA and GETMETADATA exchange.

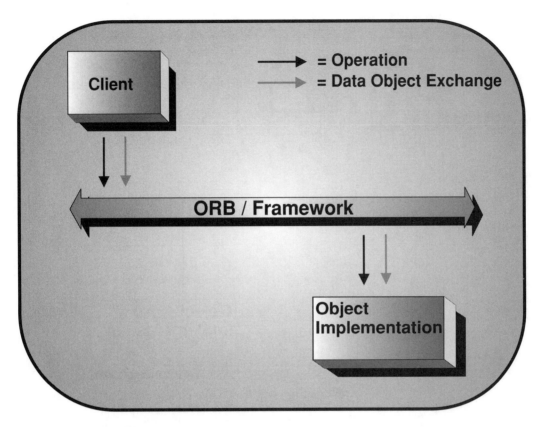

Figure 7.8. PUTDATA exchange.

- **DS_ap_OPENFRONTEND**   This exchange type may be used, for example, to send an initial object to a front-end application. When activating a map front-end to retrieve a map object, the initial exchange with the front-end may be a simple object that may have the requested map width and height but none of the other map properties (which the client may not know about yet).

```
void exchange (      in    Operation exchangetype,
                     inout dt dataobject )
                     raises ( NOT_OPEN,
                     INVALID_EXCHANGE_TYPE )
                     context ( DS_context_attributes );
```

Query   The query operation is provided to allow for the retrieval of data objects when no information is available ahead of time as to the type of objects or their properties. The query string can be made in any script language

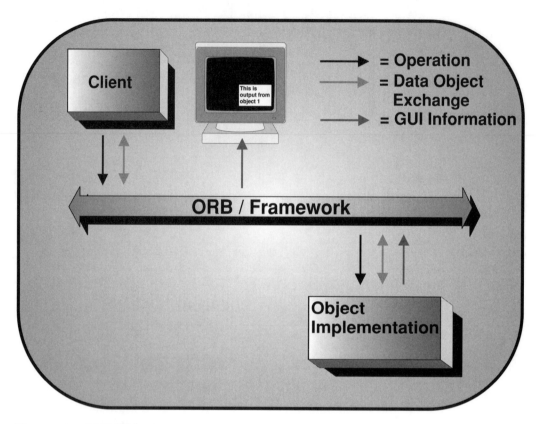

Figure 7.9.   OPENFRONTEND exchange.

and may be created by the application or retrieved from the trader or object implementation as metadata. In the last two cases, the client application need not understand the object implementation's script language in order to perform the query. (See the section titled "User Interface Functions" on page 220 for more details).

The Query operation provides a common interface to data sources (Figure 7.10). A dynamic query string parameter is tagged with the identity of the query language. The object implementation returns the results in a data object, which may contain a table object for tabular results. By convention, data source object implementations should provide a query() implementation to return data objects and an exchange() implementation to return metadata objects.

```
void query (
    in  Script query,
    out dt responsedataobject )
    raises (    NOT_OPEN, UNKNOWN_OPERAND,
```

```
                    UNSUPPORTED_QUERY, INCOMPLETE_QUERY,
                    UNSUPPORTED_LANGUAGE, SCRIPT_SYNTAX )
        context ( DS_context_attributes )
```

Convert The most prevalent problem in integration is related to data formats. Issues include proprietary formats, incompatible formats, different versions of the same format, and loss of data during conversions. The problem DISCUS addressed was simplified due to the ORB ability to convert data at lower levels. For example, integrators no longer have to worry about reverse-byte ordering between different operating and hardware systems.

The convert operation is provided to allow for the conversion between various data formats. The operation is independent from the type of data, so that conversion servers can convert between image formats, map formats, document formats, spreadsheet formats, and so on. Object implementations may choose to implement their own conversion methods (where a vendor supports multiple conversions to its own native format), or they may choose

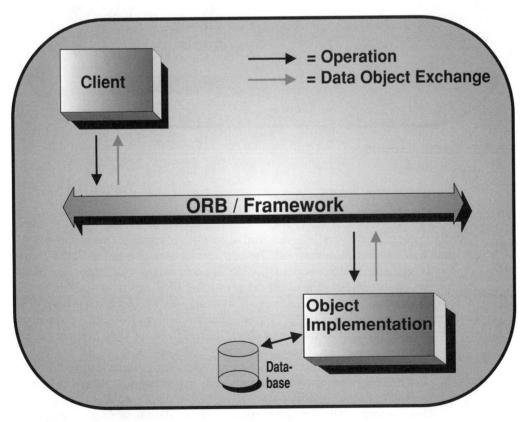

Figure 7.10. Query operation.

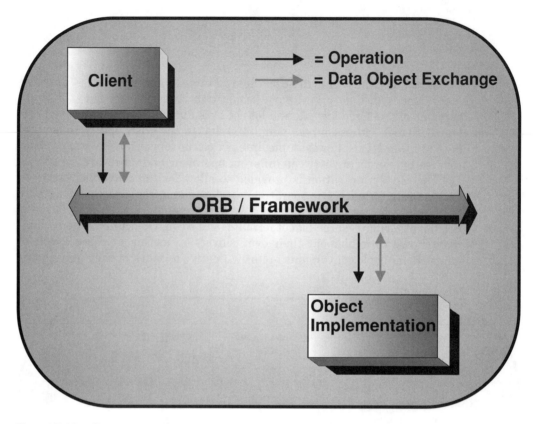

Figure 7.11. Convert operation.

to provide conversions via a conversion server that can convert between several formats.

By convention, if an application introduces a new data format, then it must provide a convert() service that allows other applications to convert the data to a commonplace format. The new service is registered with the trader to advertise its existence. All DISCUS applications should make use of the convert operation because of the large number of alternative and competing standards/nonstandard data formats available today. Usually each application has some notion of its "preferred" formats. Upon accessing a data object and a property, applications can check if the format of that property is not the one they expect. In these cases, the convert operation could be invoked automatically. Users may experience an additional slight delay; however, they are no longer required to use import or export menu options, or limited to the set of conversion filters offered by the particular application.

Upon return, if the convert is successful, the data object reference points to the same object with the modified property.

```
void convert (
        in     string  format, // desired data format representation
        in     string  propertyname,  // propery containing input data
        inout dt        dataobject ) // object containing formatted data
        raises ( NOT_OPEN, INPUT_FORMAT_UNKNOWN,
                    OUTPUT_FORMAT_UNKNOWN )
        context ( DS_context_attributes );
```

Execute   The execute operation provides a way for applications to communicate with other applications via some scripted language. The operation allows the specification of statements for operation as well as a list of input data objects to be operated upon. The operation may return one or more data objects as a result of the script. The execute operation may be used, for example, to send two input image objects to a registration algorithm and receive the output single image object as the output data object.

By convention, an object implementation's script language should provide access to functionality, by including operations accessible from legacy

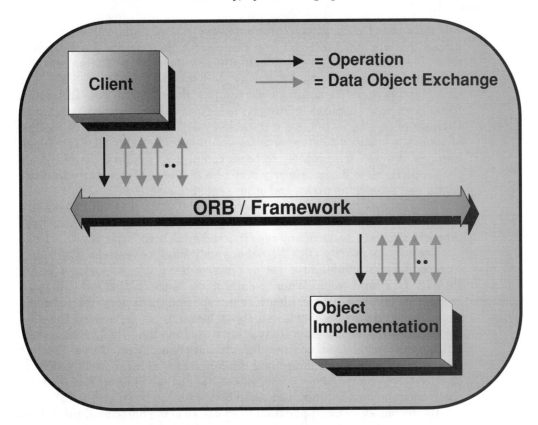

Figure 7.12.   Execute operation.

API's and any user interfaces. Object implementation metadata can contain some canned scripts. The execute operation can be used to produce combinations of other operations, such as the exchange and query. However, because excess flexibility often results in less interoperability, Execute should be used when the simpler and more direct exchange and query cannot support the desired functionality.

```
void execute (  in    Script      commandlist,
                in    SeqObject    inputdataobjects,
                out   SeqObject    outputdataobjects )
                raises ( NOT_OPEN, UNSUPPORTED_LANGUAGE,
                        SCRIPT_SYNTAX, UNKNOWN_OPERAND )
                context ( DS_context_attributes );
```

DATA AND TABLE OBJECTS

Data Objects

The data object class private attributes are sets of name-value pairs. We picked this approach in order to provide a simple conceptual approach to data objects and a simple implementation for developers. The name-value pairs are nothing more that a flat single list of CORBA Type "any". The data object is therefore nothing more complex than a CORBA NVList, and a factory can be as simple as relating NVLists to opaque data object references. Because of this approach, we were able to define a rather simple method of set/get operations to store or retrieve properties. Using CORBA Types, however, allows each property to be as complex as required. Even though the property list is flat, a property may be a sequence of structures that can contain an integer, an array, and other sequence members.

Data objects are simple containers for related data. A data object is a collection of named values; new named properties can be created, and the property may be a value of any type (passed as CORBA type "any").

For interoperability, DISCUS defines additional conventions. The framework defines an enumerated set of types of data objects, such as TEXT, IMAGE, GIS, and so on. When a data object is created (create_dat()), an enumerated type parameter identifies its type and the factory initializes the appropriate name-value fields. An object hierarchy is defined for the data object name-values. This hierarchy is separate from the DISCUS framework IDL, so that this list can be extended without changing any API's. The root class of the name-value hierarchy is a set of name-values shared by all data objects (the Common object). Specialized application classes, such as GIS, share common name-values as defined by the hierarchy (Figure 7.13).

By convention, each application supports all of the named-values defined in the hierarchy for its application class. Applications may add additional name-values, which other applications can disregard.

Figure 7.13.   Data object class definition.

The protocol for creating and accessing data objects includes the following sequences of operations:

```
create_dat()                // create the data object
open()                      // open the data object
set()....                   // one or more sets

// optional add() to create new named values
// optional delete() to eliminate named values

close()                     // close the data object

//   share with other applications using exchange(), convert(), query(),
//   or execute()
//   these perform an implicit close ,OR

destroy()
```

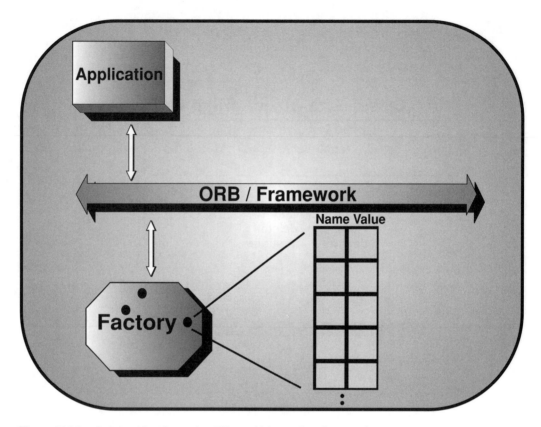

Figure 7.14.   A data object is made of Name-Value pairs of properties.

A typical sequence of operations for an existing data object may be:

```
open()                          // open the data object
get()....                       // one or more gets

// optional usage of add(), delete(), or set()

close()                         // close the data object

// optionally: share with other applications , OR

destroy()
```

Data objects are accessible to clients and object implementations only via an opaque object reference. Once the data object is created, it must be opened in order for an application to have access to its properties. When a

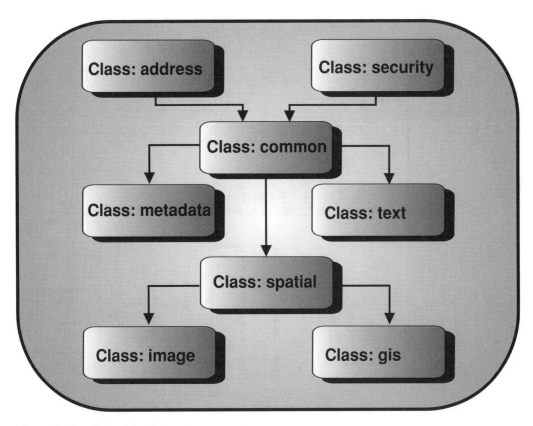

Figure 7.15. Data object hierarchy.

data object is exchanged between applications, the sending application no longer has access to the data object properties. The application cannot access the properties when the data object is destroyed or closed.

OMG IDL SPECIFICATIONS FOR DATA OBJECTS

The data object interface inherits from the common object. It defines exceptions to indicate that the object was not found, that the object already exists, that a property was not found, or that a TypeCode was not found. Data objects property lists can contain any CORBA types, including user-defined types. Properties can contain other data object references, thereby embedding data objects within data objects.

```
// DATA OBJECT INTERFACE
interface dt: DS::CommonObject {
```

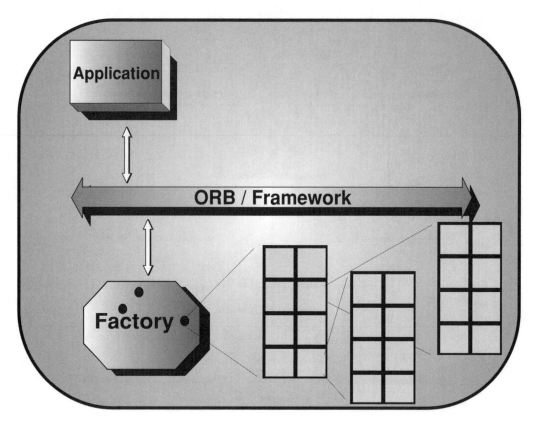

Figure 7.16.   Data objects can contain other data objects.

```
readonly attribute string objectType;
//Structure useful for storing data object properties with
//formatted values.
struct FormattedDataRep{
  string format;
  any value;
};

//Add a property to a data object
exception ALREADY_EXISTS DS_exception_body;
void add (  in string newpropertyname )
          raises ( NOT_OPEN, ALREADY_EXISTS )
          context ( DS_context_attributes );
//Delete a property from a data object
exception NOT_FOUND DS_exception_body;
void delete ( in string newpropertyname )
```

```
        raises ( NOT_OPEN, NOT_FOUND )
        context ( DS_context_attributes );

//Retrieve the names and types of a data object
typedef sequence<string> NameList;
typedef sequence<TypeCode> TypeList;
void describe ( out unsigned long numberofproperties,
                out NameList names,
                out TypeList types )
        raises ( NOT_OPEN )
        context ( DS_context_attributes );

//Set the value of a data object property
exception TYPE_NOT_FOUND DS_exception_body;
exception PROPERTY_NOT_FOUND DS_exception_body;
void set (  in string propertyname,
            in any value )
        raises (NOT_OPEN, NOT_FOUND,
        PROPERTY_NOT_FOUND )
        context ( DS_context_attributes );

//Get the value of a data object property
void get (  in string propertyname,
            out any value )
        raises (NOT_OPEN, NOT_FOUND,
        PROPERTY_NOT_FOUND )
        context ( DS_context_attributes );

}; /* end interface dt */
```

Open   The data object interface open is inherited from the common object. The reference of the object to be opened is the reference of the data object created by the factory. If the data object exists and is accessible by the application, the operation returns successfully.

Only one application object may have the data object open at any time.

Close   The interaction between the open, close, and destroy is very important. The close indicates that the application no longer requires access to the data object. A data object must be closed before it can be shared with another application through framework operations such as exchange(), convert(), query(), and exchange(); otherwise an exception is returned. The section titled "Managing Data and Table Objects" on page 205 discusses how the factory affects this interaction.

Destroy   The data object must be opened by the application in order to destroy it. Once the data object is destroyed, the reference and data associated with the object is removed. In the linked-in implementation of the framework factory, the reference count is not maintained because copies of data objects are exchanged. Data object maintenance is completely implementation dependent and can be as complex as needed. The factory or the object database can keep count of references so that when linking is available, all applications that point to the object can be notified, or the destroy will be denied until the reference count is zero.

Set The set allows the modification of a property of a data object. In order to simplify memory management, the set is destructive and copies all data. It is the responsibility of the factory or data object implementation to remove existing data, and it is the responsibility of the application to remove its copy of the data.

```
void set (  in string propertyname,
            in any value )
            raises (NOT_OPEN, NOT_FOUND,
            PROPERTY_NOT_FOUND )
            context ( DS_context_attributes );
```

The set accepts a property in the form of a CORBA type "any" so that it is self-describing. For example, for a type "any" of type "string", the value would point to a string. For a type "any" of type "integer", the value would point to an integer. For a sequence, the sequence TypeCode within the "any" describes the elements of the sequence and its length.

Get The get operation retrieves the data and type associated with a particular property. A copy of the data is given so that there is complete separation of the data object and application data. The application is responsible for removing any data it receives. The get operation implementation could be dependent on context variables that can signal whether a copy of a pointer should be passed in the case of very large data (or file pathnames).

```
void get (  in string propertyname,
            out any value )
            raises (NOT_OPEN, NOT_FOUND,
            PROPERTY_NOT_FOUND )
            context ( DS_context_attributes );
```

Add The add operation allows for the dynamic addition of data object properties of any type. While this feature is very powerful, its use should be limited. Applications should expect other applications to recognize only agreed upon properties for a given type of data object. It is possible to describe the contents of a data object dynamically. (See the section titled "Describe" on page 195.) However, code to interpret previously unknown properties may be complex. To avoid the complexity, DISCUS application code should be written to manipulate known properties of known types. Each application type has a set of specific properties (for text objects, map objects, etc.), and there is a hierarchy of properties defining the more generic common properties.

The addition of new properties is a framework capability that can be used for extensibility.

```
void add (  in string newpropertyname )
            raises ( NOT_OPEN, ALREADY_EXISTS )
            context ( DS_context_attributes );
```

Delete The delete operation allows for the elimination of a property from a data object. The property must have been added using the Add operation. An exception may be returned if the property is standard for the type of data object.

```
void delete ( in string newpropertyname )
            raises ( NOT_OPEN, NOT_FOUND )
            context ( DS_context_attributes );
```

Describe The describe operation allows an application to get a description of the metadata that comprises a data object. The operation returns the number of properties, a sequence of strings that contain the property names, and a sequence of TypeCodes that describe each property type. The information may be used to interpret the data automatically, or to display the contents of the data object to a user within some graphical-user interface (GUI) and allow the user to peruse the information or to act on it (for example, display the image contained in a Display_Rep property using some imaging display tool).

```
void describe ( out unsigned long numberofproperties,
            out NameList names,
            out TypeList types )
            raises ( NOT_OPEN )
            context ( DS_context_attributes );
```

Data Object Properties

Data object properties predate the OMG standards process for properties. Data object properties serve a different purpose than the properties defined by the OMG Properties Object Service.

The DISCUS framework supports a set of predefined properties. The framework is designed to be flexible and extensible, and we expect that the list of object properties will evolve over time and comprise industry, government, and de facto standards.

The DISCUS framework defines a strawman set of data object property lists, including the basic object, the text object, the spatial object, the image object, the Mapping object, and the metadata object.

These categories relate the data object type to the application type:

OBJ (Common)
IMAGE
GIS
SERVER_METADATA
TEXT

Future extensions:

EMAIL	Textual e-mail, attachments, active mail
DOCUMENT	Editable text with other datatype inserts
PAINT	Editable raster bitmap
OBJ_GRAPHIC	Editable object-oriented graphics viewgraphs
SPREADSHEET	Small-scale editable tabular data
DATABASE	Large-scale data—relational, browsers, etc.
VISUALIZATION	3-D data, scientific, CAD/CAM, sensor simulation
HYPERMEDIA	Linked document collections
MULTIMEDIA	Incorporating real-time media: audio, video

Table Objects

Table objects are simple containers for tabular data. By convention, a table object is referenced by exactly one data object. The table object stores a matrix of values, passed as CORBA type "any". In practice, most tables will have consistent types for each column. Table objects should never be passed as data objects to other applications.

The protocol for creating and accessing table objects includes the following sequences of operations:

```
create_tab()        // create a table object given a list of names
                    // and types, cells are empty
open()              // open the table object
set()....           // one or more times

// insert table's object reference in a data object using data object
// set operation

// share with other applications using exchange(), convert(), query(),
// or execute() ,
// these perform an implicit close, OR

destroy()              // destroys the table object and cells
```

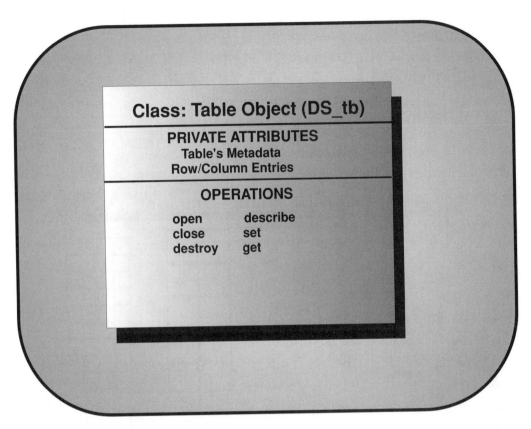

Figure 7.17.   Table object class definition.

A typical sequence of operations for an existing table object follows.

```
// get table object reference using data object get operation

open()                    // open the table object
get()....                 // one or more times

// optional usage of set()
// optionally share with other applications through a data object, OR

destroy()                 // destroys the table object and cells
```

Table objects are meant to be a part of data objects and not used as stand-alone objects. They are embedded within data objects using the object reference TypeCode. When a data object containing a table object is destroyed, the table objects it points to should also be destroyed.

Table objects rows and columns can contain any data. This structure makes table objects especially useful to exchange information about appli-

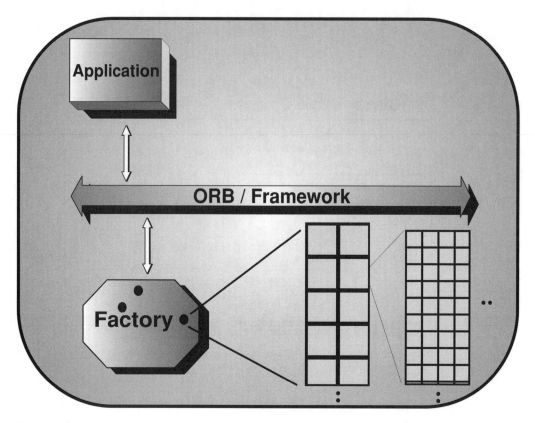

Figure 7.18.   A Table object is made of row-column cells and is part of a data object.

cations, not only spreadsheet-type data. For example, tables can be used to describe the schema of a database.

```
interface tb: DS::CommonObject {

  exception COLUMN_OUT_OF_RANGE DS_exception_body;
  exception ROW_OUT_OF_RANGE DS_exception_body;

  typedef sequence<string> ColList;
  typedef sequence<TypeCode> TypeList;

  // Retrieve the column names and typecodes of the specified table
  void describe ( out unsigned long numberofrows,
                  out unsigned long numberofcols,
                  out ColList columnnames,
                  out TypeList types )
```

```
                    raises ( NOT_OPEN )
                    context ( DS_context_attributes );

//Set a value in the table
void set ( in unsigned long row,
           in unsigned long column,
           in any value )
           raises ( NOT_OPEN, ROW_OUT_OF_RANGE, COLUMN_OUT_OF_RANGE )
           context ( DS_context_attributes );

//Get a value in the table
void get ( in unsigned long  row,
           in unsigned long  column,
           out any value )
           raises ( NOT_OPEN, ROW_OUT_OF_RANGE, COLUMN_OUT_OF_RANGE )
           context ( DS_context_attributes );

}; /* end interface tb */
```

Like the data object, the table object inherits from the common object and also can set some exceptions. In addition to the common exceptions that we may expect to find, such as ALREADY_EXISTS or NOT_FOUND, there is also OUT_OF_RANGE. This is used to signal that an application is attempting to access a data cell that is out of the bounds of the table.

Open   The open operation allows an application to open a table object. The table object must be opened before it can be accessed. In order to obtain the table object reference, the application first must perform a DS_dt_get() on the data object property of type object reference that contains the reference of the table object. Once the reference is retrieved, the application can open the table object.

Only one application object may have the table object open at one time. If an application attempts to open an already open object, it will receive the ex_DS_tb_ALREADY_OPEN exception.

Close   The close operation signals that the access to the table object is complete. A table object must be closed before it can be shared with another application through framework operations such as exchange(), convert(), query(), and exchange(); otherwise an exception is returned.

Destroy   The destroy operation removes all resources and the reference associated with the table object. All data associated with the table object cells is removed. The destruction is shallow, meaning that references to other objects are removed, but the objects themselves are not destroyed.

Set   The set operation allows an application to set a particular cell of a table by specifying the row and column index. The set is destructive and the table must have been created previously using the factory create operation. The value used to set the cell is of type "any" and must be primed with a TypeCode and value. Because of the use of the type "any", the table can contain simple or very complex data.

The set operation is destructive, the factory should remove automatically data that may already exist in the cell (or allocate the space for new sets). Applications are responsible for removing their own copy of the data.

```
void set ( in unsigned long row,
           in unsigned long column,
           in any value )
           raises ( NOT_OPEN, ROW_OUT_OF_RANGE,
           COLUMN_OUT_OF_RANGE )
           context ( DS_context_attributes );
```

Get   The get operation retrieves a copy of the data of a particular cell. The value that is returned is of type "any" and contains the TypeCode and value of the cell. The application is responsible for removing the memory associated with the copy of the data it receives. Applications can look at the column type or the "any" _type member to determine how the "any" value member should be interpreted.

```
void get ( in unsigned long  row,
           in unsigned long  column,
           out any value )
           raises ( NOT_OPEN, ROW_OUT_OF_RANGE,
           COLUMN_OUT_OF_RANGE )
           context ( DS_context_attributes );
```

Describe   The describe operation allows an application to receive information that describes the table. The information that is returned is the number of rows and columns of the table, the column names, and their respective types. The application can use the information to access the table dynamically, and/or to communicate with a user using a GUI (as appropriate).

```
void describe ( out unsigned long numberofrows,
                out unsigned long numberofcols,
                out ColList columnnames,
                out TypeList types )
                raises ( NOT_OPEN )
                context ( DS_context_attributes );
```

FACTORY OBJECT

Factory Concept

The DISCUS factory is an implementation of the life-cycle service factory concept. The factory is opened and closed by applications to gain access to services that create, destroy, and manage data and table objects. The private attributes of the class include the lists of references of managed data and table objects. The common operations that the class supports are those to open, close, and destroy the factory object. Four additional operations are provided to create and copy data and table objects. The factory inherits from the application class and therefore can support the four standard framework operations. These operations could be left unimplemented, but they can provide valuable functionality. For example, a client may want to use the query operation on the factory to receive a list or status of some data objects. The factory also can provide useful conversions.

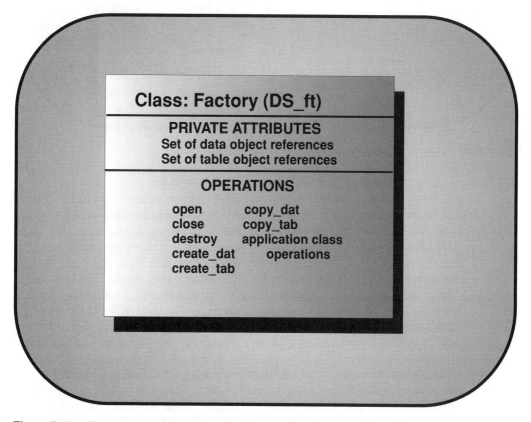

Figure 7.19. Factory class definition.

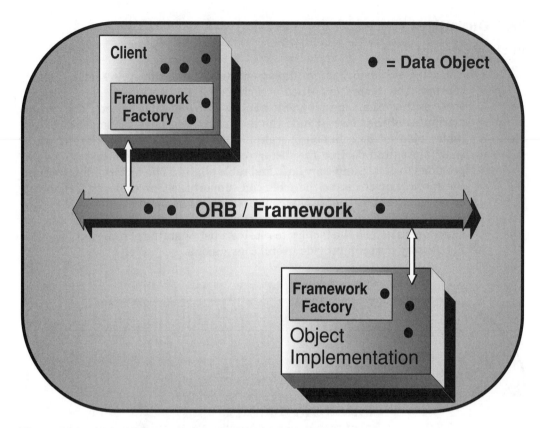

Figure 7.20. Linked-in framework and factory implementation.

The factory can be implemented in various ways.

One way is to have a separate factory object server. The data objects can be external to applications and contained within the factory. Therefore, communications between applications and data objects occurs via the ORB. Another approach is with the factory as a linked-in library. A third possibility is to have each data object implemented as a server. With this approach, a mechanism must be provided to notify the factory that a data object has been destroyed. The linked-in approach has some drawbacks, such as the need to provide data object services to applications across the ORB (other than the application with the linked-in factory). An early DISCUS implementation used a set of collaborating linked-in factories, which could migrate data objects.

The linked-in factory approach provides performance advantages for the local application. Separate factory objects, although suffering from more ORB calls, are scalable and flexible. If performance or resource management becomes an issue, it is possible to create factory objects for each system or even for each user in order to distribute the load.

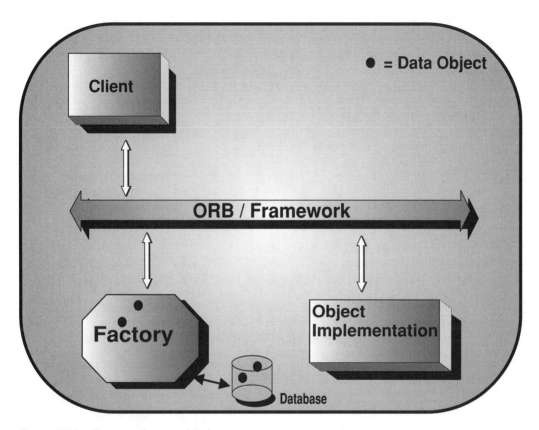

Figure 7.21. Separate factory object.

OMG IDL Specifications for Factory Objects

The OMG Common Object Services Specifications defines the concept of a factory implementation to create and manage objects [OMG, 94a]. A client using the factory receives only the object reference back from the factory; however, the factory itself has knowledge of the object internals and performs operations, such as initialization.

```
// o-----------------------------------------------------------o
// |                    -- interface ft --                     |
// |                                                           |
// | The DISCUS factory Object.  This factory creates:         |
// |         *DISCUS data objects (dt:CommonObject)            |
// |         *DISCUS table objects (tb:CommonObject)           |
// o-----------------------------------------------------------o
   interface ft: DS::ap {
```

```
// Create a DS::dt DISCUS data object
void create_dat (
        in        string   type,
        out       dt       dataobjecthandle )
        context ( DS_context_attributes );

// Create a DS::tb DISCUS table object
typedef sequence<string> ColList;
typedef sequence<TypeCode> TypeList;
void create_tab (
        in  long        maxrows, // maximum number of rows
        in  long        maxcols, // maximum number of columns
        in  ColList     columnnames, // metadata
        in  TypeList    types, // types of columns
        out tb          handle )
        context ( DS_context_attributes );

// Make a shallow copy of a DS::dt DISCUS data object
void copy_dat (
        in  dt          dataObject, // DISCUS data object to Copy
        out dt          dataObjectCopy )// The new data object
        context ( DS_context_attributes );

// Make a shallow copy of a DS::tb DISCUS table object
void copy_tab (
        in  tb          tableObject, // Table Object to Copy
        out tb          tableCopy )// The new table object
        context ( DS_context_attributes );

}; /* end interface ft */
```

Open   The factory inherits the open operation from the application class. There can be more than one factory object. DISCUS data objects are extensible, so that the factory can support additional data object properties without having to change. If other factories are introduced, it should be possible to provide a simple gateway or conversion service to convert from one factory's data objects to another's.

The DISCUS framework factory can be called in C.

```
status = DS_ft_open(factory, &Ev, &Ctx);
```

The open creates the required resources to allow clients and object implementations to create, manage, destroy, and access data and table objects.

The call initializes the internal object tables and framework resources. In the future the factory could be used to initialize various frameworks, or many factories may be available.

The framework implementation minimizes how much CORBA the programmers must know and performs standard context and object implementation registration calls whenever possible. tions move d a simple interface to the technology. Nothing prevents, however, developers from using any standard CORBA calls to interface with the ORB directly.

Close The factory close is also inherited from the application class. The object reference has to be the same one as an associated open factory object. After a close, the application cannot access any of the existing data objects.

Prior to terminating execution, the clients and object implementations should close the factory in order to release some of the framework resources. The close signals a termination of the current session.

```
status = DS_ft_close (factory,
              &Ev,
              &Ctx);
```

Destroy The factory destroy also is inherited from the application class. The object reference has to be the same one as an associated open factory object. The destroy signals the factory to remove all resources (e.g., cache storage) and data/table objects associated with the current session that an application has with the factory object. Unless specifically destroyed, objects that are stored persistently are not removed and are still accessible by the application. Depending on the implementation, this may mean that the application has the data object, or only the reference of the object, which may be stored persistently by some database.

Managing Data and Table Objects

The factory class defines four operations for the creation and copying of data and table objects. Due to the OMG IDL inheritance, each of the data and table interfaces has its own open, close, and destroy so that these operations are handled by the data and table objects themselves. The factory simply returns an opaque reference to these objects; the application can use this reference for any further access.

The create_dat operation allows an application to ask the factory to create a data object with a particular set of properties. The factory returns to the application a reference for the newly created data object, and the properties are initialized. See Section Data and Table Objects for a description of data objects.

```
void create_dat (
        in        string  type,
        out       dt      dataobjecthandle )
        context ( DS_context_attributes );
```

The creation of a table object is similar to that of a data object; however, instead of a predefined list of name-value properties, the table is created dynamically as a matrix of rows and columns. The operation accepts as input a count of the rows and columns, a list of the column names as a sequence of strings, and a list of the column types as a sequence of CORBA TypeCodes. The factory returns to the application a reference of the newly created table object. The table object may then be populated using table object operations or inserted into a data object.

```
typedef sequence<string> ColList;
typedef sequence<TypeCode> TypeList;
void create_tab (
        in   long        maxrows, // maximum number of rows
        in   long        maxcols, // maximum number of columns
        in   ColList     columnnames, // metadata
        in   TypeList    types, // types of columns
        out tb           handle )
        context ( DS_context_attributes );
```

The copy data object and copy table object operations create new objects that contain the same data. Applications can use these operations to create their own copy of objects. The new objects have new references; however, they contain the same data. This means that if a data object had a reference pointing to another data object, the new data object contains the same reference pointing to the second data object. The copy is therefore "shallow." Referenced objects are not copied themselves. Applications also can read or write data objects to a persistent store using convenience functions. (See the section titled "Convenience Functions" on page 220.)

```
void copy_dat (
        in   dt              dataObject, // DISCUS data object to Copy
        out dt               dataObjectCopy )// The new data object
        context ( DS_context_attributes );

// Make a shallow copy of a DS::tb DISCUS table object
void copy_tab (
        in   tb              tableObject, // Table Object to Copy
        out tb               tableCopy )// The new table object
        context ( DS_context_attributes );
```

FRAMEWORK SERVICES

The Trader Service and Metadata Objects

The trader service and metadata objects enable clients dynamically to discover new applications and get information about services. These facilities complement the metadata in the interface repository and the Common Object Services Specifications (COSS) Naming Service.

Metadata is used in the DISCUS framework to allow applications to learn dynamically about the format and data types that are needed to access object implementations. Metadata enables applications to learn about the services that an implementation provides and how to use the data to access them. In some cases it is even possible to make the access protocol transparent so that client code or users do not have to be familiar with the specific object implementations.

The trader service is used like a telephone yellow pages as a resource of information. The trader contains tables indexed corresponding to each one of the four DISCUS operations. A front-end client can send queries to the trader service and present options to users or act automatically. Applications can use the trader to find out what types of services and which object implementations are available. For example, an application can request a list of all object implementations that can accept an IMAGE data object. The trader also can be used to store the data object properties that are valid for certain data object types. The factory could initialize itself by reading this list. Subsequent requests for the creation of data types would use this information dynamically. In this way, versioning also can be controlled.

Under the convert table, the trader has a list of each object implementation and the conversions it supports. A client seeking a specific conversion could request the trader to perform a query and return the list of object implementations that can perform this conversion. Doing so allows the client to choose a specific conversion from a specific implementation. Furthermore, a conversion broker can be rather sophisticated and perform several recursive searches to determine if a multistep conversion can be performed when a direct conversion between two formats is not available.

The trader can be used to provide a dynamic object implementation registry. Upon installation, an object implementation may register its availability with the trader. The object implementation could create trader entries for each operation it supports.

All DISCUS object implementations are expected to be able to provide, upon request, a metadata object. The metadata object contains the list of properties that enable clients to find out about the data that the implementation supports and how to access it. Together with the trader service, this becomes a very powerful mechanism. For example, a client application may wish to retrieve an IMAGE data object. First it can access the trader to find out which implementations support IMAGE data objects. Once the client receives the list of object references for these implementations, the client can request the metadata object. In the metadata, an object implementation can provide information on internal data schemas. For example, metadata may indicate which images are available or what types of images are supported. Sample queries or scripts are some of the most useful kinds of information that can be provided.

If a client knows the language of particular object implementation, for performance reasons, it does not have to use the trader or ask for the metadata object; it can simply execute the query against the object implementation. However, sample scripts and convenience functions (described in the section "Convenience Functions" on page 220) provide a way for a client to access the information without the client code changing or the user having to understand the new language. The benefit arises from the fact that the client is guaranteed to be able to perform a known operation and receive an IMAGE object, which it will know how to access and manipulate.

This capability is the first step toward functionally oriented plug-and-play services. Imagine a graphics client that provides a menu of functions for the user. The client may provide some of its own functions, such as draw, modify line attributes, and group. However, let's assume that it does not provide its own zooming, rotation, 3-D graphics, or more sophisticated services. Upon activation, the client can access the trader to find out which services can manipulate IMAGE objects. It can then access each of the implementations and retrieve their metadata. Then the client can collect sample scripts and provide them to the user as part of its own functions menu. Users then can employ the extended functions without regard to the location of the method or object implementations that actually perform them.

Conversion Service

The DISCUS imagery conversion server has proved to be one of the most useful aspects of integration. While CORBA and ORBs solve many of today's distributed networking problems that developers face, application integration using CORBA still involves integration challenges. Applications still compete for the memory, disk space, and colormaps. Most applications use different data representations (often proprietary). These problems are prevalent for all types of applications. Today most tools offer some form of import/export capability that allows the user to convert between the native format to some other common formats. The native format always offers better fidelity and unique features compared to the common format. However, the user must be familiar with the various formats that he or she is using; often when an import or export option is not available, another third-party conversion tool must be used.

The conversion service hides these details from users and developers. Applications, both clients and object implementations, can inspect the data object formats. If they are not in the formats that they prefer, they can invoke the convert operation on the appropriate conversion server (known ahead of time, or discovered using the trader service).

Conversion servers can be built using different configurations, which usually pose performance vs. flexibility options. The first choice that must be made is whether an application should provide its own conversion or whether the conversion should be placed in a common server. This decision may be driven more by the nature of the format than by performance. A vendor may select to provide a conversion to its proprietary format to and from some other common format in order to keep the code private and secure, or because of a licensing issue.

Our first conversion service configuration was a single server that made use of several public domain and proprietary formats. The positive aspects of such a configuration are simplicity and performance. Modifications can be made to a single piece of code and clients need to make only one call to the server, or two if they need to access the trader information. A centralized configuration has some drawbacks. It is a single point of failure, and as the number of formats that it needs to handle grows, the server will be faced with increasing load.

An alternative to this approach is to have one conversion server for every conversion library or vendor. The advantage of this approach is that it does not affect the client code except for introducing additional slight delays. A client probably will need to access the trader and perhaps a conversion broker to determine which servers handle which conversions. This configuration

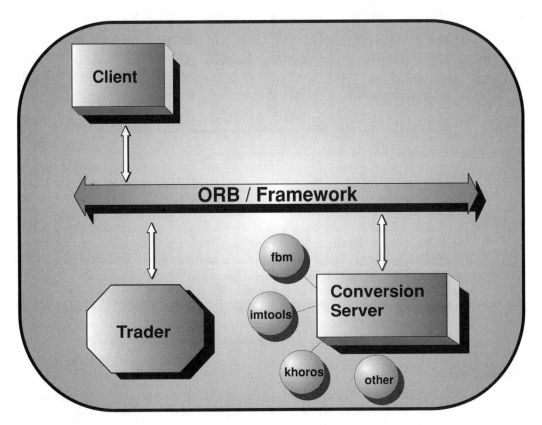

Figure 7.22. Conversion service, single server architecture.

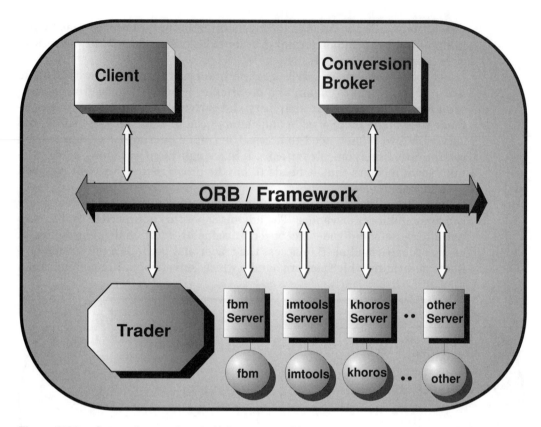

Figure 7.23. Conversion service, multiple server architecture.

is also more flexible. Modifications can be handled in small focused areas, and there is no single point of failure. The clients still make the same convert call as before, asking a conversion broker to perform the conversion as if it were the actual conversion service. The conversion broker can be as smart or as simple as required. For example, a smart broker may include a loop that can access the trader to find out how many conversions must be made if there is no direct conversion between formats A and B. The broker then can call the appropriate conversion servers to perform the conversions. While this logic could be placed within a single conversion server, extra code would have to be added to the server to search other applications for conversions it cannot handle. The broker performs this function automatically.

Public Folder

If one user creates a data object, or if the data object was owned by an application started by the same user, another user may not be able to access the data.

To address this problem, DISCUS has a public folder service similar to services provided in desktop environments today. A simple object implementation was developed that could accept data objects via the exchange operation. While most of a user's object implementations accept only the user as a valid connection, we set the server access on the public folder server to accept connections from any user. The public folder keeps a table with information on the data objects it contains. Clients can perform several queries on the public folder to learn about the data objects it contains, or they can send the exchange operation with an OPEN_FRONT_END type. The public folder will display an X window with a list of the data objects it contains, their types, creators, and other information. The user can select a particular data object and receive a copy of it.

As with most of these types of servers, reuse allows for the creation of new servers by changing only a few lines of code. The public folder could be modified/enhanced to return only object references rather than copies, depending on the type or location of the requesting client or user. Enhanced queries could allow users to search by user name and other attributes. The public folder also could be just a front-end application to existing databases and could make extensive use of the factory information and trader.

Object Gateway

During the migration of systems to the CORBA environment, we are likely to find at any given time a collection of legacy systems, new CORBA-compliant systems, and some systems in transition. In order to support interoperability with stand-alone systems that have no CORBA interface, we produced a simple yet powerful service we call the Object Gateway. The purpose of the gateway is to act as a wrapper for a particular type of data object and/or data object property. The gateway encapsulates and decapsulates properties from and to files. It makes use of a user profile that indicates the pathname of the stand-alone application to activate, the input and output fixed file pathnames to use for communication with the application, and the formats of the files. The gateway makes use of the conversion service to ensure that the properties are converted to the appropriate formats.

In a typical scenario, the gateway accepts a data object reference with an operation. It retrieves the appropriate property and writes the data to the input file. The application then is activated, and the input file is passed as a parameter. If the application does not accept command-line parameters, the user must navigate through the application menus and load or save to the appropriate file names. Once the user is finished and exits the application, the output file is read and the data placed within the data object property. The operation is then returned to the calling client.

DISCUS IMPLEMENTATION

As CORBA-compliant ORBs begin to enter the market, the DISCUS framework IDL can be simply compiled into a class repository. Developers then can develop client and object implementations and use the DISCUS-supplied factory, or create their own. Most ORB vendors plan to include some value-added capabilities, such as GUI tools to configure and administer the ORB and network. In addition, ORB vendors and object-oriented database vendors will be coming out soon with CORBA-compliant persistence storage facilities. Upcoming event services also should enable better communications between CORBA applications and windowing systems.

This section introduces how DISCUS clients and services are implemented. Implementation issues, such as support for asynchronous processing, also are covered.

Clients and Object Implementations

The DISCUS framework defines some essential conventions for providing interoperability between software applications. The framework is defined to provide this interoperability with minimal complexity and expense.

In many cases, developers' will be integrating preexisting software that was not specifically written with DISCUS in mind. The DISCUS-specific code will be a simple layer on top of existing API's and/or invoking preexisting internal functions (such as functions invoked from the user interface).

There are a few alternative ways to integrate applications through the DISCUS framework.

- *Unmodified legacy.* By applying the object gateway (a DISCUS example application), an unmodified legacy application can be interfaced to exchange DISCUS objects through the native file mechanism. This integration is fast and inexpensive but does not provide a seamless interaction since the user manually reads and writes to designated files.
- *Pure clients.* Some applications only make ORB invocations and do not provide services to other clients. It is reasonably straightforward to add this functionality through additional user interface menu options, so that DISCUS services are invoked from within the application without involving the file mechanism. This type of application can initiate activities only; because it cannot respond to external requests for DISCUS services, its roles in an integrated system is limited.
- *Pure servers.* Some back-end applications are structured to respond to other applications as a traditional "server" in client-server models. They do not have an active control flow when not servicing a request.
- *Combined clients and servers.* Some servers can have both an active client state and a server's responsiveness to external requests. Applications that maintain user interfaces usually need this capability. Threads

are an important enabling facility that makes this possible; other approaches exist, as shown in the DISCUS Map Front End to be described. Combined client-server applications will become more prevalent because they offer the most potential for interoperability.

In the standard client-server model used with Remote Procedure Call (RPC) technology, most clients are simply clients, and servers serve client requests. However, in the peer-to-peer CORBA environment, interaction is based on the interfaces and services that implementations provide. We believe that most applications in the future will act as both clients and servers. A server implementation may act as a server for a specific client, but if it needs any information from other services (such as the trader or conversion services), it needs to access these services as a client.

For example, a map front end tool can act as a client for map data but also as a server for requests for maps from other clients. In such cases, the application's main routine must register with the ORB as a server but also create the required window (e.g., X widgets) to handle the user input.

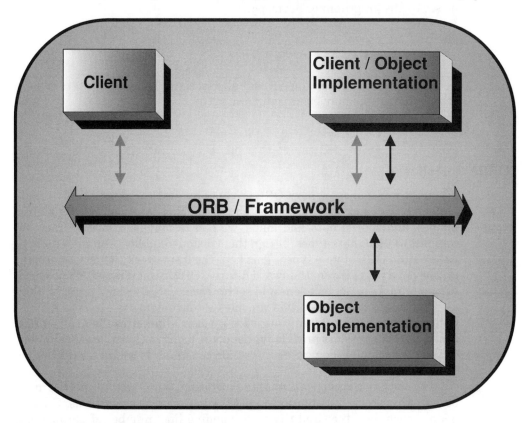

Figure 7.24.   Most applications will be both clients and servers.

When an exchange is accepted with PUTDATA or OPENFRONTEND exchange types, the application "realizes" the widget and the user enters the X window application loop to handle user input and callbacks. In some cases programmers may wish to incorporate self-interrupt timers to wake an application up and determine if any events (ORB or X windows) are waiting to be processed.

Exceptions

DISCUS exceptions are defined using the standard CORBA exceptions. DISCUS operations can raise predefined exceptions. Users may extend the exception list and define exceptions that their applications return. The Environment variable returns exception information that may be standard CORBA-defined exceptions or DISCUS-defined exceptions. A DISCUS exception comprises an exception body including an explanation of the error and other exception data. The exception data is defined as an "any" to provide for flexibility; in other words, the exception data is self-defining and can be set by the programmer/developer.

```
#define DS_exception_body { string explanation;
            any exceptionData; }
```

Each standard exception also has an associated completion status where completion_status may be an enumeration of

```
enum completion_status { YES, NO , MAYBE };
```

CORBA Compliance

When the project began, most ORB products available supported only simple data types. Because our work investigated complex data, such as documents, images, and spatial data and maps, we had to provide a facility to create complex CORBA data types, assign them opaque handles, and map them to the existing ORB simple types. This kept the framework CORBA compliant and paved a migration path toward future CORBA-compliant ORB products with minimal impact on client and server code.

The create_type() operation provides a convenient way to create TypeCode objects. CORBA 2.0 Initialization revision eliminates the need for this function. Some vendors provide type support today in this manner [SunSoft, 93]. Use of compiler-generated TypeCode constants is easier than dynamic TypeCode creation.

The operation accepts as input the requested "kind" of the type, the number of parameters it should have, and the parameters themselves. CORBA defines each data type and the corresponding line, number of parameters, and what they are. For example, simple types such as integers and longs have a kind but no parameters. They are described easily using a constant. Indeed, the create_type operation returns this constant as the type handle in such cases.

The complex type describing a sequence has two parameters. The first carries the TypeCode (another opaque type handle) of the sequence items; the second carries a number representing the maximum size of the sequence. Because each sequence can have different member types identified by the first parameter, a unique handle is generated for each sequence.

The complex type describing a structure can have a variable number of parameters. The first parameter always represents the name of the structure; the rest are pairs of parameters that describe each element in the structure. Each pair represents the element name and its TypeCode. The handle returned for this complex type is also unique.

The TypeCode tree can become rather complex because TypeCodes in the structure can point to sequences that can point to more complex data types, and so forth.

This convenience facility can be hidden behind macros. Thus, simply by changing the macro definitions, code can be easily ported to other facilities provided by ORB vendors.

For example, an "any" type is made of a type and a pointer to a value.

```
typedef struct {
TypeCode _type;
void    *_value;
} any;

any A1;

A1._type = DS_ULong; // assigns the constant typecode handle
         // for unsigned long

A1._type = DS_String_Seq; // assigns the result of a macro that
         // generates a unique sequence handle
```

Asynchronous Support

The normal way to achieve asynchronous operation in a distributed object system would be through multithreading. By using multiple asynchronous processing threads, an object implementation can conduct numerous asynchronous activities. For example, an asynchronous function call can be implemented by dedicating a thread to make a synchronous call and block until the result is returned. So, without any additional API definitions, a synchronous call interface (such as most CORBA static interfaces) can be utilized asynchronously.

Unfortunately, currently not all operating systems and ORBs support threads. Very few programming languages have adequate support for thread-based application development, and current debugging tools for threads are less than adequate. For these reasons, we anticipate that many readers will want to attempt to use CORBA without threads. The following sections detail some approaches for using CORBA and DISCUS without threads. We hope that threads technology will mature sufficiently someday soon to make this additional complexity unnecessary.

Server Asynchrony: Events and X Windows   Most server implementations enter an ORB event wait loop after registering. Clients calls then can be processed as events as they arrive. This is straightforward for servers that simply perform a simple function and then return to the loop. However, in today's computing environments, servers often have to manage GUIs and user or other input. When threads are more widely used, the servers can perform these other functions while also awaiting more ORB events. However, today's applications need to be able to handle events from multiple sources.

The map front end is a good example of such an application. In it these special requirements were handled in several ways.

Most Motif X applications require the client to enter an X main event loop. Upon a user exit indication, the proper callback is activated and the application usually terminates. In the case of a CORBA server, however, we usually should expect the GUI to terminate, but we want the server still to handle other ORB events.

```
/* own user interface main loop that allows quitting when a flag is set
*/

gisAppMainLoop(app)
XtAppContext     app;
{
XEvent           event;

    while (Global_exit_flag == 0) {
    XtAppNextEvent(app, &event);
    XtDispatchEvent (&event);
    }
}
```

Some window systems, such as the X Window system, provide the mechanism to "wake up" using internal time-out timers. This mechanism can be used to interrupt a GUI that is processing user events and perform other ORB calls.

The DISCUS asynchronous operations also can be used. When combined with time-outs, the application can gain control to process various types of events via the use of callbacks.

Server Asynchrony: Polling   The DISCUS framework also offers a mechanism by which applications may find out if they have outstanding incoming requests. For example, an application serving a user through a GUI and processing user events while also serving other applications via a back-end may need to check intermittently to discover if it has any incoming requests on its back-end. The DS_ap_PollRequest call allows the application to dispatch the request for processing.

Some ORBs offer some ORB event polling mechanism. A GUI callback can poll the ORB using the DS_ap_PollRequest operation for any outstanding requests. The DS_ap_PollRequest operation can be mapped to any vendor's polling mechanism.

The code to implement such a poll follows.

```
/* in a main routine somewhere insert code like the following line to
set up an internal timer and an associated callback */

id = XtAppAddTimeOut (Global_Gis_App_Server, 200, timeout_callback,
NULL);

/* in the file containing the callbacks, insert the callback to be
executed when the timer expires */

void timeout_callback(data)
caddr_t      data;
{
long  stat;
printf("Server Timer Expired,\n");

/* execute the poll to dispatch a request if one is waiting */

stat = DS_ap_PollRequest();

if (stat != ORB_SUCCESS)
      printf("Server Error: Cannot handle incoming request\n");

/* set the timer again */
id = XtAppAddTimeOut (Global_Gis_App_Server, 200, timeout_callback,
NULL);

}
```

Asynchronous Operations   DISCUS offers synchronous and asynchronous versions of the four main DISCUS operations (exchange, query, convert, and execute). The basic application framework operations are available in two forms:

Synchronous. The client process (or thread) blocks until the results are returned from the server object.

- *Asynchronous.* The client process receives control before the processing of the operation, so that it can pursue other activities concurrently. The operation get_response() is provided to allow the client to poll for completion and retrieve the results from the server. get_response() returns the output parameters as data objects in the same order as in the synchronous operation.

DISCUS framework operations, such as query(), may take an extraordinarily long time to complete. In one example, we are aware of a server that will routinely process operations for more than eight hours. This is not unusual for legacy systems built for processing batch jobs. The DISCUS framework provides synchronous and asynchronous calls for developers to allow them to structure their applications conveniently for these scenarios.

The choice between the synchronous and asynchronous forms of the operations is based on the programming style used. If the programmer utilizes threads for structuring the program for concurrency, then the synchronous blocking form of the operations is appropriate. A separate thread is created to send, block, and receive the results of each ORB invocation. If the programmer is not using threads, or threads are unavailable on the system being used, and the programmer needs to provide concurrency (such as when monitoring a user interface in parallel with ORB invocations), then the asynchronous operations are available. The asynchronous operations may be phased out when most programming languages, operating systems, and debugging tools use threads as a mature facility. As of the writing of this book, however, threads are still in the early phases of introduction.

The DISCUS IDL for asynchronous operations is specified as a separate interface, which can be optionally included by developers. The DISCUS core operations are extended with five new operations. The asynchronous core operations include only the input parameters and a transaction key output. These include the asynchronous forms of exchange, convert, query, and execute, and a fifth operation called get_response. This asynchronous approach is appropriate until threads are more commonly available in systems integration environments.

```
interface async : DS::ap {
exception NOT_COMPLETED except_body;
   void exchange (
      in    Operation        exchangetype,
      in    Object           dataobject,
      out   long             transactionkey )
      raises( NOT_OPEN )
      context ( context_attributes );
   void convert (
                  in    string  format,
                              // desired data format representation
```

```
                in      string   propertyname,
                                     // property containing input data
                in      Object   dataobject,
                                     // object containing formatted data
                out     long     transactionkey )
                                     // unique key to ID response
                raises( NOT_OPEN )
                context ( context_attributes );
    void query(
                in  Script   query,
                out long     transactionkey ) // unique key to ID response
                raises ( NOT_OPEN )
                context ( context_attributes );
    void execute (
                in      Script       commandlist,
                in      SeqObject    inputdataobjects,
                out     long         transactionkey )
                                     // unique key to ID response
                raises ( NOT_OPEN )
                context ( context_attributes );
    void get_response (
                    in  long         transactionkey, // key from request
                    out SeqObject responsedataobjects )
                    raises (  NOT_OPEN, INPUT_FORMAT_UNKNOWN,
                    OUTPUT_FORMAT_UNKNOWN,
                    BAD_INPUT_FORMAT,
                    UNSUPPORTED_EXTENSIONS,
                    NO_SELECTION, UNKNOWN_OPERAND,
                    UNSUPPORTED_QUERY,
                    UNSUPPORTED_LANGUAGE, SCRIPT_SYNTAX,
                    NOT_COMPLETED )
    context ( context_attributes );
}; /* end interface async */
```

Not all servers are required to support both synchronous and asynchronous forms, and the servers may return the ex_DS_ap_UNSUPPORTED_EXTENSIONS exception.

Since there is no consistent support for asynchrony across operating systems, DISCUS abstracts asynchronous operations via the use of synchronous calls. In general, the asynchronous versions of the DISCUS operations return a transaction key associated with the specific request. The transaction key must be issued by the server implementation of the operation. The call is synchronous, and the server should issue a transaction key and return immediately. The client must use the DS_ap_get_response() operation to find out whether the server has completed the requested operation. The server may return the result or a DS_ap_NOT_COMPLETED exception. In the latter case, the client may retry to retrieve the result at a later time.

CORBA supports asynchrony in the DII and in OMG IDL. OMG IDL has support for asynchrony in the form of the "oneway" operations. When an operation is declared "oneway," it cannot have any output parameters. The ORB uses its best effort to complete the request. The invocation returns immediately to the client; thus, there is no predefined mechanism for returning exceptions.

Convenience Functions

Convenience functions are defined as libraries of functions that build on documented interfaces and provide developers with additional abstraction and simplified usage. DISCUS includes several convenience functions that simplify operations, such as initialization, persistence, and user dialogs.

Convenience functions always can be provided for increased value by ORB vendor libraries, third-party vendors, or by application developers. Because they are not part of the OMG IDL framework, developers should not expect them to be available across multiple languages and platforms.

Use of "convenience functions" should always be optional; they should be thought of as simplifications of functions that can be otherwise programmed using a combination of the basic framework operations. DISCUS convenience functions provide generic, simple interfaces to frequently used operations in the DISCUS environment. Since these functions rely on the same DISCUS framework interface, they always can be reused or adapted for specific purposes.

Miscellaneous convenience functions include metadata processing and GUI interaction, exception handling, object inspection, persistence, and others. Most of these can be categorized as Object input/output functions. They can be further grouped into User Interface functions, Screen Interface functions, and File-System Interface functions.

In the following sections we explain some of the most useful convenience functions provided with the DISCUS framework.

User Interface Functions   The User Interface functions are routines that use a GUI to communicate with the user. They present information to the user and accept the user input.

Pop-up Lists   Pop-up lists are useful functions for creating user dialog boxes containing any selection lists. This capability can be provided by many window system support libraries or ready-made widgets. The DISCUS support pop-up lists are a little more specialized for handling information returned in table objects, such as a list of server handles from the trader service, or a list of sample queries in the server metadata object. The dialog boxes are displayed using X Windows and Motif. As event services become available, these functions could be separated into a specialized window server that can provide common look-and-feel across a system, operating system, local area network (LAN), or collection of systems. An application should be able to send an event to pop up a window; if the client and user are running on an MS-DOS system, the window could be an MS-Windows window. If the client and user are running on a UNIX system using X Windows, the window should be an X window.

The pop-up list function **ds_get_action** pops up a menulike row column widget where the buttons are labeled with strings given by the calling function. The pop-up list function returns the string and index chosen by the user.

Input to the pop-up list function is a structure containing an array of character pointers, a count of the number of items in the array, and a character array to contain the returned value.

The input structure is defined in C as:

```
typedef struct {
char **action_list;  /* array of strings to be displayed */
char   choice[MAXSTING];  /* array to contain user selection */
int    index /* index of the choice */
} action_struct'
```

The parameters for **ds_get_action** are:

```
void ds_get_action (a_struct, win_name)
     action_struct    *actions /* pointer to the structure
                        containing input list, count, and
                        user choice */
     char *win_name;  /* name to be displayed as menu title */
```

In order to use this function, the calling program must have set up an X window environment. The **ds_get_action** function is not a callback.

Parsing Query Strings   Generating queries for multiple servers using different query languages and dialects is a key interoperability challange. Sophisticated middleware products are available that address this issue for major Structured Query Language (SQL) dialects. DISCUS needed to cover a wider, flexible range of languages. Here we describe how DISCUS can use metadata to provide basic interoperability in the presence of multiple query languages.

Query string parsing functions are useful for interpreting server metadata tables that contain prototype queries. These functions parse a sample query and pop up a type-sensitive form that accepts parameters to be inserted in the query prototypes. By using these functions, clients and users are insulated from the details of query syntax, for a limited set of queries. This powerful facility enables clients that discover new applications to interoperate seamlessly. These functions are unnecessary in applications that generate their own query language statements. For performance reasons, clients may know a preferred server's language ahead of time and could communicate with it directly. However, in the cases when services are added dynamically, the parsing facility can be used to display a set of predefined sample queries to the user. When a client selects one, the query is parsed using a server-specified delimiter and a form is popped up on the screen. The form includes the names and DISCUS types found in the query string. The user can then fill in the blank, and the query is sent to the server.

This facility may save costs because applications do not have to be rebuilt and users no longer have to learn the syntax of new query languages. Even though a client is not familiar with a server's query language, it is still guaranteed to be able to communicate with it using familiar DISCUS operations, and it will be able to interpret the returned DISCUS data and table objects.

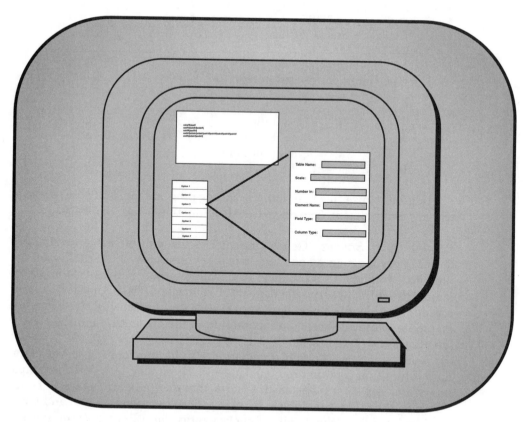

Figure 7.25. Convenience functions: Pop-up lists and forms.

The format for the **ds_get_query_dat** function is :

```
ds_get_query_dat (buttons, count, in_query)
      char **buttons; /* array of pointers to button names */
      int    count;   /* number of items in button array */
      query_struct   *in_query;   /* query structure */
```

The **ds_get_query_dat** function parses a query string into field names and types and displays a form to the screen for the user to fill in values. The function also validates that the values are of the correct type for the field. The query string is then rebuilt with the user-chosen values filled in.

The format of the query string can be (using sql as an example):

```
select from * <table_name> <type>* where <field_name> = *<field_label>
<field_type> * [and <field_name> = *<field_label> <field_type> * ...]
```

The '*' is a delimiter; it can be replaced by any other character as long as that character is not used elsewhere in the query string.

The **ds_get_query_dat** function is set up to be called as a callback for some event in the calling program, such as a button press or menu selection. The data structures are set up in the calling program and are passed to **ds_get_query_dat**.

Arguments to **ds_get_query_dat** are an array of pointers to button names, the number of items in the button array, and a pointer to the query structure.

The structure used to pass in the query information is:

```
typedef struct {
      char     *selection_string;  /* input query string */
      char *new_selection_string;  /* output query string with
                                           values */
      char delim_char;  /* delimiter for query string */
      int num_count;  /* number of parsed items used
                             internally by the function */
  } query_struct;
```

When the **ds_get_query_dat** function is complete, **query_dat.new_selection_string** will contain the new query string that can be sent to the server using the query() or execute() operations.

Screen Interface Functions   Screen interface functions provide the ability for applications to display information on the screen without requiring a window system or user input.

The call

```
status = ds_check_status (&Ev);
```

checks the _major component of the environment and displays the system or user exception value as appropriate.

The call

```
ds_display_discus_obj (dataobject);
```

accepts an opaque object handle as its argument and displays to the standard output the properties of the object and their type and values. This function is useful for debugging purposes.

File System Interface   These functions provide a simple persistence storage capability for DISCUS data objects. The state of the CORBA technology and lack of Object Database support, combined with the linked-in factory approach, present several interesting obstacles.

Ideally, all clients and servers would exchange only the handle of the data object in the data object argument of the OMG IDL interface calls not the data object itself. Data objects could then be stored in a single location, perhaps in a database. A separate factory or life-cycle service could provide such a capability.

Our first implementation approach simply saved a data object to a flat file. Each property name and its type and data were stored. In this very basic service, only predefined properties were supported. Dynamically added properties were not supported, and the type of the data object determined which properties would be saved.

In the next incarnation of the framework and supporting libraries, the persistent object file also contained a header with information as to the number of properties found in the object and their types. This enabled the service to support any data object with varying number and types of properties, and with properties in different orders.

The most difficult challenge in supporting CORBA in a persistent service is the support for complex CORBA types and type "any". CORBA types are self-defining; a property containing a sequence of different types that could also be complex, such as structures or other sequences, is difficult to handle generally. When writing a complex structure or a linked list to a file, the data can be traversed and written contiguously. However, in order to read it back as an object to memory, the application that is reading the file must be able to interpret the type information in order to be able to piece the data back correctly. This is not an easy task; it would require a complex file structure that would enable saving of the type information and indexes into the data file to indicate where data for a particular type is held.

Relevant OMG standards addressing these issues include the Object Persistence Service, the Object Externalization Service, and the Object Query Service. (See Chapter 3.) The persistence service allows alternative persistence protocols, such as the one defined here.

Because our model dealt with storage of the actual data and not just with object references, we had to develop rules to handle specific states of the object. For example, when a data object is written to a file, the data object handle is written with the object. When the object is read into an application, the memory copy is created using that same object handle, not a new one. The factory tables are checked to ensure that the object does not already exist in the memory of that same application. In the latest implementation of the framework, there is increased support for user-defined types via the ability to add read/write callbacks for the new types.

The call

```
ds_writedataobj(filename, dataobject);
```

writes the data object to the file specified by filename.

The call

```
ds_readdataobj(filename, &dataobject);
```

reads the data object found in the file specified by filename.

DISCUS ISSUES AND FUTURES

Specializations of the Framework

To maintain its relative simplicity, DISCUS supports only a moderate range of functionality. DISCUS is intended to be a subset of a complete architecture solution, the subset that provides horizontal interoperability across multiple functional areas. In addition to the horizontal services, there is also a need to provide specialized vertical services within functional areas. An extensive analysis of horizontal and vertical service architectures is presented in Software Architecture Patterns in Chapter 4.

Where specialized access is not needed, DISCUS could provide a low integration cost. There are many potential reasons why the DISCUS framework would need specializations and extensions. For example, for handling large data objects, a fine-grained set of data interchange operations could be added to allow incremental transfer of data. DISCUS does not particularly optimize copying of data, such as data caching and replication.

DISCUS can be readily extended in several ways. It has some built-in extensibility, for example, supporting new conversion services for new data formats, new data object properties, and new query or script languages. DISCUS also can be extended through OMG IDL subtyping. Using subtyping, the application object interface could be specialized for particular types of applications with their own unique sets of operations, in addition to the common operations defined by DISCUS.

In general, we recommend that OMG IDL extensions to DISCUS be designed in an application product-independent manner. (See Chapter 4.)

Simple, product-dependent service extensions can be provided through the DISCUS Execute operation. For example, electronic control of a product's user interface is highly product dependent and best implemented using Execute.

Scalability

The features of available ORB products and their implementation vary greatly. In addition, a variety of tools and configuration files must be used and maintained to manage the ORB and clients and servers.

During the testing phase of a new implementation, it takes only a short time to realize how easy it is to run into memory and resource management issues on the various workstations that make up the user's testbed. For example, if a server does not exit gracefully, it may leave behind a running process that takes up valuable system resources. In the case of an experimental testbed, this issue does not have a severe impact. However, in an operational environment where hundreds or thousands of applications and data objects may be involved, this issue is critical. We have found it useful to enable servers to catch certain signals that allow them to execute cleanup code upon termination. Upon exit, the servers can disconnect from the ORB and release other framework and system resources. A server could be created whose sole purpose is to find defunct servers and remove them and their resources.

While the ORB environment provides exceptional capabilities for managing a system and network resources by devising rules that determine where a server should run, problems can arise if one is not already running. For example, if a server is running on machine B, but the default to start it up is on machine C, whenever problems occur between a client and the server on B (e.g., comm problem or server crash), the next client operation will start up another server on C. The client and user may not even realize that another server has been started; however, now there is a defunct server on B and possibly multiple servers on C.

The default configuration of most ORBs is to have a server or implementation per client or user. While this is the simplest configuration to support (in terms of security and resource allocation and session control), it is not necessarily the most efficient. For example, the conversion server is widely used by most applications on the testbed, and it provides generic capabilities. One server is usually sufficient to handle the conversion requests of several applications. Depending on system and network load, it may make sense to start up several such servers (one handling several systems), or even one per system. However, we have found that one conversion server per user uses too many system resources. It is valuable to be able to configure an ORB to allow various clients run by different users to have the ability to connect to the same single server. The server must be able to perform some session control and could provide synchronous or asynchronous services.

For testing purposes, users and developers may find it useful to begin development without involving the complete network and ORB. The essential element of CORBA technology that enables application to communicate is the framework interfaces defined in OMG IDL. These interfaces allow a phased-in approach where testing can begin with the client and server linked together. This approach allows for the ORB to be brought in at any time. The client and server can then be separated even though they are not aware that they are running in a distributed manner.

When this approach is used for testing, if a linked-in factory is used, developers should comment-out code that handles data object deletion until termination. This is because the client and server are linked in together with a single factory. Deleting a data object will make it unavailable to the other side of the interface. The code can be reactivated when the ORB is introduced.

Security

The DISCUS framework assumes that some security will have to be performed by the applications that have access to data objects. The OMG security model concentrates on providing security at the ORB or Basic Object Adapter (BOA) level. This will enable control of access across ORBs and applications; however, applications that exchange data may require additional security mechanisms to control the data itself. While the applications may be able to use some of the same security services, such as the Generic Security Service Application Programming Interface (GSS-API), to perform their security checks, each DISCUS data object carries security information to enable such checks. Each data object inherits from a security object that contains such information as the CLASSIFICATION or label of the data object, the RELEASE MARKINGS, and CAVEATS. Applications may make use of other available information passed within the Context object (such as User Id) to determine whether a certain user, using a certain application, has access to a data object.

Today some security mechanisms are needed at each level.

The ORB itself may be able to use available system security mechanisms (e.g., DCE, Kerberos, etc.) and internal configurable access control lists to determine whether a particular user has access to start a particular server. Proxy information on different workstations can assist so that user 1 on machine 1 requesting a service on machine 2 will get his own new process, if user 2 on machine 2 already has the same server up using his own process id.

Interoperating ORBs may need a security gateway between their domains unless some common mechanism is agreed upon that can provide consistent policy between ORB domains. CORBA 2.0 provides a general capability to build a gateway using the DII and the Dynamic Skeleton Interface (DSI). These DII/DSI gateways can be used as software firewalls to provide isolation between ORB domains. In the future, software firewalls may be used to replace dedicated hardware firewalls, commonly used for protection.

In the cases where objects are stored persistently in a centralized location, such as an object-oriented database, it may be simpler to perform security checks and concurrency control in the factory. However, with implementations that move data objects around, some security must be performed by applications at the application level.

DISCUS Futures

The DISCUS framework has been ported to the Object Broker 2.5 by DEC and IONA Orbix 1.3. These ORBs support CORBA complex and user-defined types and have compliant OMG IDL compilers.

An important DISCUS goal is the commercial standardization of the DISCUS framework interfaces. OMG is planning to standardize the following service interfaces in 1995 and 1998: the Trader Service, the Query Service, and the Data Interchange Service. DISCUS may become part of such services, or it may evolve to using these when they are standardized. Regardless of the standards outcome, DISCUS provides an upwardly compatible technology transition path for applications supporting the DISCUS framework.

COMMENTS

The DISCUS framework was initially designed about two years before the widespread availability of OMG IDL compilers in CORBA products. During this time, we were able to refine the framework to a design point that was as well matched as possible to the integration needs of the end users. In this experience, we found that technical merit alone is not a sufficient motivation for suppliers and consumers to adopt a framework. Some in-house people must champion the architecture in other organizations before it will be considered worth using. Follow-on activities to the DISCUS project are focusing on this ownership/championship issue to promote community wide adoption.

Even though DISCUS is a simple architecture, it still requires a nontrivial amount of documentation and training to transfer the architectural concepts. For example, this chapter is one of the longest in this book. This was surprising to us, DISCUS's architects and developers, and raises some important concerns about the adequacy of documentation and technology transfer of more complex architectures.

DISCUS was pioneering research in the use of object technology for systems integration. Several years of DISCUS research focused on the general problems of data interchange and the realization of practical solutions. DISCUS already has had an impact on the OMG standards process, in terms of influencing the Object Query Service toward more general support of multiple query languages.

OMG Common Facilities is scheduled to begin the adoption process for the Data Interchange Facility in mid-1995. As we learned from the Object Query Service experience, the DISCUS interfaces are quite generic, in some respects generic enough to meet the requirements of general-purpose standards. With the assistance of our colleagues from other organizations, we hope to impact the OMG process in some substantial way regarding the use of DISCUS-like interfaces as horizontal OMG standards for data interchange. In this way, we can help realize the DISCUS vision of ubiquitous commercial and end user plug-and-play interoperability.

8

Object Wrapper Techniques

Object wrapping is the practice of implementing a software architecture, given preexisting components. Developers are faced with a diverse array of new and preexisting components from future systems, new systems, old systems, and obsolete systems. In this chapter, we use the term legacy systems to describe all forms of preexisting components. Wrapping techniques provide a natural way of integrating legacy systems with each other and with new software. Legacy systems usually involve complex objects; object wrapping provides key techniques for managing complexity. The developer may have limited control over a legacy system, but an object wrapper reencapsulates the system in a controllable form. Object wrappers also provide isolation between complex subsystems, enabling more adaptable systems.

Object wrapping is related to new systems integration concepts, including layering, migration, reengineering, reverse engineering, and forward engineering. In this chapter we introduce some of these concepts and describe how they can be applied to object wrapping.

There are various levels of wrapping, some involving tighter coupling than others. For example, wrappers may employ multiple integration mechanisms such as files, sockets, remote procedure calls (RPCs), scripts, and others. Later in this chapter, we present an extended example of how object wrappers mask differences between object implementations built using different mechanisms. We describe the detailed object wrapper implementations for each mechanism and explain how they are integrated using CORBA.

INTEGRATING LEGACY SYSTEMS

Object wrapping is a practice that is well suited to the integration of legacy systems for several reasons:

- Legacy systems often are closed systems with no access to source code or documentation.
- Object wrapping allows for information hiding.
- Wrappers provide access to a legacy system through abstract application program interfaces (APIs), regardless of the internal implementation complexity of the legacy system.
- Wrappers provide technology migration paths for legacy systems, allowing component upgrade without affecting the rest of the system.

A developer faces various design options depending on the characteristics of the legacy system. For example, the system may have an existing API, it may provide some scripting interface, or it may be a completely closed system. We look further at these examples in Wrapping Examples on page 238, after we define several useful concepts.

Types of Wrapping

Object wrapping allows us to provide access to a legacy system through an encapsulation layer. The encapsulation exposes only those attributes and operation definitions desired by the software architect.

The wrapper serves as an interoperability bridge between a legacy system and a software architecture. On one side of the bridge, the wrapper communicates using the legacy system's existing communication facilities. On the other side of the bridge, the wrapper presents other applications a clean interface that provides abstract services.

One of the key benefits of wrapping is that services may be provided by a legacy system or by a new object. The clients cannot distinguish between the implementations, nor should they care (except possibly for performance or security). If we take the example of the DISCUS framework in Chapter 7, the wrapping of a legacy system may mean the mapping of some of its functions onto the framework Object Management Group Interface Definition Language (OMG IDL) operations and the encapsulation of the legacy system data within data object representations. The wrapper functions as a customized gateway between the legacy system and the software architecture.

The approaches comprising object wrapping can be divided into categories, as described in the following sections:

- Layering
- Data Migration

- Reengineering Applications
- Middleware
- Encapsulation
- Wrappers for Architecture Implementation
- Wrappers for Mediators and Brokers

Layering   Layering is the most basic level of wrapping. A layer is a mapping from one form of application program interface (API) to another. For example, OMG IDL interfaces could be layered over some C++ classes as in Fresco (page 132). Layering can be done without modifying the underlying API design—for example, layering a CORBA-based interface over RPC services. Layering might involve substantial mapping changes between the layers, as in mapping one set of operations onto a completely different set. A prime example is the layering required for OpenDoc parts to interoperate with OLE2 components. (See Chapter 6.)

The functionality of the interface provided by layering depends on the sophistication and availability of APIs to the legacy system. We can extend the legacy system capabilities by adding additional wrapping code to the layer.

Layering also can be used to aggregate multiple legacy systems. Several systems can be wrapped together to provide another layer of functionality. Inversely, layering can be used to partition a complex system into manageable components.

Data Migration   Many legacy systems revolve around large amounts of data and are actually very large database applications. Systems often have anomalies in their schemas, such as overlapping database tables. Such systems may be migrated or wrapped. Migration involves moving the data to another data model, for example, relational, extended relational, or object-oriented database systems. Wrapping involves adding layering code to provide access to the legacy database. The sophistication of this layer can range from a simple API layer, to a limited query interpreter, to a full Structured Query Language (SQL) interpreter. The last option may require a middleware product. (See section titled "Middleware" on page 235.)

One of the challenges in migrating legacy databases to the object-oriented databases is the impedance problem. Most older databases contain simple data types. The primary benefits of object-oriented databases occur with the use of complex user-defined types and specialized access operations. The data types must be mapped between the relational database and its object-oriented counterpart, and this often causes data coupling. Further complications arise when due to the fact that inheritance must be taken into consideration and that operations must be stored somehow [Jacobson, 92].

From a CORBA perspective, a persistent storage of data objects should be independent of the type of database or mechanism used to store the objects. Furthermore, operations that access the data objects should be free of the knowledge of whether the object is persistent or transient.

To transition older databases to object-oriented representations, it is useful to start by mapping tables into classes. The attributes can become columns and each instance can be represented by a row. Keys or handles can be used to index into the table. Tables also can be created to represent associations, and inheritance can be represented by a table for the abstract class, or all inherited attributes can be copied to the appropriate subtables [Jacobson, 92].

Object-oriented databases can help bridge the semantics gap. The available programming language can be used directly to solve the impedance problem. User-defined data types can be used directly as types within the database [Jacobson, 92]. In order to provide a CORBA-compliant interface where data objects and NVLists can be stored directly, an object-oriented database should support complex objects and complex data types, object handles, encapsulation, and inheritance, and it should be extensible.

Extended relational databases eliminate many of the limitations of ordinary relational databases and mitigate the programming burden required by object-oriented databases. Although extended relational databases are relatively new, they should be evaluated as an alternative to object-oriented databases.

Reengineering Applications   Once an application is wrapped, it can be reengineered one piece at a time if needed. Usually reengineering is performed to reduce costs, to increase performance, and to enhance maintainability of the system. As the system architecture improves, it can be adapted more easily to new needs.

There are two types of engineering processes, forward engineering and reverse engineering. Forward engineering is the implementation of a system change using ordinary software development techniques. Reverse engineering comprises system analysis and reimplementation.

Reverse engineering is the process in which the software is analyzed in order to gain a better understanding of how it operates. The abstract description of how the system operates is mapped onto subsystem components. In the process of reengineering, a system is first reverse-engineered, then a change is made to the system at the abstract level and the system is reimplemented [Jacobson, 91]. Changes to the system can be functional ones (modifications or additions), a reimplementation of the system with no functional changes, or a combination of both. The decision to reengineer a system depends on the business value and the level of changes that can or need to be made to it. Domain analysis may be employed in reverse engineering. For example, in Jacobson [91] the application domain is modeled as objects and associations.

The system model maps the application domain to elements of the existing system. Analysis is made and an analysis model is created. Mapping of the analysis model is made to the existing system to determine which parts of the system will be reimplemented using object-oriented techniques. After iterations of the process are complete, a new subsystem is designed and the old system is modified to interface to the new system. The two are then integrated. Wrapping allows for the replacement of the old system components with object-oriented components.

Middleware   The term middleware is used to describe a wide range of commercial system integration software. Key categories of middleware include:

- Distributed processing middleware (lower middleware)
- Database and user interface middleware (upper middleware)

The distributed processing middleware is migrating toward CORBA. Perhaps the most successful independent vendor in that market is Expersoft, whose Xshell product is now CORBA compliant. Most other distributed processing middleware vendors have announced CORBA futures.

Database middleware includes software that mediates between various database products and provides a common access mechanism. Several such products are available. These products enable an application to send a single query to the middleware software, which, in turn, accesses several other data sources, usually of the same type but from different vendors and syntax.

CORBA can be used in conjunction with database middleware. Several products have direct CORBA support (i.e., Bluestone, Forte); other products can be utilized through object wrapping techniques, such as layering.

Some database middleware products are closed systems that have vertically integrated user interfaces and minimal support for external software interfaces. A key indication is the lack of a well-documented client/server API, which would support the use of CORBA and an end-user software architecture. These products are difficult to wrapper properly.

In a CORBA-based software architecture, database middleware should be wrapped like other legacy systems. For example, wrapped middleware can become a data brokering service registered with the trader service. Similar to data conversion services, database middleware provides a commonality among different data sources using different formats and query language dialects.

Encapsulation   Encapsulation is the most general form of object wrapping. An encapsulation is a black box abstraction in which the interface hides the details of the underlying implementation. No direct memory access operations are allowed; every direct and indirect access to state variables is performed through controlled functions defined by the object implementation.

Encapsulation is a separation of interface from implementation. Among object technologies, CORBA provides the most comprehensive form of separation via encapsulation. CORBA encapsulations hide differences in programming language, location, operating system, algorithm, and data structure. OMG IDL is a key tool enabling the definition of encapsulations free of implementation dependencies.

Encapsulation includes the wrapping of non–object-oriented systems. In the cases when the legacy code is inaccessible, the legacy system does not need to be modified; all access can be provided via the wrapper through access to files or other mechanisms. If code access is available, the wrapper can provide more direct communication between the legacy system and the object-oriented environment.

Encapsulation can be used to partition and componentize a legacy system. Each component can be encapsulated separately, and then the system can be reintegrated using object-based communications. The benefits of this approach is that each component can now be reused, and system upgrades can occur incrementally. This approach is often referred to as "Divide and Unite."

Encapsulation is wrapping for wrapping's sake. In general, we wish to utilize wrapping to build architectural components for CORBA-based systems, as in the following section.

Wrappers for Architecture Implementation   The purpose of object wrappers can be understood best in the context of an architecture-based systems integration. At the architecture level, a wrapper needs to be more than just a simple encapsulation layer. The wrapper must implement the architecture design in all aspects. The wrapper provides interoperability between the architecture and the legacy subsystem. It also should provide value-added functions and information, such as metadata, data conversions, and other architecture features.

Metadata beyond the trader service capability is an often-overlooked feature that greatly enhances architecture flexibility. (See Chapters 4 and 7.) Since most legacy systems have limited metadata, metadata is a key responsibility of the object wrapper. Metadata allows applications to discover detailed information about the object implementations they wish to utilize. Metadata can include key interoperability information, such as supported data formats and the schema of information sources. The applications also can find out detailed information, such as the methods of communication supported by the implementation (such as scripts) and the syntax for this communication.

Using CORBA for object wrapping provides some key advantages. CORBA provides a strong encapsulation. It minimizes the need for rewriting object wrappers for different clients and configurations. CORBA provides runtime architecture flexibility, allowing the flexible allocation of clients and object implementations. CORBA hides activation state and minimizes the need for custom integration, since it effectively hides implementation details behind the wrapper. A wrapper can satisfy the needs of any set of existing and future clients, regardless of language, location, or platform.

The API of a legacy system can aid object wrapping. The legacy API is the software access path to the implementation's supported functions. A simple layer mapping from the legacy APIs to OMG IDL provides for a quick and powerful wrapping and distribution of the services through CORBA.

If the legacy API is hidden behind a more abstract architectural wrapper, then clients can utilize various implementations that provide the same services, without tying into any implementation's specific legacy API.

A software architecture or framework, such as the one described in Chapter 7, provides many benefits. Some of them are:

- Single simple extensible interface
- Local control of the interface
- Horizontal integration and data exchange between different domains
- Application object polymorphism

An application client that communicates with implementations that are compliant with the framework can access these implementations regardless of the way they work internally. In the next section we show how a single client can communicate via the framework with object implementations that use various mechanisms (such as RPC, Sockets, scripts, etc.) to communicate with legacy or proprietary software.

Wrappers for Mediators and Brokers The increasingly diverse array of processing services introduces a requirement for mediator or brokerage services to aggregate various types of functions, such as:

- Access to disparate information sources
- Access to diverse value-added processing services
- Sophisticated search and data presentation algorithms to reduce client complexity and simplify the user interface
- Conversion of data between incompatible formats

Brokers can access multiple services through CORBA to provide a consolidated access to services. For example, a client may request a data conversion broker to perform an arbitrary data conversion. The client does not know whether the broker performs the conversion itself or whether the broker calls other services to perform the conversion. A particularly complex conversion could require searching through the trader service data and access to multiple conversion service interfaces. The broker can hide all this complexity from the client.

For example, the conversion service, discussed in Chapter 7, allows the data to be converted to each object implementation and client's native data mode. The simple Data Object interface, combined with the seamless conversion of data is key to interoperability. The trader service allows for applications to find details about services not found in the Interface Repository. Rather than just finding out about the syntax of an interface, the trader can be searched for specific services that perform certain functions. A naming service is an essential counterpart to the trader for converting service names to object references. Most ORB vendors support the naming service.

WRAPPING EXAMPLES

Object wrapping is a practice that transforms a component's software interfaces from one form to another. There may be value added in this process—for example, enhancing interoperability and system flexibility through metadata.

The process of wrapping involves different implementation techniques depending on the accessible elements of the legacy system. In the best-case scenario, access to legacy system source code is available. In this case, it is possible to integrate the legacy system directly to the object wrapper code. If it is possible to bypass the file system and exchange data in memory, performance is greatly improved. Ideally, the legacy system has a clean API and services that are well documented. It is then possible to define a direct CORBA interface that should be minimally impacted when any changes occur. It is also possible to reengineer and modularize the system over time without affecting clients. This idealized case is seldom encountered in the real world of systems integration.

More typically, systems integrators have limited access to legacy system code. Each legacy system presents a uniquely constrained integration problem. The legacy system may have no API at all, a limited API, or an extensive proprietary API. The legacy system may use sockets, RPCs, or any number of access mechanisms. The object wrapper hides these idiosyncrasies and presents an interface that is consistent with the desired software architecture. The following table lists some of the key ways that object wrapping changes a component interface.

Before Object Wrapping	After Object Wrapping
Unique API	Desired API
Unique access mechanism	Uniform access mechanism
Nonexchangeable data format	Exchangeable data format
Limited metadata	Complete/uniform metadata
Inadequate interoperability	Meets Interoperability Needs
	System-component independence
Limited/proprietary security and management interfaces	Uniform/comprehensive security and management interfaces

Object wrapping is best understood through examples. In the following sections we give examples of many different mechanisms that we have encountered in our systems integration experience. Many more exist, and there are various flavors of the ones we describe. We provide these examples to show what steps are needed to integrate these mechanisms into a CORBA-based software architecture.

The benefit of wrapping quickly becomes apparent. Wrapping greatly simplifies and empowers client access to services. Each of the object implementations uses a different mechanism internally, but the mapping onto the IDL framework interface hides the unnecessary details of individual servers.

In the following examples, the client uses the C binding of the DISCUS framework described in Chapter 7. The client has an object reference to a data object that it may have retrieved from an earlier query operation. The data object comprises a name-value list of CORBA type "any" properties that include the Image identifier, the size of the image, the region of interest in latitude/longitude, the image bitmap display, and so on. The client sends the data object reference with the exchange() operation to the object implementation with the DS_ap_OPEN_FRONT_END flag. The object implementation then uses the framework interface to access the data object bitmap display property and extract the data. It then uses its internal mechanism to import the data into its environment and present the user with its graphical user interface (GUI). Upon the GUI exit, the object implementation captures any user modifications to the image and updates the bitmap property and any other related properties, such as the image size. When the exchange() operation completes, the control is returned to the client, which can access the updated data object. The following is the example client code in C. (Note that for simplification some code, such as repetitive checks for exceptions, has been omitted and marked with "...")

```c
#include <orb.h>
#include "discus.h"

main (argc, argv)
int argc;
char **argv;
{
    CORBA_Environment    client_ev;              /* The environment */
    CORBA_Context        client_ctx;             /* The context */
    CORBA_Status         status;                 /* ORB status */
    DS_dt                dataobject;             /* Data Object Reference */
    CORBA_any            temp_any, result;       /* CORBA Any type */
    CORBA_Object         factory;
    CORBA_Object         SERVER;
```

```
/* Get the default context. */
status = CORBA_ORB_get_default_context(  CORBA_ORB_OBJECT,
                                &client_ev,
                                &client_ctx );

if (status !=SUCCESS)
   fprintf(stdout, "Exception from getting context\n");

GetObjRefFromNameService("DISCUS_FRAMEWORK", &factory);

DS_ft_open(factory, &client_ev, client_ctx);

/* Display exception if returned */
ds_display_status(&client_ev);

/* Get the dataobject from some image archive */
....
/* Get the Image application server object reference */

GetObjRefFromNameService("IMAGE_SERVER", &SERVER);

/* open the server */

DS_ap_open(SERVER,&client_ev, client_ctx);

/* Call the server with the Exchange operation and pass the dataobject */
DS_ap_exchange (   SERVER,
                &client_ev,
                client_ctx,
                DS_OPEN_FRONT_END,
                &dataobject);

....
/* Upon successful return, open the data object */
DS_dt_open(dataobject, &client_ev, client_ctx);

/* Access the properties */

DS_dt_get (dataobject, &client_ev, client_ctx, "Display_Rep",
        &temp_any);

/* do something with it, e.g., display it, write to file, etc. */

....

/* close the server */

DS_ap_close(SERVER,&client_ev, client_ctx);
```

```
/* destroy the server */

DS_ap_destroy(SERVER,&client_ev,client_ctx);

/* we are done with the dataobject */
DS_dt_close (dataobject, &client_ev, client_ctx);

/* close the factory */
DS_ft_close(factory, &client_ev, client_ctx);

}
```

This client code is the same for accessing all of the example object implementations. The object wrappers provide this client/service isolation. The following sections describe the implementations of multiple servers. The servers vary with respect to the legacy interface and thus the wrapping techniques.

Wrapping with Remote Procedure Calls

Remote procedure calls are a mechanism that allows clients to execute code that resides in a server, regardless of whether the server is executing locally or remotely. RPC is similar to CORBA, but at a more rudimentary level. RPCs have client and server stubs that package the arguments of the function call and marshall them between the processes and across the network. They extend the function calls that clients can make to allow for distribution. There are a few de facto standard implementations available, such as SUN Open Network Computing (ONC), and many developers like RPCs due to their availability.

RPCs, though, have some limitations. They are synchronous and require threads technology or callbacks to provide asynchronous capabilities. This adds a high level of complexity for programmers. Both the sender and receiver must be available, both applications must be RPC cognizant, and no dynamic binding or routing is available.

Most systems that use the RPC mechanism as their API provide an RPC server and the calls and data structures that it supports. The way to communicate with these systems is by creating RPC clients. In the next example, the object implementation communicates on one side with the OMG IDL framework and on the other with the RPC mechanism. The wrapper comprising the object implementation in this example is an RPC client that can communicate with a legacy RPC server.

Using the rpcgen compiler, the external data representation (XDR) defines the data structure. In this example we wish to send a stream of data representing an image, so we represent the data as an opaque variable length data type. The rpcgen compiler generates the data type as a structure with a buffer and an associated length parameter. The program specification itself defines two calls, a get_buf to retrieve data through the RPC mechanism, and a put_data to send data through the RPC mechanism. Once the code is generated, it can be interleaved with framework code. In this case the framework CORBA server uses the RPC client stub code to communicate with the legacy application. The first step is to create the client handle. Once this is accomplished, the data object is opened and the data of the display property is retrieved. The data is placed within the opaque buffer, defined as temp_buf and the length set to the length of the octet sequence that was read from the data object. Then the put_buf call is executed and the data is sent. Upon return, the get_buf call is executed to retrieve data from the server. The result is placed into another temporary buffer. Finally, the data is placed in a CORBA_any structure and the data object property set with the new data. When all processing is complete, the data object is closed.

```
/* let us assume that the rpcgen specification file looks like: */

typedef opaque buffer<>;

program GET_BUF_PROG{
  version GET_BUF_VERS{
    buffer get_buf(void) = 1;
    long put_buf(buffer) = 2;
  }=1;
} = 0x31111111;

#include <orb.h>
#include "DS_server.h"
#include <stdio.h>
#include <stdlib.h>
#include <rpc/rpc.h>

DS_ap_exchange(
        Object,
        Ev,
        Ctx,
        exchangetype,
        dataobject)

CORBA_Object       Object;
CORBA_Environment *Ev;
CORBA_Context      *Ctx;
CORBA_Int          exchangetype;
DS_dt              *dataobject;
{
```

```
CLIENT *cl;
int *result;
char *server;
int length;

ORBStatus status;
any temp_any;
buffer temp_buf;
buffer *result_buf;

/* call to create the client handle */
/* server is the server name          */
/* PROG is the program as generated by the rpcgen compiler */
/* VERS is the version as generated by the rpcgen compiler */

cl = clnt_create(server, GET_BUF_PROG, GET_BUF_VERS, "tcp");
if (cl == NULL) {
  /* Couldn't establish connection with server. */
  clnt_pcreateerror(server);
  exit(1);
}

DS_dt_open(dataobject, Ev, Ctx);

DS_dt_get(dataobject, Ev, Ctx, "Display_Rep", temp_any);


temp_buf.buffer_len = ((CORBA_sequence_octet*)(temp_any->_value))
                        ->_length;
temp_buf.buffer_val = malloc(temp_buf.buffer_len);
memcpy(temp_buf.buffer_val,
       ((CORBA_sequence_octet *)(temp_any->_value))->_buffer,
       temp_buf.buffer_len);

if ((result = put_buf_1(&temp_buf, cl)) == NULL) {
  clnt_perror(cl, server);
  exit(2);
}

/* now get the data back */
if (result_buf = get_buf(NULL, cl)) == NULL {
  clnt_perror(cl, server);
  exit(3);
}

memcpy(((CORBA_sequence_octet *)(temp_any->_value))->_buffer,
       result_buf.buffer_val, result_buf.buffer.len);
```

```
((CORBA_sequence_octet*)(temp_any->_value))->_length
                        = result_buf.buffer_len;

((CORBA_sequence_octet*)(temp_any->_value))->_maximum
                        = result_buf.buffer_len;

DS_dt_set(dataobject, Ev, Ctx, "Display_Rep", &temp_any);

DS_dt_close(dataobject, Ev, Ctx);

}
```

Wrapping with Files

The worst case of legacy (or proprietary) systems integration involves a system that provides no API, no access to code, and no scripting interface. Usually such tools are started by executing them and then exercising their user interfaces to load and save files. Manipulation of the data occurs within

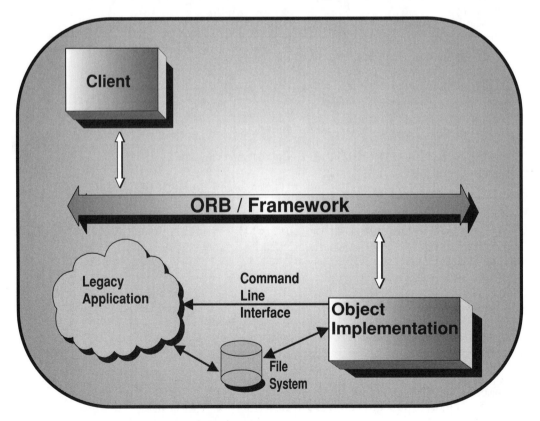

Figure 8.1. Wrapping without direct integration.

the closed system using that system's menus, user interface, and toolset. In such cases, we have found that a simple object gateway encapsulator provides powerful and quick integration with minimal effort required. Such a server communicates on one side via objects with other object-oriented applications and via files with the legacy applications. The gateway strips from the object the required data and saves it to prearranged files. The legacy system is then started, and the user can load the file. Once the data is saved and tool is quit, the data is reencapsulated into the object and returned to the client that invoked the server. The major drawback of this method is that it is left up to the user to read and save the files in the appropriate locations. The benefit is that such a gateway can be made very generic and reused to integrate new applications within minutes.

The code sample illustrates the implementation of an exchange operation receiving a data object reference. After the data object is opened, the application retrieves the data by specifying the appropriate data object property within the get operation. A local function call can then be executed which writes the data to a specified file name. Usually such a routine has understanding of the data structure it is writing and can cast the type "any". The file name is usually a "known" fixed or temporary file name to allow the user simplified maneuvering through the file system. Because of the simplicity of such an interface, the UNIX system call can be executed to launch the required application. In some cases the file name can be passed to the application on the command line. In others, the user may have to load the file. Upon exit from the application, it is assumed that the user saved the result into the same or other prespecified file name. Another local function or routine can be called to read the data and place it within an "any" structure. The framework set operation is then called to store the data back into the data object and the data object is closed.

```
/* Skeleton for exchange operation */
DS_ap_exchange (
        Object,
        Ev,
        Ctx,
        exchangetype,
        dataobject)

CORBA_Object        Object;
CORBA_Environment   *Ev;
CORBA_Context       *Ctx;
CORBA_Int   exchangetype;
DS_dt *     dataobject;
{

   ORBStatus   status;
   any   temp_any;
```

```
/* Open the incoming data object */
DS_dt_open(dataobject, Ev, Ctx);

/* Get the property of interest */
DS_dt_get (dataobject, Ev, Ctx, "Display_Rep", temp_any);

/* Write the property data to a file */
write_to_file (temp_any, filename);

sprintf(command, "%s %s","/pathname/executable",filename);

/* execute a program with the filename as an argument */
system(command);

/* upon return re-encapsulate the output file */

read_from_file (filename, &temp_any);

/* Set the read-in data into the data object property */
DS_dt_set (dataobject, Ev, Ctx, "Display_Rep", &temp_any);

/* Close the data object and return to the calling client */
DS_dt_close(dataobject, Ev, Ctx);

}
```

Wrapping with Sockets

Sockets were developed at Berkeley to provide programmers with an API to networking that is somewhat analogous to standard UNIX file input/output [Stevens, 90]. The socket interface provides system calls to set up or destroy a connection and to send and receive data across it using various networking protocols. In this example, the object implementation must manage the socket interface and the marshalling of the data object properties.

In this example, the exchange operation implementation begins with opening the data object and retrieving the data using the get operation. Using standard socket calls, the application then attempts to open the socket and then fork. Code must be provided to handle the fork and the pid is checked to separate the child code from the parent code. The client code begins by writing to the socket the size of the contiguous buffer that will be sent. The data buffer is then written to the socket. The parent process is able to receive the returned data and reads first the size of the data that will be received. Then the process reads the data from the socket and writes it to the buffer. Upon completion, the socket is closed and the data object property is set.

```
#include <stdio.h>
#include <sys/file.h>
#include <sys/types.h>
#include <sys/socket.h>
#include <sys/un.h>
#include <sys/stat.h>
#include <errno.h>

#include <client_ex.h>
#include <log_mgr.h>
#include <socket_lib.h>
#include <ioutil.h>

main (int argc, char *argv[])
{
char send_file[256], receive_file[256]; /* file names */
int     sf_fd, rf_fd;                   /* file descriptors */
int     sockfd, childpid;               /* socket desc. and child pid */
struct  sockaddr_un     serv_addr;      /* socket */
int n;                                  /* num bytes */
char sendline [MAXLINE];                /* send buffer */
char recvline [MAXLINE + 1];            /* receive buffer */
struct stat buf;                        /* file info structure */
int receive_size, num_read;             /* byte counters */

/* Open the data object */
DS_dt_open (dataobject, Ev, Ctx);

/* Get the property of interest */
DS_dt_get (dataobject, Ev, Ctx, "Display_Rep", &temp_any);

        /* open the socket */
        if ((sockfd = setup_client(SOCKET)) == -1)
                {
                perror ("client");
                log_event(FATAL,"client: could not open client socket

%s\n","SERVER");
                exit (ERROR);

                }

        /* fork the client */
        if ((childpid = fork()) < 0)
                {
                perror ("client");
                log_event(FATAL,"client: could not fork %s\n","SERVER");
                exit (ERROR);
```

```
            }

/* if child */
 if (childpid == 0)
        {
        /* client child writing file */
        /* write the size of the file to the socket */
        write (sockfd, &((CORBA_sequence_octet*)(temp_any._value))
               ->_length, sizeof(long));

        num_read = 0;

        /* write buffer to the socket file descriptor */

        while ((n = buffer_read(((CORBA_sequence_octet*
        )(temp_any._value))->_buffer,sendline, MAXLINE)) != 0)
                {

                if (writen (sockfd, sendline, n) != n)
                        {
                        printf("client: child could not write to
                                socket  %d\n",n);
                        exit (ERROR);
                        }
                log_event (INFO, "Client child wrote %d bytes to
                        socket\n",n);

                /* increment byte count and stop if wrote whole
                        buffer */
                num_read += n;
                if (num_read == ((CORBA_sequence_octet*)(temp_any.
                        _value))->_length)
                        break;
                }

        /* close descriptors */
        close (sockfd);
        exit (SUCCESS);
        }
 else
        /* parent */
        {
        log_event (INFO, "Client parent\n");

        /* read buffer size */
        read (sockfd, &receive_size, sizeof(long));
        log_event (INFO, "Client parent will read
              %d\n",receive_size);
        num_read = 0;
```

```
                    /* read data from socket into receive buffer */
                    while (num_read < receive_size)
                          {
                        n = readn (sockfd, recvline, MAXLINE,
                              receive_size);
                         if (n < 0)
                                {
                                log_event(FATAL,"client: parent could
                                    not read from socket %d\n",n);
                                exit (ERROR);
                                }
                        recvline[n] = 0;

                        /* write to receive buffer */
                        write_to_buffer ((((CORBA_sequence_octet*)(temp_any.
                            _value))->_buffer, recvline, n);
                        num_read += n;
                        log_event (INFO, "client: parent num_read
                                    %d\n",num_read);
                          }

                /* close the descriptors */

                close (sockfd);

                /* wait for the child */
                if (wait (NULL) == -1)
                        exit (ERROR);
                }

        /* Set the property with the read-in buffer */
        DS_dt_set (dataobject, Ev, Ctx, "Display_Rep", &temp_any);
        /* Close the data object */
        DS_dt_close(dataobject, Ev, Ctx);
}
```

Wrapping with a C API

The mechanism that provides the best integration is usually a well-defined
software API. A few of the packages we integrated provided a C language
API. At first glance, it might seem tempting to convert all of the functions
provided by the API into IDL. While doing so is usually a rather simple me-
chanical process, the only benefit is that the API can now become distributed
and clients can make calls to an object implementation on different systems.
The pitfall becomes apparent when we consider integration of $N \times N$ clients
and services. If each server API is simply converted to IDL, clients still need

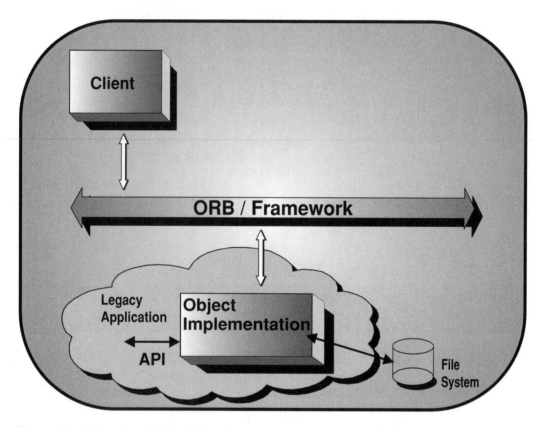

Figure 8.2.   Wrapping with direct integration.

to know about the hundreds of unique function calls and encounter many overlapping ones. In addition, while an API may contain many separate calls, usually they can be grouped into a few services. It is possible to map major services onto common framework operations, while leaving room and flexibility to extend the framework with more specific services. In this example, we show how a set of legacy APIs might be wrapped behind common framework interfaces.

The framework code and API code are often interleaved. Upon the data object opening and retrieval of the data using the get operation, some initialization function is often called. Such calls can sometimes be called prior to the framework calls or even placed in the server's main routine. If the software package or application being used supports a GUI front-end, the appropriate API calls can be used at this time (represented by the pkg_set_up_window call). Before the data is loaded into the application, the server can call a conversion server if the format of the data is not in its preferred format. If successful, the conversion server converts the data and stores it in the data object. The get operation can be called again to retrieve the converted data. The buffer is then loaded using the API's pkg_load_image call. Often, applications allow control of various functions via their API. The example assumes that the application here allows loading of an image and automatic zooming by setting a scale variable using a pkg_scale call. The appropriate data object property value representing the image scale is retrieving and passed using the API call. Because GUIs usually have their own event loops, once the GUI is started, the server must enter some wait event loop that enables proper processing of the GUI events. When the GUI is exited and control is returned to the server, the proper API calls are executed to retrieve the updated or new image and scale and their values set within the data object. It should be noted that different APIs may require a different sequence of interleaving. For example, it may be required to retrieve the image data prior to the GUI exiting (if retrieved from a display related buffer). Alternatively, the API may provide a read function to read a file that was saved during the process.

```
....
/* access the dataobject and required fields */

DS_dt_open(dataobject, Ev, Ctx);
DS_dt_get (dataobject, Ev, Ctx, "Display_Rep_Format", &temp_any);

/* call the package API */
pkg_initialize();

/* set up GUI */
if (pkg_set_up_window() != NULL)
     {
     /* check image type and call convert if needed */
     if (temp_any._value->Format != own)
          {
          /* Call the image convert server */
          DS_ap_open(CONVERT, Ev, Ctx);
          DS_ap_convert(CONVERT, Ev, Ctx, "Display_Rep",
                        "my_own_format", dataobject);
          .... /* check for errors */
          /* Get the returned converted property */
          }
     }
          DS_dt_get(dataobject, Ev, Ctx, "Display_Rep", &temp_any);

/* Call the API to load the image to the display window */
pkg_load_image((CORBA_sequence_octet)(temp_any._value))->_buffer);
/* Get the scale factory from the data object */
DS_dt_get(dataobject, Ev, Ctx, "Scale", &temp_any);
/* Call the API to scale the displayed image */
pkg_scale (*(long *)(temp_any._value));
```

```
....
....
....
/* Enter package event loop */
while (!exit_flag)
     pkg_loop();

/* Get image output when done */
pkg_get_image_from_buffer((CORBA_sequence_octet*)(temp_any.
_value))->_buffer);

/* Set the property in the data object for return to client */
DS_dt_set (dataobject, Ev, Ctx, "Display_Rep", temp_any);

/* Get the display scale in case it was changed by the user */
pkt_get_current_scale(&scale);

/* Set the new value in the proper property */
temp_any._type = TC_long;
temp_any._value = scale;

DS_dt_set (dataobject, Ev, Ctx, "Scale", &temp_any);

/* Close the data object and return to client */
DS_dt_close(dataobject, Ev, Ctx);
  .
  .
  .
```

Integration with Common Lisp

Integration using Common Lisp programming is complicated by the fact that interoperability is product-specific and supported selectively by existing technologies. Heterogenous computing with various language compilers provides a major challenge for Common Lisp developers. Yet Common Lisp applications, such as simulators, play an important role, and a mechanism must be provided to integrate them with other applications [Mowbray, 95]. A team at MITRE has leveraged existing work and has proposed an OMG IDL to LISP mapping that leverages the Common Lisp vendors toward a future OMG standard.

The binding maps CORBA types onto Common Lisp types and IDL interfaces into Common Lisp object system classes. This sort of object encapsulation supports subtyping and inheritance. The team demonstrated how a server could be written to communicate with the ORB on one side and with the Common Lisp application on the other.

Integration with Smalltalk

Smalltalk provides an interesting integration case because it has an independent environment and language. Smalltalk is an object-oriented programming language that provides a runtime class and type definition capability. During our work we developed two interfaces to a package running under Smalltalk. The first interface was rather simple; the second evolved into a more mature interface.

The first interface did not instantiate any new classes within the Smalltalk package. The object implementation simply extracted the image data from the data object, wrote it to a file, and then used the Smalltalk stream class to read in the file. Once in the Smalltalk language, an image object was created. The next interation of the interface did not use the file system. Instead, the socket class interface was used and the buffers were transferred directly to their Smalltalk object counterparts. This provided a simple wrapping capability using the two main methods of interface that were available with Smalltalk at the time.

Using a more sophisticated Smalltalk-to-C interface the framework operations and data object access operations could be developed into stubs. To do this, a lot of Smalltalk would have to be written to create the appropriate classes and instances and then call the C code that talks to the ORB.

The OMG has adapted a CORBA binding for Smalltalk that will be supported by multiple vendors.

Wrapping with Scripts

Legacy systems that provide some sort of command-line or scripting interfaces are one step above integration via files. Instead of simply encapsulating object data retrieved from files, the server can implement a more sophisticated seamless interface. The server may still need to use the file system for some data; however, it also can execute some commands to the legacy system to act on the data. The server in this case is simulating a user, with minimal user interaction.

An example of a scriptable application is a product called Rapport from Clarity. Rapport is an integrated package that offers object-oriented capabilities with a word processor, e-mail, spreadsheet, graphics, and so on. Rapport offers complete control of all of its functions via a detailed script API. We wrote a server that extracts the Display_Rep property of the data object and writes it to a file. The server then connects to Rapport and sends two simple script commands. One opens a word processing window, the other loads the file. The result is that the Rapport window pops up and the image is read in. Rapport also offers its own image conversion filters. The server could have used the conversion service to convert the image to a format Rapport prefers, or it simply can pass the file to Rapport and hope that it possesses the proper filters to complete the conversion.

The scripting implies that the client wishes to indicate certain actions that go beyond the purpose of the DISCUS exchange() operation. The purpose of the exchange() operation is to provide for simple data exchange. To use scripts directly, the query() or execute() operations should be used instead.

Wrapping with Events

Some applications make extensive use of events. Events may be part of a windowing system, such as X window events, or they can be system signals, such as the UNIX SIGUSR1 signals. Many integrated applications today provide event-based interprocess communications in proprietary ways. Often these mechanisms are similar to the functionality offered by an ORB but were developed before ORB technology was available. The API of these applications usually allows a client, in this case the object implementation, to register with an event mechanism and ask to receive or capture certain events. The way in which the object implementation processes these events is actually very similar to the way in which the ORB activates the skeleton. It is as if the object implementation is talking with two different ORB types, one CORBA and one proprietary.

On the CORBA and DISCUS framework side, the object implementation may receive an exchange operation with a data object. It can then communicate with a GUI via a combination of events and C API calls (Figure 8.3). When the user presses certain event-generating buttons on the GUI, the object implementation is interrupted and a callback is executed (previously registered with the event mechanism for a specific event type). The object implementation then can process the data or make more API calls.

Sometimes the GUI actually resides in the object implementation, as an X Windows GUI might. In these cases, the object implementation needs to be able to process ORB and X Windows events. Because ORB vendors may deal with their event loops and X window loops differently, we found it useful to allow the application to control the X loop. The code in the section "Server Asynchrony: Events and X Windows" on page 216 allows the X GUI to exit the X event loop rather than quit the whole application. In addition, we made use of X self-interrupts to interrupt the X event loop from time to time to check whether any ORB events are waiting to be processed.

Wrapping with Shared Memory

Shared memory usually is used when performance and speed are of the utmost importance. Shared memory allows two processes on the same machine to share a memory segment. This reduces the number of copies of the data that are required compared to other common mechanisms, such as message

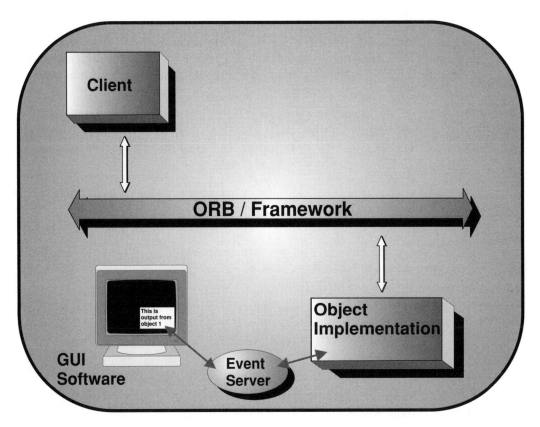

Figure 8.3. Event server configuration.

queues and PIPEs. Standard shared memory has some major limitations in distributed environments. The processes have to reside on the same machine, and many systems have limits on the size of the shared memory segment. Thus, large images or other type of data may not be supported.

It is very common for integrators to encounter shared memory legacy applications because the older systems, running on slower hardware, required all the performance improvements that were possible when they were implemented. Combined with the CORBA technology, object implementations can be developed to communicate with the ORB on one side and shared memory on the other. We will assume for this example that the segment can support the image file buffer that we will write and read to it.

This example is similar to the socket and RPC examples, in that it retrieves the data by opening the data object and using the retrieve operation to get the data. The shared memory area must be set up and a key assigned. If the connection to the area is successful, the data is written to the area using a subroutine (code not provided). To handle concurrent use of the area by different applications, semaphores could be used. When the data is available, another routine can be called to read the data from the shared memory area (code not provided) and the property within the data object set. Finally, the UNIX shared memory destroy and removal calls can be made.

```
char file_name[256];      /* file name containing data */
FILE *fp;                 /* file pointer */
sh_data *sh_ptr;          /* pointer to the shared memory area */
int index, interval;      /* index and time interval read in */

int n;                    /* number of items read in by fscanf */
```

....

```
/* Open the data object and get the property of interest */
DS_dt_open (dataobject, &Ev, Ctx);
DS_dt_get (dataobject, &Ev, Ctx, "Display_Rep", &temp_any);

  /* get the shared memory area */
  if ((sh_ptr = (sh_data *)connect_shm (SHMKEY,
          sizeof(octet)*((CORBA_sequence_octet*)(temp_any._value))
     ->_length)) == NULL)
          {
          log_event(FATAL,"install_data: could not
                  connect_shm \n");
          exit (ERROR);
          }

/* call routine to write buffer to shared memory area */
write_data_to_shm(sh_ptr, ((CORBA_sequence_octet*)(temp_any._value))
                ->_buffer)

/* wait for some processing by other side and check semaphores */
```

...

```
/* When read, read the data from the shared memory into buffer */
read_data_from_shm(sh_ptr,
                ((CORBA_sequence_octet*)(temp_any._value))->_buffer)
/* Set the property */
DS_dt_set(dataobject, &Ev, Ctx, "Display_Rep", &temp_any);
DS_dt_close(dataobject, &Ev, Ctx);

  /* we are done, get rid of the shared memory area */
  if (destroy_shm (SHMKEY) == ERROR)
          {
          log_event(FATAL,"install_data: could not
                  destroy_shm \n");
          exit (ERROR);
```

```
                }

}

/* Standard routine to connect to shared memory */
void *connect_shm (int key, int size)
{
        int i;

            sh_info.key = key;

        /* get the shared memory area */
        if ((sh_info.shmid = shmget ((key_t)key, size ,  IPC_CREAT  ))
            < 0)
                {
                perror ("connect_shm: shmget");
                return (NULL);
                }

        /* attach to the area */
        if ((sh_info.sh_ptr = (sh_data *)shmat (sh_info.shmid, (char *)
                0 , 0)) == (sh_data *) -1)
                {
                perror ("connect_shm: shmat");
                return (NULL);
                }

        /* return the pointer to the area on success */
        return (sh_info.sh_ptr);
}

/* Standard routine to remove shared memory when not needed */
int destroy_shm (int key)
{

        /* check if request fits our stored info */
        if (key != sh_info.key)
                {
                printf("destroy_shm: invlid key %ld\n",key);

                return (ERROR);
                }

        /* call to detach the area */
        if (shmdt ((char *)sh_info.sh_ptr) < 0)
                {
                perror ("destroy_shm: shmdt");

                return (ERROR);
```

```
        }
/* call to remove the area */
if (shmctl (sh_info.shmid, IPC_RMID, (struct shmid_ds *) 0) < 0)
        {
        perror ("destroy_shm: shmctl");
         return (ERROR);
        }

    return (SUCCESS);
}
```

An alternative wrapping approach is a layer of OMG IDL functions that directly access the shared memory (bypassing the ORB). With this approach, performance advantages are retained.

Wrapping with Dynamic Queries

Dynamic queries are very similar to scripts in that they provide for communication with a system that provides a rich query and update mechanism via some other language. The language can be standard, such as SQL92, or a vendor's proprietary language. Query languages differ somewhat from general scripting languages because they usually have a complex syntax, act on some schema or database, and support a wide range of data types.

Integration with systems that support query language access often involves some sort of parsing capability, regardless of whether the client or the object implementation generates the query. In DISCUS, if the client generates the query, the client either knows the language or has used the metadata object to retrieve sample scripts from the object implementation. The client then can parse the scripts and, using a simple GUI, prompt the user for input. (Alternatively, the client may insert the proper values without user intervention.) In this case, the client must use the query or execute operations.

If the object implementation generates the query, the client still may use the simpler exchange operation as in the examples just cited. The object implementation must then extract the appropriate properties from the data object, create and fill the script, and use the proper query mechanism provided by the legacy or database application to manipulate the data.

Today many middleware products provide their own dialect query language. In turn, middleware products convert queries into other dialects that enable communication with different database products (e.g., Sybase, Oracle, Informix, etc.). These products usually offer a rich API. Instead of developing separate servers for each database product, a system integrator can develop one implementation that wraps the middleware product and accesses all of the databases. With the proper metadata object support, which product it is communicating with can be transparent to the client.

Wrapping with IPC

Systems use many more mechanisms to provide for interprocess communication (IPC). For example, IPC can be in the form of streams, first-in first-out (FIFOs), semaphores, and message queues. These mechanisms can be handled similar to the way we have handled sockets, RPCs, or shared memory. They all provide some mechanism for reading or writing data. We have purposefully not discussed them in great detail here because they usually are used exclusively for control. As a result, they often have size limits that preclude using them for data interchange.

Wrapping with Macros

During one of our integration efforts, we wrapped a commercial off-the-shelf application by providing a macro interface. Using the DISCUS framework and data objects of different types, the macro interface differentiates between different types of data and handles them seamlessly.

The application was Applix by Applixware. This product is an integrated package that provides word processing, graphics, spreadsheet, e-mail, and other services. In our testbed the product was intended to provide the user with report generation capability using the word processor portion. The primary requirement was to allow the user to import data objects of different types (e.g., text, images, maps, etc.) into the word processor.

Applixware provided several features that made the integration simpler—an API, a rich macro language, an IPC mechanism using sockets, and a linking service. The linking service enables the linking of imported items to files in the file system.

To complete the interface, clients and servers had to be developed. The server communicates with the ORB on one side and with the Applix user interface on the other. When the server receives a data object, it checks its type and stores the object persistently using a randomly generated filename. Depending on the type, the appropriate property is "stripped out." The property data is extracted from the object and written to a file with the same name, but with a different suffix. If the data object is of type Image or Map, the display representation is extracted; if the object is of type text, the textual field is extracted. The server then activates the internal Applix socket interface and passes the filename of the extracted property and its type. Applix macros then receive the data, filter it through the proper conversion filters, import the data into the open document, and link the data to the file in which it resides on the file system. A listening macro is always running in the background when a word processing window is active. The background macro is ready to receive incoming requests from the server.

When a user double-clicks on an item, Applix can activate a macro that uses a file linked to the item. This feature allowed us to activate a client that reencapsulates the linked file back into the data object and send it via to the ORB to the application that created it.

These capabilities can be implemented in other ways. For example, it is not always possible for an implementation to have a back-end server waiting for incoming data. In this case, similar functionality can be added with the addition of menu picks within the application. Each menu pick can activate a client that is data object-type dependent. The client then can connect to another application, retrieve a data object, and import it as appropriate into the application using the correct macro. A developer can choose from almost endless combinations. Another variation could make use of both configurations and provide a menu pick that incorporates most of the server code to handle different types of incoming data objects that the client may bring back.

```
/* Various variables to support socket set-up */
    int             sockfd;
    struct stat     stat_buf;
    char            *response;
    int             size;
    char            *filename;
    char            *message;
    char            *env_var;
    char            *hostname;
    int             portnumber;
    struct  {
    long    msg_type;       /* Applix required structure */
    long    type;           /* Applix type of data */
    long    size;           /* the size of the data */
    char    string[256];    /* the file pathname */
    } msg;

    msg.msg_type = 0;       /* always zero */
    msg.type = 2;           /* type string */

....

    /* Open the data object */
    DS_dt_open(dataobject, Ev, Ctx);

    /* Get the property */
    DS_dt_get(dataobject, Ev, Ctx, "Display_Rep", &temp_any);

    /* Write only the property data to a file */
    write_to_file(temp_any, filename);

/* copy the object filename into a message structure */
        msg.size = strlen(filename) + 1;
```

```
        strcpy(msg.string,filename);
        }
/* Get APPLIX_SERVER_PORT */
        env_var = (char*) getenv("APPLIX_SERVER_PORT");
        portnumber = atoi(env_var);

/* Create Client Connection */
        sockfd = create_client_socket(hostname, (unsigned short)
                        portnumber);
        if (sockfd == -1)
        {
        fprintf(stderr, "client: create_client_socket() failed\n");
        exit(-1);
        }

/* send the message structure across the socket to Applix */
        write(sockfd, &msg.msg_type, sizeof(msg.msg_type));
        write(sockfd, &msg.type, sizeof(msg.type));
        write(sockfd, &msg.size, sizeof(msg.size));
        write(sockfd, msg.string, strlen(msg.string)+1 );

/* Close the socket */
        close(sockfd);
}
```

Wrapping with Header Files

The CORBA and framework technology provide a very effective integration capability, and we have been very successful in integrating applications in a very short time (days or weeks). However, an ORB cannot always be used. For example, the integration may require working on an older platform for which there is no ORB support. Or it may not be cost effective for a project to purchase an ORB product. The project may require a simple integration between two applications on a single system and may not even require distribution. In such cases, even IDL by itself provides a tremendous benefit in creating a well-described and controlled interface between the two pieces of software.

One of the outputs of the IDL compiler are the header files that define the prototypes appropriate for the particular language. Developers can use these header files when building their clients and servers simply to define their API. In some cases it is beneficial to use the header file even if the entire application is in a single executable. For example, an application may have a data retrieval back-end and a user interface front-end. If the interface between the two modules is well defined using IDL, when distributing the application is required, the modules can be separated into a client and an object implementation with minimal or no impact on the code.

IMPLEMENTATION TRADE-OFFS FOR OBJECT WRAPPING

In the CORBA environment, developers are presented with a myriad of configuration possibilities. Often the major trade-offs are performance vs. flexibility. As an example, a choice exists between a single server versus multiple servers for a partitionable service, such as data format conversions. In this example, the single server can be used to wrap several conversion libraries. Alternatively, each conversion library can have its own wrapper.

Using a common framework API enables this flexibility. Here's why. Consider these two alternative configurations. First a single server for multiple libraries must act as a conversion broker sort of middleware solution. Each library's API must be translated into a new single API that allows various clients to ask for conversions. This single API may be yet another proprietary API. Second if each library has its own server, each library's API may be simply translated into IDL to make it distributed. With many different APIs, clients are faced with an interoperability problem that forces developers to write custom code.

The availability of a framework with a consistent conversion API provides a common thread that makes the configuration completely transparent. With either type of service, the translation between a library's API is to the common API. It is therefore transparent whether the client is talking to a middleware broker or to a single library server, because in both cases the API is identical. The greatest flexibility is provided when each library has a different server because each server can now be run on a separate machine.

We can analyze several versions of this example and rate their relative flexibility and performance. Each configuration can be given a simple flexibility rating from one to five, with five being most flexible, and each configuration performance can be described by the number of ORB hops.

Each of these server configurations has several alternative performance and flexibility options. Table 8.1 presents a comparison of the options. Because a client may call a known conversion server directly, the table displays results for that case and for the case in which the Trader Service is called at least once to select a conversion service. The column labeled "Convert from A to C via B" takes into account the case where a direct conversion between two formats is not available and another conversion has occurred in between. This case can be extended by adding more intermediate steps.

Table 8.1. Flexibility vs. Option table.

Convert from A to B without trader, with	Convert from A to C via B without trader, with	Flexibility
Option 1 1, 2	1, 4	Poor
Option 2 1, 2	2, 4	Good
Option 3 2, 3 + (?)	3, 4 + (?)	Very Good
Option 4 2, 3 + (?)	3, 4 + (?)	Excellent

Option 1 is a simple conversion server that runs on a single machine. All the conversion libraries are collocated and therefore present very poor configuration flexibility. To convert between two formats, only a single ORB hop is required; two hops are required if the trader is involved. If the conversion is not direct and more formats are involved, this form is most efficient. No matter how many steps are required, if no trader is involved, the server can process all the required conversions immediately and return the final result. If a trader is involved, the number of hops is doubled for each additional conversion.

Option 2 provides somewhat better management because each conversion server is separate and can be placed on different systems. For the case of a single conversion, it is as efficient as Option 1 because only a single server is involved. For multistep conversions without a trader, there is a slight cost to access each separate server; however, if a trader is involved, there is no added cost to access each server or to access the same server multiple times.

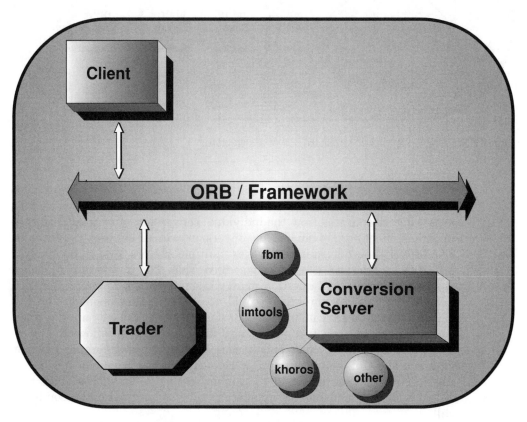

Figure 8.4. Conversion service, single server architecture.

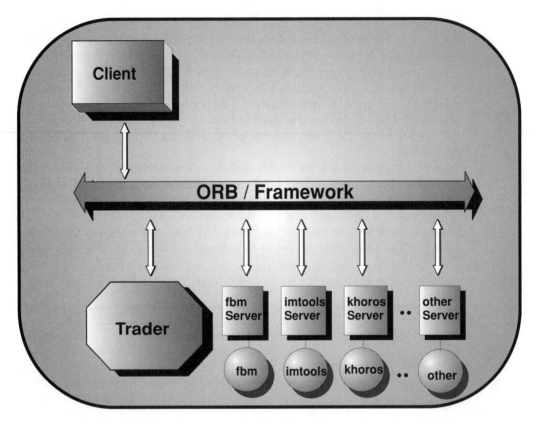

Figure 8.5. Conversion service, multiple server architecture.

Options 3 and 4 involve the addition of a conversion broker (Figures 8.6 and 8.7). The broker provides more flexibility because the service selection reasoning is separated from the individual conversion servers and from the clients. A client simply can ask for conversion to occur between two formats. The broker then determines whether multiple servers need to be involved and if the conversion is a multistep conversion. The number of trader accesses is followed by a question mark to denote that it is implementation dependent. A conversion broker could access the trader upon startup and cache all the necessary information, or it could access the trader each time a conversion is required. Option 4 is most flexible because it allows the placement of conversion servers on separate systems. The difference between Option 4 and Option 3 is extra network overhead and the delay in completing an ORB request between two systems instead of an ORB request on a single system. Often this cost amounts to several hundred milliseconds per call.

Table 8.1 presents only some of the wide range of possible configurations. System administrators and managers can determine which servers can be colocated or replicated in order to improve performance and reduce the number of ORB and network hops.

COMMENTS

Object wrapping is an eclectic practice involving many integration mechanisms. The selection of an object-wrapping technique is driven by the characteristics of the preexisting component and the integration goals. Generally, we follow the path of least resistance, seeking to utilize preexisting entry points before resorting to modification of legacy software. If substantial modifications to legacy are required, it may be more cost effective to create an entirely new module. Object wrapping enables the use of more preexisting software. This can have substantial cost benefits compared to the develop-

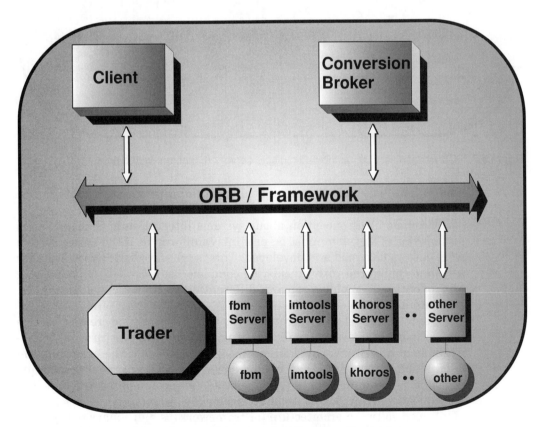

Figure 8.6. Conversion service, multiple server architecture with a broker.

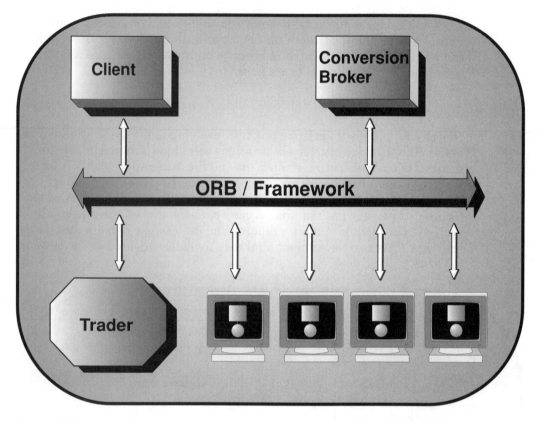

Figure 8.7. Conversion service, distributed multiple server architecture with a broker.

ment of new software. For example, accreditation and testing costs can be saved.

A common misconception about systems integration is that interfaces at all levels of a system must be pristinely uniform, as if the entire system were custom designed and developed. This is an unrealistic expectation for a system configured with preexisting components. Most sets of preexisting components will employ a range of different integration technologies, APIs, and data formats.

A successful system integrator works with diversity and creates the system without extensive software rewriting. Software architecture and frameworks help this process by defining the design goals for the encapsulation of each subsystem. Instead of implementing the mapping from one unique component to another, the integrator builds to a common abstraction that embodies the life-cycle goal architecture for the system.

A good software architecture (or framework) is a visionary design that should never be compromised for the convenience of a particular component integration. If it were compromised, the architecture could become component dependent and embody characteristics such as brittleness, premature obsolescence, and lack of component isolation. Architecture design issues should be addressed, but not in a component-dependent manner. Since each preexisting component has its own unique way of integrating with other software, object wrappers provide the impedance match between component-specific integration approaches and the uniform integration approach defined by the software architecture.

9

Systems
Integration
Guidance

This chapter is an overall summary of some key lessons learned and advice for executives, managers, architects, and developers for the use of CORBA. The advice is applicable to non-CORBA architectures.

This information is for those people who have accepted the benefits of CORBA and are seeking the next steps toward CORBA usage. We wish to provide timely guidance that will help them avoid pitfalls and maximize their successes.

Many managers, architects, and developers are just becoming aware of CORBA. They have heard CORBA briefings, seen convincing demonstrations, but they are unsure as to how to proceed. More important, they are concerned about the risks involved, and they have basic questions and concerns, such as:

- Is CORBA technology ready for operational system development?
- Which CORBA product should I use? What if that vendor changes the product?
- What is the maturity of this technology and what are its shortcomings?
- What problems does CORBA really solve?
- How can I utilize CORBA standards? Emerging new standards?
- What should we do now? in the future?

THE IMPORTANCE OF SOFTWARE ARCHITECTURE

Guideline #1: Improve your *software architecture* during your migration to CORBA; improved software architecture will provide the primary benefits.

The primary benefit of the migration to CORBA is software architecture reengineering. Migration to a well-designed software architecture has many potential benefits and can provide qualities such as:

- Interoperability between components and with external systems.
- Extensibility through the system life cycle to add, modify, and replace capabilities.
- Component interchangeability including insulation from product-specific dependencies and proprietary implementations.
- Integration and operations and management cost savings—the architecture's key role is to minimize these costs.

The creation and installation of well-designed software architectures are essential activities in the development of information systems with long life cycles. Over a long life cycle (six years or more), it is reasonable to expect that

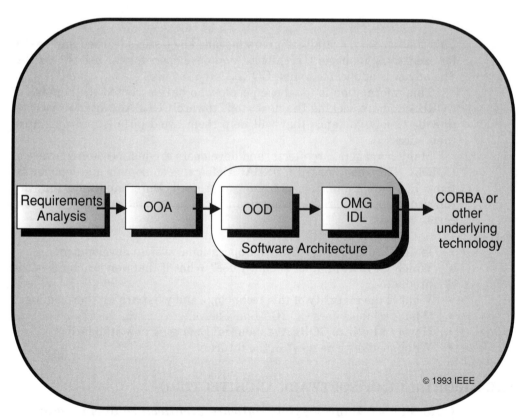

Figure 9.1. Insertion of OMG IDL into design process.

hardware and software components will be replaced as technology evolves toward higher performance and greater functionality at lower costs. The software architecture is that "integration glue" that remains in the system, regardless of how the external components are modified, interchanged, and extended.

Architecture Relation to Cost

Software architecture design is intimately related to life cycle cost. A well-designed software architecture represents a valuable investment that yields adaptability to new requirements and technologies over a system's life cycle. A poorly designed or ad hoc software architecture is a hidden liability that will demand payment whenever the system evolves. Undocumented or poorly designed systems have numerous interdependencies (i.e., spaghetti code) that make them costly to modify, maintain, and extend. For example, there could be two implementations of a set of requirements that differ in the quality of their underlying architectures. These systems could appear identical to the end users, but they could have dramatically different life cycle costs.

CORBA Relation to Architecture

CORBA is an implementation technology and a set of related standards. If used wisely, it can help achieve many software architecture benefits. CORBA provides encapsulation tools, such as Object Management Group Interface Definition Language (OMG IDL), that support the realization of good software architectures. CORBA-based software architectures support process relocation, automatic server activation, and other implementation features. However, just as it is easy to create bad programs with good programming languages, it is not at all difficult to create bad architectures and poor integration solutions using CORBA.

CORBA Reengineering Process

The migration to CORBA can be part of a larger software reengineering activity, as shown in Figure 9.1. The requirements analysis and object-oriented analysis processes can provide the analysis of business processes independent of automation decisions. The object-oriented development and OMG IDL processes can define custom modules and the software architecture. OMG IDL is an appropriate notation for software architectures whose usage is independent of underlying CORBA implementation. CORBA is utilized during the code development phase because it is an implementation technology as opposed to a design process.

MARKET AND STANDARDS-BASED DECISIONS

Guidance #2: Make decisions using *market and standards awareness;* lack of awareness can easily lead you to dead ends.

You can gain substantial leverage by aligning your technology strategies with commercial market directions and standards initiatives. By aligning your strategies, you can leverage the commercial market's investments in products and technologies that you can incorporate into your activities as they are introduced. If you stray too far from the prevailing trends, then your investments must stand on their own; in this age of increasingly complex technologies, that's too much exposure for all but the most generously funded high-risk activities.

Making Objective Decisions

Product selection should almost always be based on an objective process as opposed to a subjective process. It is very easy to make technology decisions based on subjective influences, and this is almost always a mistake. In fact, certain marketing strategies are directed specifically at capturing subjective influences, such as executive management biases toward a product and its competitors.

Objective processes include the brainstorming of criteria and alternatives that are scored and compared. With access to the right expertise, a simple trade-off can be conducted in less than a day for most product selections. More elaborate decision processes are possible and necessary based on the importance of the decision, such as the amount of resources at risk. Electronic meetings are a particularly effective mechanism for gathering requirements, ranking criteria, and scoring alternatives, but other technology-independent processes are available, such as Kepner-Tregoe. We have conducted such trade-offs for advanced parallel processors, groupware products, CORBA object request brokers, and other technology markets. These markets were immature when these trade-offs were undertaken, and other organizations used immaturity as a rationale for subjective product selection—even though the immaturity of the technology is precisely why a systematic selection is required.

One important result of the objective process is that it clarifies subjective influences quickly, as evidenced by objections to the recommendations. Conscious decisions then can be made to accept any resulting risks. The objective process also provides a documentation trail for these decisions, which can be leveraged into other decisions.

Standards and Technology Cycle

There is a strong correlation between the market directions and ongoing standards activities, as shown in Figure 9.2. We are not limiting our discus-

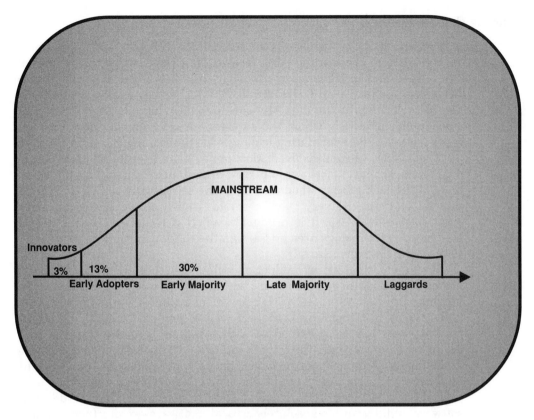

Figure 9.2. Standards and technology adoption cycle.

sion to formal standards groups, but also consider voluntary standards (such as CORBA) and alliances (such as the Common Open Software Environment [COSE]). A technology moves through various phases of acceptance during its market cycle [Halliwell, 93]. Initial innovators are the first to accept the technology. The most important phase of technology acceptance involves the early adopters, who are the first to deploy technologies to end users. These early adopters are organizations that first experience the benefits of the technology and use it to gain a technological advantage in their systems [Halliwell, 93]. They provide the first case studies of technology payoffs and educate the mainstream market as to its benefits. The early adopters also work with the commercial market to put standards activities in place. Mainstream adoption proceeds in parallel with the first standards adoptions. Finally, the laggards extend the life of post-mainstream technologies. In this context, this guidance addresses the early adopters and early majority, who are the key groups assessing CORBA in this phase of its acceptance.

Leading Edge Awareness

It is important to know where your component technologies are positioned with respect to the leading edge. The leading edge is the initial technology release that is accepted by the early innovators who experiment with technology for its own sake [Halliwell, 93]. Technology readiness can be assessed by looking at the date of technology introduction, the market size, the supplier offerings, whom the suppliers are, whom the users are, and other factors. When evaluating leading edge positioning, consider the complete set of technologies involved. Most projects can tolerate very few leading edge technologies (at most two or three) without incurring unacceptable risk; most of the technologies should come from the mainstream. The risks can interact and escalate very quickly as additional leading edge technologies are incorporated. Also, it is prudent to select a technical backup in each leading edge technology area and design the software architecture to adapt to the technical backup easily.

When adopting a new product or technology, there is an implicit commitment of substantial resources. The least of the costs may be the actual purchase price of the product; this investment is almost irrelevant compared to the real costs. Depending on the scale of your project, formal training costs for developers can easily exceed an order of magnitude more than the product price. End-user training is perhaps two orders of magnitude or more. Including development, system extension, and operations and management, total life cycle costs might exceed three or more orders of magnitude more than the product price. This is one of the key reasons why a well-designed software architecture is absolutely critical. Software architecture can mitigate your risks by isolating the potential negative consequences of individual products and leading edge technologies. Because of the substantial costs involved in product and technology adoption, it is important to invest upfront in a thorough product assessment.

If a technology is too close to the leading edge, then investment is very risky. In our experience, it is likely that product-dependent code will be throwaway because early offerings are not likely to be supported in an upwardly compatible manner. Technologies that are too far in advance of the market do not yield any commercial leverage because the industry has not committed to a specific direction. Technologies in this category are acceptable for basic research and very early prototyping efforts that are known to be throwaway.

An appropriate leading edge technology, for an early adopter, is one that can produce real benefits without too much risk and cost due to the technology's immaturity. Typical inconveniences due to immaturity include product bugs, inadequate development tools, product instability, inadequate documentation, and so forth. These inconveniences can lead to project delays, unpredictable labor costs, and potential lack of functionality.

An expedient way to evaluate a specific product is to request and peruse its technical documentation, such as reference manuals, developer's guides, and user's guides. A software product description or release notes that list configuration requirements should be scrutinized very carefully and compared to the target platform environment. Also, most suppliers maintain a bug list for each product; in some cases it can be obtained through nondisclosure.

A more thorough way to evaluate a product is through the vendor's training course. Two training perspectives are required: architecture impacts and development environment. A competent software architect can cover both perspectives, but if budget allows, an architect and a developer together make up the ideal product assessment team. An architect can determine how the technology fits within the system, how it impacts architectural issues, and how it might be exploited best in multiple applications. The developer can assess the maturity of the product at the programming level. In

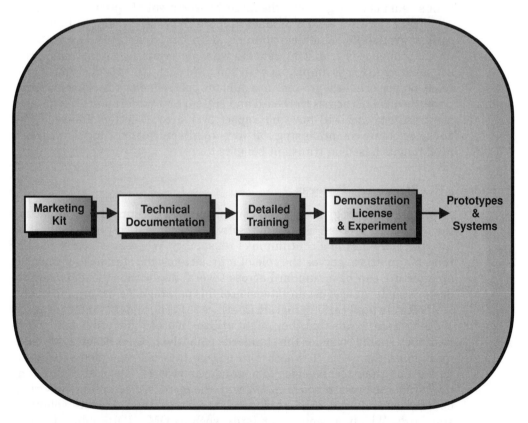

Figure 9.3. Leading edge product assessment.

our experience, this level of product assessment cannot be obtained through briefings, demonstrations, demo disks, and literature review. In fact, this level of marketing information is intended to influence management decision makers and sometimes can be misleading. A product demonstration license is an appropriate follow-up to the product training course. Once the architecture issues have been resolved and a development capability has been established, a product demonstration experiment will yield additional details that are specific to the application environment, such as interproduct compatibilities.

Mainstream Awareness

With respect to non–leading edge technologies, it is appropriate that technology selections gravitate toward the mainstream. What we are talking about here are choices such as operating systems, programming languages, versions/releases, standards, and other such selections. In most cases, the mainstream choices give you the largest assortment of options, the best independent software vendor product support, the best development tools, the earliest availability of new capabilities, and other advantages. Beware of the undue influence of transient benefits when determining mainstream product selections. For example, as with software architecture, decisions based solely on performance grounds are dubious, as technology performance continues to advance across the board and any current performance advantages are transient and will have no impact over a total system life cycle. We advise avoiding compromising software architecture or risking mainstream investments based on transient benefits.

Impacting the Standards Process

An advanced strategy goes beyond simple market alignment into impacting the standards process. Standards, software architectures, and application interfaces are part of a continuum of reusability. Whereas a locally popular reusable interface serves the role of a project-specific standard, a reusable architecture can be a standard across several application systems, and industry standards are just an extension of this paradigm across organizations.

Software application program interface (API) designers should be aware of existing standards that they might utilize. In areas that are not standardized, they should consider the standards potential of their designs. Management must choose as to whether to pursue the risk-reduction strategy of forwarding their technologies to a standards process. The cost of pursuing the standards processes is dropping with the increased acceptance of virtual enterprises and consortia-based standards bodies that generate voluntary standards. Widely accepted standards, such as OMG IDL, reduce the cost of generating specifications, and streamlined acceptance processes, such as the OMG's request for proposal (RFP) and request for comments (RFC) processes, have reduced the time of standards adoption from many years to one year or less.

Standards investment is a commonplace activity in the commercial community, and it is an emerging activity across end-user communities. Very few commercial software producers do not have standards involvement at some level. Many end users have unique technology leadership and potential for standardizing specialty markets.

The processes required to specify and develop application architectures are very much like those required to develop a quality standards specifications. A good software architecture will provide the robustness benefits of a good standard. For specialty market areas, high-quality software architectures probably should be evolved into standards because they provide technology bridges between the commercial components and the application needs. If a consistent architecture is deployed across multiple application systems, then it enlarges the market for a given technology solution and reduces risks for potential suppliers as well as providing an economy of scale. The elevation of application architectures to standards is the ultimate seal

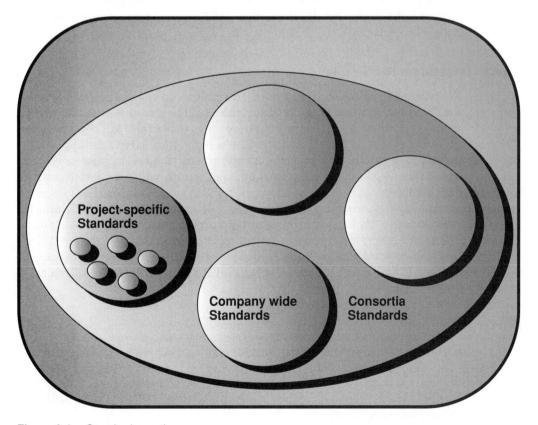

Figure 9.4.   Standards continuum.

of credibility and risk reduction for both the consumers and suppliers in a specialty market.

The OMG is pursuing the adoption of specialty market specifications in its Common Facilities Task Force and end-user track.

PRODUCT INDEPENDENCE

Guideline #3: Depend on the standard, not the product

The primary role of standards is risk reduction for both suppliers and consumers of a technology. Standards enhance the credibility of a technology market; interoperability and portability are secondary priorities. Structured Query Language (SQL) is a prime example, where the credibility benefits of the standard created a major market, but the interoperability and portability gaps are so significant that they have created a niche market for middleware vendors bridging the gaps.

In the case of CORBA, there is significant movement toward an interoperable and portable technology market. X/Open is creating an interoperability test suite, and virtually the entire UNIX and PC market has pledged to support CORBA.

How to Depend on the Standard

We advise CORBA users to write their application code based on the standard and not on proprietary product features. The goal is to insulate investments in application software from product specifics that will change as the products evolve; the standard provides a more stable basis for application code. Users should identify product-specific extensions or gaps in compliance, then develop layering code that isolates application code from product dependencies.

We have successfully implemented this approach in DISCUS, and its usage has greatly increased our ability to port to other ORB products and to successive generations of the same product as it evolves (see Chapter 7). This layering approach has even been used successfully on several occasions to support DISCUS API interfaces layered over RPCs, sockets, shared memory, and so forth.

USING OMG IDL

Guideline #4: Use OMG IDL for Specifying Software Architecture

Start using OMG IDL for specifying software architectures now. It is a highly portable, technology-independent tool that yields many benefits for the software architect.

OMG IDL is a key component of the CORBA standard. We believe that OMG IDL is as fundamental and significant as Backus-Naur Form has been as a computing standard. Some people have called OMG IDL the "standard for writing other standards." OMG IDL enables the specification of APIs in a language- and platform-neutral manner and allows an architect, library writer, or standards author to define implicitly multiple programming language bindings for a specification. OMG IDL has gained mainstream acceptance from groups such as the X Consortium, the Open Software Foundation, the International Standards Organization ODP Trader working group, X/Open, and many others.

OMG IDL has many advantages compared to a typical interface control document (ICD). OMG IDL is independent of Computer Aided Software Engineering (CASE) notations. OMG IDL defines error handling, including user defined errors and operation specific errors. OMG IDL has a complete type definition system compatible with modern programming languages. It is also object oriented, supporting encapsulation, polymorphism, and multiple inheritance. The OMG standards defined in OMG IDL provide a set of baseline definitions for commonplace operations such as event notification and name retrieval that can be reused and extended for use in application architectures.

The utilization of OMG IDL is independent of the underlying implementation technology. IDL interfaces can be layered on top of library functions, remote procedure calls (RPCs), object request brokers (ORBs), and other underlying approaches. For example, a well-defined mapping exists between the CORBA and the Distributed Computing Environment (DCE), as adopted in the CORBA 2.0 combined submission. Layering code can be reused readily by multiple client and service applications. The advantages of uniformly defined, technology-independent architectures can greatly outweigh the cost of taking the precaution of using layering code to provide isolation.

QUALITY SOFTWARE ARCHITECTURE

Guideline #5: Strive for a well-designed software architecture

We advise having a software architecture and investing in the quality of the architecture; such investment is likely to pay for itself many times over the system life cycle.

A simple analogy can explain these concepts effectively. Consider the case of a household closet. A bad architecture is like a messy overcrowded closet. The contents are put together in an ad hoc manner; it is difficult to separate the pieces; and there is no obvious way to add new components without exacerbating the mess. During the life cycle the mess just seems to get worse until you are ready to put in a substantial investment of time to clean it up. A good architecture is like a well-organized closet, replete with

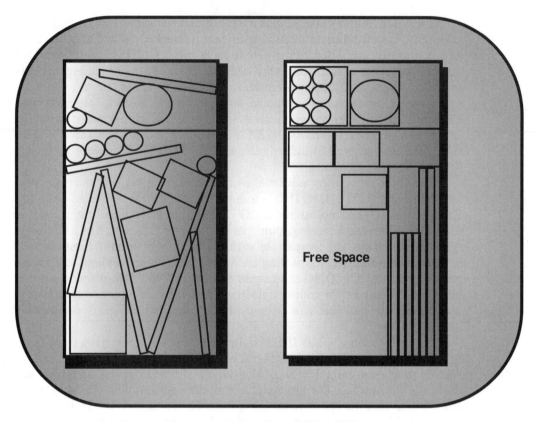

Figure 9.5. An architecture analogy: Messy closet vs. clean closet.

shelving systems and various storage containers that organize the space. A well-organized closet is easy to use and easy to maintain. It can accommodate more items than a closet without space organizers, and if it's done properly, it can flexibly support changing needs of the users as the contents evolve (as seasons, fashions, and hobbies change).

Key Architecture Qualities: Stability and Cost Minimization

The two most essential characteristics of a good architecture are stability and cost minimization.

A stable design implies that the architect has successfully supported the application functionality without overdependency on the component implementation specifics. The architecture should have a plan for system evolution that specific documented features supporting extensibility exhibit. Extensibility needs to be balanced with other factors; many architectures also go too far in supporting flexibility.

Minimizing cost is the primary benefit of software architecture. The software architecture minimizes cost by providing clean, well-documented interfaces between system components and by isolating components from unnecessary interdependencies. The architecture first reduces cost during the initial system development by simplifying the complexity of component integration. Good architecture simplifies system interfaces that need to be understood by each developer, minimizing programmer training and the size, cost, and complexity of the integration code. The architecture continues to moderate costs as the system evolves during the life cycle. Each time the system needs to be extended or maintained, the architecture is a living design that limits the effects of changes across component boundaries.

Iterative Design

A good architecture must be developed iteratively in concert with prototyping. The prototyping experience provides essential lessons learned that help shape the architecture. The architecture evolves as the application problem is better understood, through successive prototype iterations. A top-down specification process is an inadequate approach to architecture design that will lack robustness when implemented.

SYSTEMS INTEGRATION PRIORITIES

Guideline #6: Keep architecture priorities in focus

Keep your architecture goals in perspective with respect to methodology priorities and know how and where to accept compromises in the system implementation.

The purpose of technology is to satisfy application needs in a cost-effective manner. Object orientation is a technical and research field that has many ardent proponents, and many conflicting notations, and is based on many alternative viewpoints. Outspoken object methodologists dictate the values of our technical culture. We have met many engineers who are intimidated by this, and it is easy for them to be more concerned about the methodological correctness of their solution than the true technical benefits that it provides. In our viewpoint, the question "Does it save development and maintenance costs?" is much more important than the question: "Is it really object oriented?" Object orientation someday will have a successor, most likely within the life cycles of end-user systems that we are architecting today. We believe that architectures should not be wholly dependent on a single methodology but should represent good commonsense design and implementation judgments that will survive changes in methodology trends.

Another misconception concerns CORBA. Many people believe that when you adopt CORBA, you can forget everything you know about remote procedure calls, sockets, and other networking layers; that all software will have a clean and nice interface directly to the object request broker. In the far-distant future, this might well be possible. In practice, this has not been our experience. In any integrated architecture comprising a mixture of new and preexisting components, there will be some (perhaps a great deal of) inelegant integration code. For example, different vendors choose different API approaches (open network computing, distributed computing environment, sockets, language specific APIs, no APIs); these must be dealt with on their terms in order to build a system. CORBA's role in the software architecture is to allow the developers to hide the differences between these implementations, so that access to disparate services is consistent, regardless of the component-specific technologies involved. For example, a system comprising six components typically will require six product specific integration approaches; but CORBA enables the architect and developer to map them all to one consistent level, so that integration of a seventh component will require only integration with the CORBA-based architecture, not the six other unique API approaches.

Acronyms

ANSI	American National Standards Institute
API	Application Program Interface
ASCII	American Standard code for Information Interchange
BNF	Backus-Naur Form
BOA	Basic Object Adapter
CASE	Computer Aided Software Engineering
CCITT	Consultative Committee for International Telephone & Telegraph
CLOS	Common Lisp Object System
CMW	Compartmented Mode Workstation
COM	Common Object Model
CORBA	Common Object Request Broker Architecture
COSE	Common Open Software Environment
COSS	Common Object Services Specifications
DAC	Discretionary Access Control
DCE	Distributed Computing Environment
DDE	Dynamic Data Exchange
DII	Dynamic Invocation Interface
DISA	Defense Information Systems Agency
DLL	Dynamic Linked Library
ECMA	European Computer Manufacturers Association
EEI	External Environment Interface
FIPS	Federal Information Processing Standards
GIS	Geographic Information System
GKS	Graphics Kernel System
GSS-API	Generic Security Service Application Programming Interface

ICD	Interface Control Document
IDL	Interface Definition Language
IEEE	Institute of Electrical and Electronics Engineers
IETF	Internet Engineering Task Force
IR	Interface Repository
ISO	International Standards Organization
ISO ODP	ISO Open Distributed Processing
MAC	Mandatory Access Control
MLS	Multi Level Security
MVC	Model View Controller
NIH	National Institute of Health
NIST	National Institute of Standards and Technology
NSA	National Security Agency
OA	Object Adapter
ODMG	Object Database Management Group
OGIS	Open GIS Interoperability Specification
OLE	Object Linking and Embedding
OMAG	Object Management Architecture Guide
OMG	Object Management Group
ONC	Open Network Computing
ORB	Object Request Broker
OSF	Open Software Foundation
PHIGS	Programmer's Hierarchical Image Graphics System
POSIX	Portable Operating System Interface for Computer Environments
RFC	Request for Comments
RFP	Request for Proposal
RPC	Remote Procedure Call
SCO	Santa Cruz Operation
SOM	System Object Model
SQL89	Structured Query Language 1989
SQL92	Structured Query Language 1992
TCB	Trusted Computing Base
TCP/IP	Transmission Control Protocol / Internet Protocol
TCSEC	Trusted Computer System Evaluation Criteria
UDT	Uniform Data Transfer
VMS	Virtual Memory System
WAIS	Wide Area Information Services
XPG	X/Open Portability Guide

Appendix:
ORB Products

Many CORBA-compliant object request broker (ORB) products are available today. CORBA-compliant products that the authors have used and evaluated include:

- Digital Equipment Corporation's ObjectBroker, formerly called Application Control Architecture Services (ACAS)
- SunSoft Distributed Objects Everywhere (DOE)
- IBM System Object Model (SOM)
- IONA Technology Limited's Orbix™
- HP ORB+

The history of these products dates from the origins of CORBA. The authors of the Object Management Group's (OMG's) CORBA standard included DEC, SunSoft, Object Design, NCR, HyperDesk, and Hewlett-Packard. Early in the CORBA proposal process, DEC and HyperDesk submitted a joint proposal to the OMG for the dynamic invocation interface (DII). The other CORBA authors submitted the static interface features based on the Interface Definition Language (IDL). The OMG formed a consensus by including both static and dynamic interfaces into CORBA. As expected, the early products from DEC and HyperDesk supported only the DII. The market has matured since that time. To be competitive, all current CORBA products support OMG IDL and have static interfaces. SunSoft facilitated OMG IDL adoption by offering the source code for an OMG IDL compiler front-end in the public domain, as distributed by the OMG (via Internet ftp from omg.org).

Hyperdesk was one of the early entries into the ORB market. Compared to today's ORB products, the HyperDesk product, the Distributed Object Management System (HD-DOMS), was never more than a proprietary middleware solution, since it had no support for OMG IDL. HyperDesk's product was withdrawn from the market in the spring of 1994. The product had some serious deficiencies: for example, it lacked robustness and stability, due to many product revisions during migration toward standards compliance. Because HyperDesk was a relatively small company (about 25 people) and its product really never gained acceptance, the product had to be withdrawn. This event offers us some important lessons. Because HyperDesk required extensive dependence on proprietary APIs, application code developed for the product was not portable to other ORBs. Companies that made substantial code investments in proprietary HyperDesk interfaces had to discard and rewrite virtually all of their code.

In fact, Anderson Consulting has estimated that it requires about 18 months of calendar time to migrate from one proprietary middleware package to another. Interestingly, Anderson's 1994 top pick for the best middleware product, Expersoft's Xshell, now has comprehensive CORBA support.

In the same timeframe as the HD-DOMS product introduction, the authors were building the initial prototypes of DISCUS. (See Chapter 7.) At that time, we had the option of choosing HyperDesk or DEC ACAS for any level of commercial CORBA support. Our initial choice was ACAS. It was an obvious choice based on our exposure to both products in the vendors' programmer training courses. Although the level of CORBA support for both products was similar in 1992, DEC clearly had a more stable, mature product that would provide the best support for system development. HyperDesk had superior support for object-oriented concepts, which was the key product discriminator for some users.

In order to protect our DISCUS code from proprietary dependence, we took the extra step of writing our own OMG IDL compiler based on CORBA's specifications for the C binding [OMG, 92a]. This step would not be necessary today because OMG IDL is bundled with all CORBA ORB products. We also created an OMG IDL layer on top of all exposed proprietary product features. These precautions paid off in both the short and the long term. In the short term, DISCUS's OMG IDL framework enabled parallel development of DISCUS applications and legacy integration using object wrappers. In the long term, DISCUS has been highly portable between CORBA-compliant ORB products. Fully operational DISCUS systems exist on both IONA Orbix and DEC ObjectBroker. Applications port easily between the ORBs. The DISCUS framework has been compiled and tested on other ORBs as well, such as SunSoft DOE.

In general, software architectures should be specified in OMG IDL, and most of the code should rely on these APIs. Where direct ORB interfaces are exposed, standards compliance should be evaluated and layering code

Table A.1. CORBA ORB products and OLE platform support.

Product	MS Windows 3.1	Mac System 7.0	IBM O/S 2	DEC VMS	MS Windows NT	UNIX				
						SunSoft Solaris	IBM AIX	HP-UX	DG UX	SGI IRIX
Sunsoft DOE EDR-2.0β										
DEC ObjectBroker 2.5										
HP ORB Plus β										
HP Distributed Smalltalk										
IBM SOMobjects 2.0		β								
IONA Orbix										
Microsoft OLE2										

Key β = Beta and Pre-Beta Test

should be provided as needed to protect application software. It is preferable to be dependent on custom interfaces (that you control) than on proprietary nonstandard interfaces (that vendors control). To maximize portability and multilanguage support, custom interfaces should be specified in OMG IDL.

Table A.1 compares some existing ORB implementations. It shows that there is strong support for CORBA standards. Object services are an emerging standards area that is important to technology users.

SUNSOFT DISTRIBUTED OBJECTS EVERYWHERE (DOE)

This section reviews SunSoft's Distributed Objects Everywhere (DOE) project's Early Developer's Release #1 (EDR-1). SunSoft's first CORBA technology release, DOE EDR-1, was available to selected early developers. EDR-1 was a pre-beta test technology. SunSoft has had subsequent technology releases based on EDR-1, including a second version, EDR-2, and an Object Development Framework (ODF). SunSoft is also working in an alliance with NEXT corporation to develop a CORBA-based version of the NEXTSTEP application development framework, called OPENSTEP.

SunSoft's DOE's significance is due to the importance of Sun's workstations to end-user organizations. Some organizations are reluctant to use CORBA until it is available as bundled technology—delivered as an integral part of the operating system. When SunSoft announced DOE, it promised to deliver a quality implementation of CORBA bundled with the Solaris operating system. Similar plans announced by other major UNIX vendors involved the Common Open Software Environment (COSE) alliance, including HP, IBM, SCO, Univel, and DEC.

SunSoft has been an influential supporter of the OMG process from its inception. SunSoft was an original author of the CORBA specification, and it continues to be a major player in OMG activities. This implies a substantial investment on SunSoft's part, and Sunsoft has assembled an impressive team of computer scientists to create the DOE technology. In EDR-1, this team has proposed some revolutionary innovations to the software environment. DOE EDR-1 is a preliminary view into SunSoft's vision for distributed object technology. In the long term, OMG standard interfaces could supplant all application software interfaces, including the operating system, the windowing system, and software standards. EDR-1 is an interim realization of the vision, which requires the mastery of both old and new paradigms, the legacy software interfaces (UNIX, X), and the CORBA interfaces that allow access to new distributed capabilities. SunSoft held back some capabilities, such as desktop services, from EDR-1 to reduce the overall complexity of the release.

This section assesses some of the key aspects of Sun's revolutionary vision for distributed object computing as embodied in EDR-1. Many of these innovations, such as static interfaces and object services, are defined explicitly in the OMG standards. Other aspects are implicit requirements of the technology that not all vendors have interoperated in their implementations such as threads and support for fine-grained objects. As a whole, DOE EDR-1 is an intriguing experiment into the future of computing.

Some of the interesting issues that EDR-1 raises include:

1. Does the object paradigm provide enough benefits to justify the associated changes in the computing environment?
2. Is CORBA a process simplification for distributed computing, or is it a complete process reengineering for sofware development?

Static Interfaces

Static interfaces use compile-time specifications written in the CORBA Interface Definition Language (IDL). OMG IDL is a syntax for specifying object interfaces that are independent of programming language, operating system, and physical process allocation. An interesting aspect of CORBA is that it does not constrain the underlying implementation behind the IDL interfaces; thus, IDL can be used in a variety of ways: for library function interfaces and for distributed object interfaces. EDR-1 enables utilization of both approaches.

DOE EDR-1 provides IDL static interface support for C and C++. Of the two languages, C++ is the more fully supported interface. The C++ interface is a relatively seamless integration of the C++ object system and CORBA. The EDR-1 IDL compiler generates a header files containing client and server class definitions for the IDL interfaces. One or both header files may be included for implementation of client program, server program, or a combination of client and server functionality. The only area where the CORBA functionality diverges from C++ is in object construction. EDR-1 supports a factory object approach; a special server object is instantiated that has responsibility for creating other objects.

```
// IDL Example
interface obj {
    void func(inout long parm);
    };

// Static Invocation in C++
    objRef server;
    CORBA::Environment ev;
    ....
    server->func(ev, parm_value);
    ....
```

Substantial code simplifications in the client software can be realized by using static interfaces rather than dynamic ones. Static interfaces also provide compile-time checking, which can result in faster development, more reliable code, and more architectural control of the implemented system. In C, static interfaces greatly simplify parameter handling. Compiled IDL can be used to define the native C data structures for the program that are supplied in parameters without conversions to predefined types. The true potential of static interfaces becomes apparent when they are used with C++. Since C++ already supports an object paradigm, IDL interfaces interoperate seamlessly with the C++ object system. In EDR-1, CORBA objects are defined with C++ class definitions, and ORB method invocations are syntactically the same as C++ function invocations. HP's Distributed Smalltalk provides a seamless CORBA IDL static interface in the Smalltalk object environment. Because the CORBA static interfaces are much less expensive to utilize than dynamic interfaces, in practice, 90 percent or more of all programs would probably use static interfaces.

Fine-Grain Objects

Efficiency concerns were a primary consideration in the EDR-1 architecture. Efficiency trade-offs are observable in many aspects of EDR-1. Because EDR-1 was engineered for efficiency, it enables the realization of a wide range of distributed object granularities.

ORB performance is considerably faster than RPC performance levels for comparable operations because DOE is based on a lower, more efficient layer, the Transport Layer Independent (TLI).

The EDR-1 internal architecture includes a Distributed Object Management Facility (DOMF) daemon that resides on each network node. CORBA object handles are opaque, in that the ORB implementor can include product-dependent information and applications should not utilize handle contents.

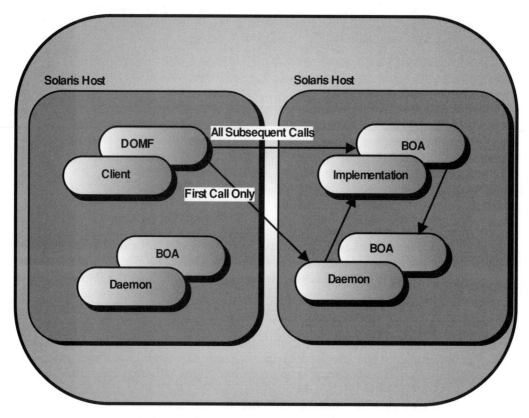

Figure A.1. DOE Distributed Object Management Environment.

In EDR-1, object handles contain node information, internal object references, and implementation definitions (server executable pathname, etc). This enables the DOMF daemons to route invocations transparently, regardless of whether the request is local or remote. An object handle with NULL reference data is a seed pattern for new object instances and is called a DNA object (in reference to its genetic counterpart). EDR-1 object handles are approximately 1KB in size; sample programs typically retain DNA and object handles persistently in flat files. Object migration between nodes is not supported directly in EDR-1 but can be implemented using the EDR-1 utilities for DNA and instance creation.

CORBA object adapters provide the server's interface to the ORB. CORBA 1.1 specifies one object adapter among many possible adapters. The CORBA V1.1 basic object adapter (BOA) comprises a minimal set of server/ORB interfaces. Choice of object adapters is transparent to the clients, and there are a wide range of adapter interfaces tailored to the needs of applications programmers. CORBA minimizes the need for server portability because object location is transparent to clients.

The EDR-1 object adapter supports several forms of object implementation. Single-object servers are supported through the CORBA BOA interfaces. A shared server implementation, called group objects, allows each server process to register several embedded objects with the ORB. Group objects are activated implicitly upon server process activation. Alternatively, individual group objects can be deactivated and reactivated on demand. Another form of shared server, called subobjects, allows a server to manage clusters of light weight objects that share the same interfaces and implementations. Subobjects within in a cluster are deactivated and activated together. Both shared server approaches require the management of a lookup table, which the object adapter uses to match object identifiers with object methods and states.

The trade-off between the different object adapter approaches is due to efficiency. Embedded objects utilize machine resources more efficiently than separate servers, and embedded objects can communicate among their siblings with the efficiency of a shared process and address space. Embedded object facilities require an underlying threads infrastructure.

Threads

Threads are lightweight concurrent processes that execute within a shared address space. Threads are a popular emergent operating system facility with significant impacts for software developers. The Institute of Electrical and Electronics Engineers' POSIX has a draft standard for threads interfaces [POSIX, 93]. One of the POSIX threads implementations, the OSF DCE threads library, is available on several operating systems. POSIX threads are a bundled capability in SunSoft's Solaris 2.X and a pervasive facility in DOE EDR-1. DOE is the first major Sun program to utilize threads.

Threads are a necessary infrastructure for the realization of distributed objects. Future distributed object systems will comprise numerous interoperating objects that will communicate in unanticipated, recursive manners. For client simplicity, most distributed object invocations are synchronous (i.e., blocking); thus, each embedded object must provide an active state to service requests in a timely manner. Without active objects, a distributed object system could deadlock quite easily. Threads are a near-term infrastructure facility that readily provides multiple flows of control.

Threads represent a major paradigm shift for programmers. In a threads environment, programmers use existing languages (i.e., C++) but with dramatically altered semantics: concurrency. To the uninitiated, many new types of errors are possible, such as deadlocks and race conditions [Brinch Hansen, 76]. Causes usually involve subtle changes in code ordering that affect only the program's dynamic behavior. State-of-the-art debugging tools support sequential processing, a much simpler model; and debugging technology to support threads is still in its infancy.

Threads also require new ways to handle libraries and legacy software. Code that is *threads safe* generally can be used without special handling. By default, all other legacy code is unsafe, including important libraries such as libc and MOTIF. Code restructuring for threads safety is expensive. An inexpensive way to integrate unsafe legacy code is with a drastic approach: Use a code-lock operation to block the other threads entirely.

Solaris 2.X and DOE EDR-1 have come a long way toward realizing a comprehensive threads development environment. They provided a threads safe libc and a version of the dbx line-oriented debugger that supports threads. They also provided a graphical memory inspection tool, called mspy, which provides a higher-level view of a complex multiobject application.

Object Services

DOE EDR-1 provides implementations of the OMG's Naming Service and the Event Notification Service. EDR-1 also provides other service implementations that are targeted at future OMG standards, including an association service and a property service. The EDR-1 object services are described in more detail later.

The EDR-1 naming service is a straightforward implementation of the OMG's IDL interfaces. EDR-1 also provides a command-line facility for factory object registration and a convenience function for the retrieval of the initial naming context. These additional capabilities are implemented using the published naming services interfaces, which is consistent with the Object Management Architecture Guide approach of providing services without hidden interfaces.

The EDR-1 event service utilizes event object interfaces from the OMG's Object Event Notification Service and an additional interface for an event channel factory. EDR-1 provides an implementation for the event channel and the event channel factory. EDR-1 event channel servers can support any number of supplier and consumer applications.

The EDR-1 association service provides a capability for defining relationships between objects. The service comprises server objects that retain the object handles of the linked objects. Associations are a fundamental service that can be used to implement many types of object links. For example, associations can be used for desktop object linking and embedding. The association service is useful in combination with other services, such as events to manage relationships.

The EDR-1 properties service is a facility for attaching dynamic information to an object. A set of properties of any type can be attached to an object without changing the object's implementation.

DIGITAL EQUIPMENT OBJECTBROKER

DEC's ObjectBroker is an ORB product that runs across nearly a dozen platforms, such as: DEC Ultrix, DEC VMS, the DEC Alpha's OSF/1, IBM AIX, HP-UX, SunOS, Macintosh System 7.0, and MicroSoft Windows. ObjectBroker has a sophisticated method binding and server binding facility that supports dynamic process allocation in heterogeneous environments. ObjectBroker has facilities that directly support integration with MicroSoft's OLE.

Experience with DEC ObjectBroker

DEC's Application Control Architecture Services (ACAS) was one of the earliest object request brokers (ORBs) on the market. The product has been renamed ObjectBroker.

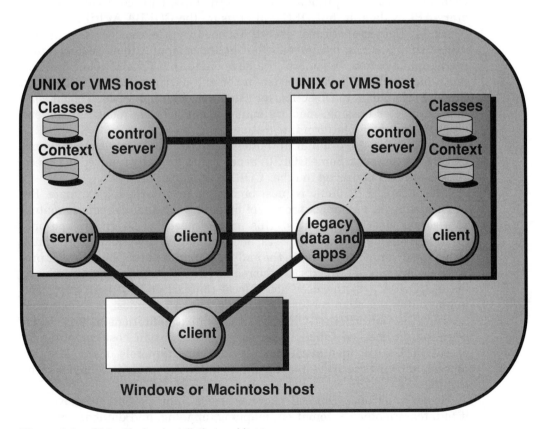

Figure A.2. ObjectBroker installation architecture.

Internally, ACAS uses Transmission Control Protocol/Internet Protocol (TCP/IP) or DECNET networking protocols. Because ACAS is layered on top of sockets instead of remote procedure calls (RPCs), there is added flexibility compared to pure client-server architectures. Server applications that are also active clients can be built easily without using multithreaded code.

ACAS Version 2.1.2 provided two alternative application program interfaces (API). The first is a proprietary DEC API that predates CORBA. The second is a CORBA-compliant API that implements the CORBA Dynamic Invocation Interface. In the ObjectBroker release of ACAS, DEC delivers a fully CORBA 1.2 compliant product, which contains an IDL compiler and supporting IDL static interfaces. Future ObjectBroker releases will again support two APIs, CORBA 2.0 and the MicroSoft Common Object Model.

For the programmer, ObjectBroker training is essential. ObjectBroker training is a five-day hands-on program that teaches ObjectBroker and CORBA programming fundamentals. In the past, DEC covered the proprietary API by default, but DEC will focus on the CORBA API if requested. A five-day class cannot cover everything one needs to know; class examples utilize simple string parameters, but end-user applications require much more sophistication. In general, we have found that ObjectBroker provides much more flexibility than needed in the end-user application framework. Students should go to ObjectBroker class armed with questions about complex parameter passing, memory management policies, reentrant servers, security, and cross-platform integration.

DEC, one of the original authors of CORBA, had significant influence on CORBA contents. Some CORBA aspects that are fully realized in ObjectBroker are still maturing in other CORBA implementations.

ObjectBroker dynamic request binding is an interesting example. Request binding is a complex process of matching the client's request context to a server objects' attributes. This process needs to be understood only for design and debugging purposes; once configured it works transparently, providing dynamic flexibility in the end-user architecture. ObjectBroker provides a hierarchy of contexts: (1) the request has attached context attributes (as in CORBA); (2) the user has a local context; and (3) each host computer contains system-context definitions. When a request is issued from a client, the ObjectBroker ORB uses the context definitions as criteria for selecting the method function, server application, and host computer for execution. User-defined attributes play an important role in the selection process, allowing the system integrator to tailor the dynamic behavior of the architecture.

In our experience, ObjectBroker has been a stable product. We have used it to integrate office automation, mapping, imaging, and database applications across a network. Our ObjectBroker-based prototype has been easy to extend with new application functionality. DEC has provided runtime messages to make debugging straightforward. The ObjectBroker ORB uses a sophisticated method/server binding algorithm, and these messages make it easy to determine what ObjectBroker is doing.

IONA TECHNOLOGIES' ORBIX

IONA Technologies, Ltd. is the developer of Orbix, a CORBA-compliant ORB product. Orbix was the first ORB product released on the market with support for OMG IDL-based static interfaces. Currently Orbix provides only a C++ language support. Orbix was formally produced and delivered in June 1993. Since then the product has built an important niche market in cross-platform CORBA support. The product is unique in that it is the only ORB supporting both Solaris 1 and Solaris 2. In addition, it supports Silicon Graphics IRIX, Windows NT, HP-UX, and IBM AIX.

Underneath CORBA, Orbix is implemented on top of Open Network Computing Remote Procedure Call (ONC RPC). Since ONC is almost universally available, Orbix could be ported quickly to a very wide range of platforms by the vendor. Like DCE, ONC is a relatively high-level layer, with some corresponding performance consequences. ONC and DCE-based ORBs probably will have performance slightly less than the base RPC. Other products, such as DOE, ObjectBroker, and SOM, are built on lower-level layers with correspondingly improved performance. Early benchmarks indicate that ORBs built upon low-level layers can perform at least twice as fast as basic RPC.

Orbix's CORBA support is relatively complete, but Orbix does have a number of proprietary extensions available to developers as well. The primary extensions include a proprietary naming service and custom filters that allow user-specific implementations of stubs and skeleton code.

Architects and developers should be aware that any code dependent on proprietary features will not be portable to other ORBs and will be dependent on the commercial success of a single supplier. This is especially critical with Orbix because some of its key product discriminators are in this category. We have presented this precaution elsewhere in the book, but we cannot overemphasize it. We have talked to many developers who are unable to appreciate this precaution; architects and developers need to work together to implement this guidance.

IONA Technologies, Ltd. (Dublin, Ireland) is a small company and is therefore vulnerable to market downturns. Because of its niche market positioning, it enjoys a rapidly growing customer base. SunSoft has a silent partner investment stake in IONA that guarantees interoperability support between DOE and Orbix. In so doing, SunSoft can focus DOE on Sun Microsystems workstation hardware, and Orbix will provide cross-platform interoperability. This alliance may be critical only until the CORBA 2.0 interoperability specification is productized by the industry.

IBM SYSTEM OBJECT MODEL (SOM)

IBM System Object Model (SOM) is a CORBA-compliant ORB supporting C, C++, and Smalltalk across a wide range of platforms. SOM is delivered with some preexisting frameworks. In particular, the Replication Framework is of interest here, but we need to lay some groundwork on the features of the SOM ORB to put this framework in context.

Interesting features of SOM include the language bindings, SOM's use of the Interface Repository, the base class SOMObjects, SOM Class Objects and Metaclasses, Distributed SOM, and, finally, the Replication Framework. SOM language bindings include C, C++, Smalltalk, and others under development. The language bindings are extensible through the SOM Emitter Framework. SOM provides a universal base class, SOMObject, and facilities for class objects and metaclasses. The Interface Repository is a central element of the SOM implementation and plays a much more important role in SOM than in other ORB products. Distributed SOM (DSOM) is the distributed version of SOM, providing a slightly different set of APIs and performance characteristics. The Replication Framework is another distributed implementation of SOM that provides a generic mechanism for distributed replication of objects that could be very useful for groupware applications.

A major benefit of SOM is that it reduces the need for multiple software builds because it transparently supports integration of multiple languages. The purpose of the language bindings is to encapsulate the underlying details of the SOM implementation by providing abstract APIs. Bindings also support user-defined method signatures, which are mapped into normal APIs and parameter types of the target programming languages. This provides a transparent calling mechanism between object implementations and their users that may be local, distributed, or replicated.

SOM has three kinds of language bindings: client usage bindings, object model bindings, and implementation bindings. The usage bindings are the normal OMG IDL mappings defined by the Object Management Group. For non–object-oriented languages, usage bindings are implemented as macro calls, and for object oriented languages usage bindings are implemented as proxy class definitions. Proxy classes are client-side usage classes that act as substitutes for the object implementation, which might be remotely located. Although the proxy mechanism is transparent in SOM, it is used pervasively in the implementation, and it is useful for understanding how SOM and DSOM operate internally. The SOM object model bindings are a future feature that will allow subclassable proxy classes.

Some details of SOM IDL must be understood to understand the SOM object implementation bindings. SOM IDL is a compatible extension to OMG IDL. SOM IDL extends OMG IDL with "PRIVATE" and "implementation" clauses that are surrounded (by convention) by conditional precompiler directives that will remove the nonstandard clauses in non-SOM environments.

```
// SOM IDL
#include >>somobj.idl>
interface example: SOMObject
{
    attribute string exattr;
    void publicMethod();

#ifdef __PRIVATE__
    void privateMethod();
#endif

#ifdef __SOMIDL__
    implementation
    {
        somInit: override;
        exattr: noset;
    };
#endif
};
```

In the preceding SOM IDL example, the SOM compiler will not generate usage bindings for the method in the PRIVATE clause, but it will generate a binding for the object implementation. The implementation clause indicates that an inherited function, somInit, will be redefined by the object implementation. The attribute will have a custom set function, as opposed to the default set, and get implementations provided automatically by SOM. The SOM compiler will generate method function headers in the object implementation bindings source file for the overridden and custom attribute handling, as well as the new method signatures for both public and private methods.

As already described, the SOM IDL compiler has many features not generally found in IDL compilers. A feature unique to SOM is implementation inheritance. Implementation inheritance is a very useful capability that supports software reuse. It is particularly helpful in the creation of specializations of existing classes, because a small amount of code can be added to a class to achieve new behaviors. The IDL extensions also give the developer a great deal of control over the behavior of the compiler and implementation without resorting to separate configuration files, as seen in some other ORB products.

SOM's IDL compiler is extensible through the Emitter Framework. The Emitter Framework is a high-level compiler generator for creating custom IDL compilers. It is useful for creating new language bindings, class browsers, pretty printers, and other tools. The SOM IDL compiler is delivered with multiple emitters, which generate the usage bindings, the object implementation bindings, the header files, the interface repository data,

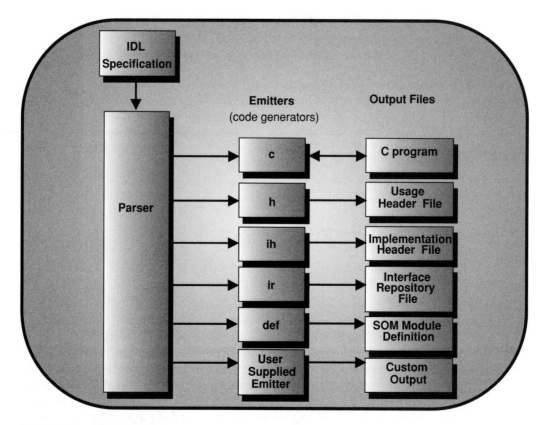

Figure A.3. SOM compiler

and so forth. Through the Emitter Framework, the user can extend the set of outputs as desired to create new tools and language mappings.

The Emitter Framework is customizable at two levels: the template file level and the emitter source code level. Each emitter uses a template file that specifies the output patterns to be generated. Output patterns can contain predefined tokens from the IDL syntax tree. A comprehensive set of tokens is available, including scoped names from the existing language bindings. Using these predefined tokens, it is relatively easy to create new emitters. A second level of customization is available at the emitter source code level. At this level, the number and order of code generation scans can be selected. The default implementations of the compiler classes also can be overridden to produce any extent of customizations to the IDL compiler. This second level of customization is for expert compiler developers; most programmers can perform the template level of customization. The emitter features provide useful tools for both types of developers.

The SOM implementation supports three types of method resolution: offset resolution, name resolution, and dispatch function resolution. Offset resolution is essentially a function call implemented through a calling table. This has the best performance (similar to C++ virtual functional calls) but is basically a static compile-time binding. Name resolution is a dynamic binding process that binds to functions in a dynamically linked library through a comparison of method signatures. Dispatch function resolution is used by Distributed SOM and can be used to create customized binding approaches.

DSOM is a separate API framework within SOM that extends SOM's capabilities across distributed environments. In informal benchmarks run by Raleigh Systems on an 80486-based OS/2 system, about 166K static invocations/sec were measured using SOM and about 24 invocations/sec using DSOM, regardless of whether the DSOM processes were local or distributed across a network. This performance is within the range of the performance of RPC technology, so the DSOM ORB is not introducing any significant overhead. In some applications that use local calls exclusively, use of the nondistributed SOM would be appropriate, and the only difference is in the system APIs; the user-defined OMG IDL APIs are identical between the two implementations.

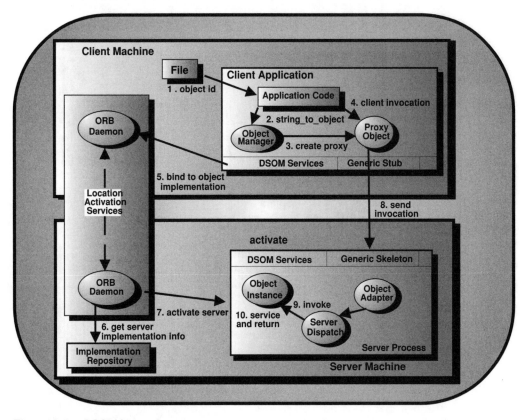

Figure A.4. DSOM invocation process.

The DSOM invocation process is an interesting example of under-the-hood workings of an ORB implementation. What we are describing here is transparent to the application program. On each DSOM host machine, there is an ORB daemon that provides the location and activation services. Each application program has a DSOM object manager and library DSOM service routines that administrate invocations. Each time a client application obtains a new object handle, a proxy object is created within its address space that provides local method handling for the object implementation. The DSOM implementation must peruse all method parameters for embedded object handles so that proxy object creation can occur transparently. The CORBA Interface Repository plays a key role in the creation of proxy objects, providing the interface descriptions necessary for parameter marshalling. This is in contrast to most other ORBs, which use static compiler-generated stubs and do not rely on the Interface Repository in the invocation process.

A method invocation on the proxy object causes the following chain of actions. A copy of the request is forwarded to the Location/Activation services daemon, which uses the Implementation Repository dynamically to deter-

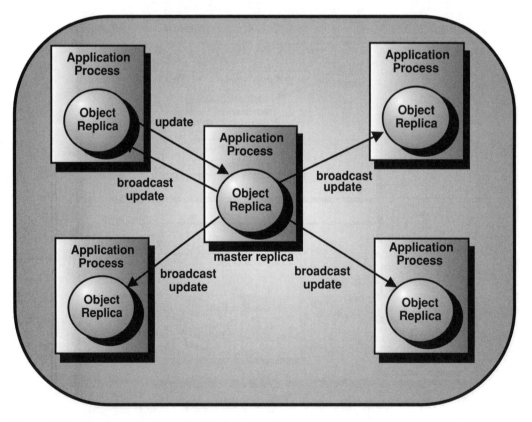

Figure A.5. Replica group in replication framework.

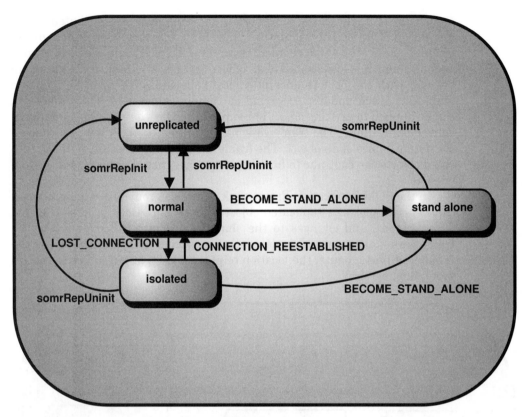

Figure A.6.   Replica state transitions based upon directives.

mine a server binding. If necessary, the server process is activated. The binding information is returned to the client process, and a direct connection is established between the proxy object and the server object through the server's object adapter. This connection is at the MPTN networking layer, the underlying network layer utilized by DSOM. MPTN is a protocol-independent layer that supports NETBIOS, TCP/IP, and Netware IPX transparently. To complete the invocation, the method call is then given to the proxy object for parameter marshalling, dispatching across the network, performing the service, and returning the results. This final sequence is the normal method invocation process for DSOM that will occur on all subsequent messages to this proxy object.

DSOM method invocation is unique in that it is a completely dynamic process on the client side through its heavy reliance on the Interface Repository. Through this process, DSOM achieves a level of isolation between client and server that supports independent recompilation. There is also a version-numbering mechanism in the SOM IDL implementation definition that enables runtime checking of versioning.

The SOM Replication Framework is a special-purpose distributed implementation of SOM. The framework is useful for creating distributed group-oriented applications that require fast update of shared data. The framework supports multiple local copies of an object that are synchronized. Copies can be read with the performance of a local call, and a copy can be modified with distributed updates occurring as rapidly as possible. The framework can be applied to existing object implementations with relatively minor software modifications. The framework has a locking protocol that guarantees consistent copies of an object. The framework is fault tolerant, so that replicated objects can continue to function in the presence of network and system crashes.

In the SOM Replication Framework, a replica group is a set of processes that share copies of a replicated object (Figure A.5). Each process is called a participant, and changes to the shared object are called updates. The framework makes various implementation aspects transparent, such as the number of participants, the location of participants, and changes in replica group membership.

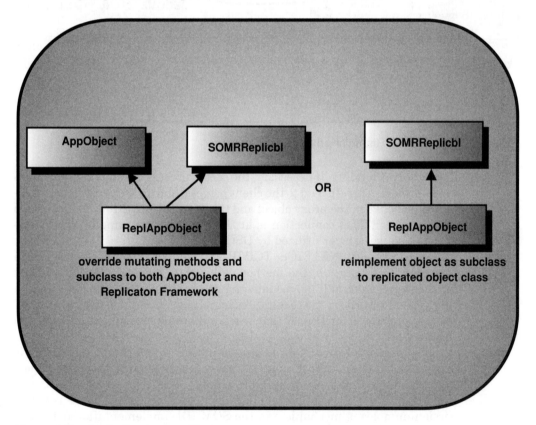

Figure A.7. Replicating legacy objects.

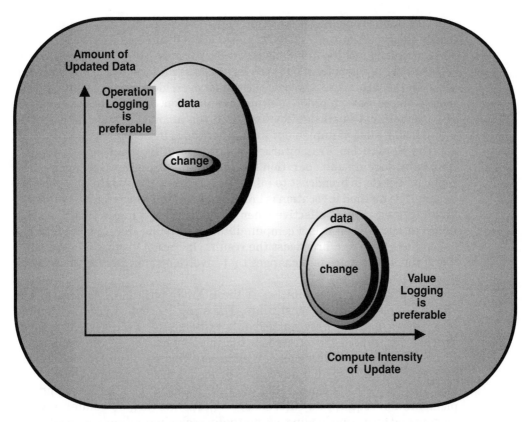

Figure A.8. Selection of value logging vs. operation logging.

The underlying framework implementation is organized in terms of a master object and slave copies (Figure A.5). Participants can read their copy without informing the group. All shared object updates are propagated through the master object.

Various framework messages (called directives) have been defined to notify the participants in case of failures (Figure A.6). The framework provides default implementations of these messages, but they can be overridden for custom handling. If a nonmaster participant crashes, there is no effect on the other participants, and no directive is issued. If a communication failure partitions the network, then the slave copies become isolated from the master and receive the BECOME_STANDALONE directive, which signifies an unrecoverable partitioning of the replicated copies. If a recoverable error occurs, such as the failure of the master process, the framework issues the LOST_CONNECTION directive when the error is detected and the CONNECTION_REESTABLISHED directive when service is restored. In all cases the replicas will continue to function normally, operating in an isolated mode until replicated updates are restored.

The Replication Framework provides two principal ways to replicate legacy objects (Figure A.7). The framework can be inherited directly into the class requiring modification of legacy code. Alternatively, a new class can be created that inherits from both the legacy class and the Replication Framework. In the latter case, the new class must override all legacy methods that modify object state in order to support replication. The process of coversion of legacy objects is straightforward, and the amount of code necessary is minimized by use of implementation inheritance in SOM.

The Replication Framework supports two different modes of replication: value logging and operation logging (Figure A.8). In value logging, the replicated state is broadcast to all the copies for every update. In operation logging, the method invocation is broadcast to all the copies for every update. Value logging is most effective when updates affect a majority of the state information or when it is a compute-intensive update that is more efficient to complete once and broadcast the result. Operation logging is more effective if the updates are fast changes that involve a small portion of the state information.

The current implementation of the SOM Replication Framework has various implementation constraints. The size of a replica group is limited to 14 participants. These participants must share a file system because at least one shared file is used in the implementation of the Replication Framework. (Future versions will eliminate this requirement.) Operation logging currently does not allow user-defined types in method parameters, and update methods cannot allocate new memory. The value-logging implementation requires an externalized object state (i.e., no pointers). Value logging and operation logging are mutually exclusive and cannot be mixed in a replicated implementation, although replication can be utilized with other SOM frameworks. The SOM Replication Framework is a potential candidate technology for the future Object Replication Service standard in the OMG's Object Services Architecture.

Bibliography

The following sources are cited in the text using the name-date notation, as in [Katz, 93].

Anderson, D., and Venkat Rangan, P. "A Basis for Secure Communication in Large Distributed Systems." *Security and Privacy* vol. 2, IEEE Computer Society Press, 1990.

Brinch Hansen, P. *Operating Systems Principles*. Reading, MA: Addison-Wesley, 1976.

Brockschmidt, K. *Inside OLE2*. Redmond, WA: Microsoft Press, 1994.

Cargill, C. F. *Information Technology Standardization: Theory, Process, and Organizations*. Digital Press, 1989.

Chalmers, L. S. "An Analysis of the Differences Between the Computer Security Practices in the Military and Private Sectors" *Security and Privacy*, vol. 2, IEEE Computer Society Press, 1990. Washington D.C.

Clark, D. D., and Wilson, David R. "A Comparison of Commercial and Military Security Policies," *Security and Privacy*, vol. 2, IEEE Computer Society Press, 1990.

Connell, J. et al. *Rapid Structured Prototyping*. Reading, MA: Addison-Wesley, 1987.

Coplien, Object World Briefing on Design Patterns, Hillside Group, 1994.

Cornwell, D., Katz, M., Mowbray, T., and Zahavi, R. DISCUS Technology Transfer Package, MITRE Technical Report, 1994.

Digital, HP, Hyperdesk, IBM, NEC, and OSF. "Joint Submission to the ORB 2.0 Task Force Interoperability and Initialization Request for Proposals," OMG Document 94.3.5 (OSF CORBA 2.0), Framingham, Massachusetts, 1994.

Defense Intelligence Agency, *Compartmented Mode Workstation Evaluation Criteria*, Ver 1, DIA Document DDS-2600-6243-92, 1991. [CMW, 91]

Department of Defense. *Trusted Computer System Evaluation Criteria (TCSEC Orange Book)*. DOD 5200. 28-STD, NCSC, Dec 1985.

Elements of Security Computing, Office of Security Information Systems Group, August 1992.

Fairthorne, B. et al., eds. "Security White Paper." OMG TC Document, 1994.

Fellows, J. et al. "The Architecture of a Distributed Trusted Computing Base." *Advances in Computer System Security* Vol. 3. ed. Rein Turn. 1988. Artech House, Norwood MA.

Gamma, E., Helm, R., Johnson, R.,and Vlissides, J. *Design Patterns*. Reading, MA: Addison-Wesley, 1994.

Goldberg, A. *Smalltalk-80: The Interactive Programming Environment*. Addison-Wesley, 1984.

Goldberg, A., and D. Robinson. *Smalltalk-80: The Language and Its Implementation*. Addison-Wesley, 1983.

Gupta, S. "Object-Oriented Security in the Trusted Mach Operating System." Workshop on Security in OO Systems, OOPSLA Conference Proceedings, 1993.

Hagmann, R. *Concurrency Within DOE Object Implementations*. SunSoft Microsystems, May 27, 1993.

Halliwell, C. "Camp Development and the Art of Building a Market through Standards." *IEEE Micro*, vol. 13, no. 6 (December 1993).

Horowitz, B. M. *Strategic Buying for the Future*. Libey Publishing, 1993.

Hutt, A., ed. *Object Oriented Analysis and Design*. John Wiley & Sons, Inc., 1994.

Institute of Electrical and Electronics Engineers. IEEE P 1003.0. Draft Guide to the Posix Open System Environment. New York, 1993.

Institute of Electrical and Electronics Engineers, POSIX Working Group P1003.4a/D6. "Threads Extension for Portable Operating Systems." 1993.

Internet Engineering Task Force. "RFC 1510 Internet Security," 1992. [ISO, 92]

International Standards Organization. *ISO 7498-2 Security Architecture*. 1988.

Jacobson, I. *Object Oriented Software Engineering*. Reading, MA: Addison-Wesley, 1992.

Jacobson, I., and Lindstrom, F. "Reengineering of Old Systems to an Object-Oriented Architecture," OOPSLA Conference Proceedings, 1991. ACM Press, New York SIGPLAN NOTICES vol. 26, NVMII Nov 1991.

Janssen, W., and Spreitzer, M. "Using ILU with Common Lisp." Technical Report, Xerox Corporation, January 1994.

Katz, M., Cornwell, D., and Mowbray, T. J. "System Integration with Minimal Object Wrappers." Proceedings of TOOLS 93, August 1993.

Kohl, J., and Neuman, C., *The Kerberos Network Authentication Service*, ACM Press, 1993.

Linn, J. "Generic Security Service Application Program Interface." RFC 1508 Geer Zolot Associates, September 1993.

Linton, M. *An Introduction to Fresco*. Tutorial W7, XWorld Conference, New York, June 1994.

Malamud, C. *STACKS Interoperability in Today's Computer Networks*. Englewood Cliffs, NJ: Prentice-Hall, 1992.

McMahon, P. "An Extended GSS API." Ms., May 1993.

Microsoft Corporation. *OLE2 Programmers Reference, Volume One Working with Windows Objects*. Redmond, WA: Microsoft Press, 1994a.

Microsoft Corporation. *OLE2 Programmers Reference, Volume Two Creating Programmable Applications with OLE Automation*. Redmond, WA: Microsoft Press, 1994b.

Mowbray, T. J. "Distributed Objects Everywhere: An Early Assessment." *Object Magazine* (January 1994).

Mowbray, T. J., and Brando, T. "Interoperability and CORBA-based Open Systems." *Object Magazine* (September 1993).

Mowbray, T. J., and White, K. L. *Towards an OMG IDL Mapping to Common Lisp*. ACM Lisp Pointers, Volume VII, Number 2, April-June 1994.

Mowbray, T. J., and Zahavi, R. "Distributed Computing with Object Management." ConneXions—The Interoperability Report, Vol. 7 No. 112 Dec 1993 The Interop Company.

Nessett, D. "Factors Affecting Distributed System Security." *Advances in Computer System Security* vol. 3, ed. Rein Turn. 1988.

Object Management Group. *The Common Object Request Broker: Architecture and Specification*. John Wiley & Sons, Inc., 1992a.

Object Management Group, *Object Services Roadmap*. OMG TC Document. Framingham, Massachusetts, 1992b.

Object Management Group. *Object Management Architecture Guide*. John Wiley & Sons, Inc., 1993.

Object Management Group. *Common Object Services Specifications*. John Wiley & Sons, Inc., 1994a.

Object Management Group. *Object Services Architecture*. OMG Document 94.11.12, November 1994b.

Object Management Group. *Common Facilities Architecture*. OMG Document 95.1.2, January 1995a.

Object Management Group. *Common Facilities Roadmap*. OMG Document 95.1.32, January 1995b.

Roetzheim, W. H. *Developing Software to Government Standards*. Englewood Cliffs, NJ: Prentice-Hall, 1991.

Rymer, J., et al. "Microsoft OLE 2.0 and the Road to Cairo." *Distributed Computing Monitor*. Patricia Seybold Group, vol. 9, no. 1, January 1994.

Saydjari, O. S., et al. "Synergy: A Distributed, Microkernel-based Security Architecture." National Security Agency, November 22, 1993.

Shaffer, Steven L., and Simon, Alan R. *Network Security*. AP Professional, 1994.

Shaw, M. "Software Architecture for Shared Information Systems." Carnegie-Mellon University, Software Engineering Institute, Technical Report No. CMU/SEI-93-TR-3, ESC-TR-93-180, March 1993.

Stallings, William. *The Open Systems Interconnection (OSI) Model and OSI-Related Standards*. Macmillan, New York 1987.

Stevens, Richard W. *Unix Network Programming*. Englewood Cliffs, NJ: Prentice-Hall, 1990.

Stroustrup, B. *The C++ Programming Language*, 2nd ed. Reading, MA: Addison-Wesley, 1991.

SunSoft, Inc. "Distributed Objects Everywhere: A White Paper." September 1993.

Taylor, D. A. *Object-Oriented Information Systems*. John Wiley & Sons, Inc., New York, 1992.

Ting, T.C., and Demurjian S. A. "Shouldn't the OO Paradigm Influence and Guide the Approach for Security?" Workshop on Security in Object-Oriented Systems, OOPSLA 93 Conference, 1993.

National Computer Society Center, Trusted Network Interpretation of the Trusted Computer System Evaluation Criteria, NCSC-TG-005, Version-1, July 1987.

Wray, J. "GSSAPI: C-bindings." RFC 1509, IETF Dec, September 1993.

Zahavi, R. "Compartmented Mode Workstations." MITRE Technical Report, 1993.

Index